Wired-Up
Young People and the Electronic Media

Edited By

Sue Howard

First published in 1998 by UCL Press

UCL Press Limited
1 Gunpowder Square
London EC4A 3DE
UK

and

1900 Frost Road, Suite 101
Bristol
Pennsylvania 19007–1598
USA

The name of University College London (UCL) is a registered trade mark
used by UCL Press with the consent of the owner.

British Library Cataloguing in Publication Data
A catalogue record for this book is available from the British Library.

Library of Congress Cataloging-in-Publication Data are available

ISBNs: 1–85728–804–1
       1–85728–805–X

Typeset in 10/12pt Times
by Graphicraft Typesetters Ltd., Hong Kong

Printed in Great Britain by T. J. International Ltd., Padstow, Cornwall

Wired-Up

Media, Education and Culture
Series Editors: David Buckingham is Reader in Education at Institute of Education, University of London, UK and Julian Sefton-Green is Media Education Development Officer at Weekend Arts College, part of Interchange Trust, UK.

In response to the increasing diversity of contemporary societies and the significance of the electronic media, cultural studies has developed rigorous and exciting approaches to pedagogy, both in schools and in higher education. At the same time, research in this area has begun to pose fundamental questions about the political claims of much cultural studies theory, and about the relationship between academic knowledge and lived experience. *Media, Education and Culture* will extend the research and debate that is developing in this interface between cultural studies and education.

Also in the series:

Teaching Popular Culture: Beyond Radical Pedagogy
edited by David Buckingham

Digital Diversions: Youth Culture in the Age of Multimedia
edited by Julian Sefton-Green

Teen Spirits: Music and Identity in Media Education
by Chris Richards

Forthcoming:

Schooling the Future: Education 'Youth' and Postmodernity
by Bill Green and Lindsay Fitzclarence.

Contents

Contents

Series Editors' Preface

Media and Cultural Studies are currently expanding areas of the curriculum at all levels of the education system, not merely in English-speaking countries but in many other parts of the world. Cultural Studies has made a radical contribution to the study of education, particularly in terms of its emphasis on 'popular' knowledge and on the political dynamics of young people's leisure cultures. Yet in the context of anxieties about the apparent decline in traditional cultural values, it also challenges much current thinking about the aims and methods of core areas of the curriculum such as English. In response to the growing significance of the electronic media and the increasing diversity of contemporary societies, media educators have developed rigorous and exciting new approaches to pedagogy both in schools and in higher education. At the same time, research in this area has begun to pose fundamental questions about the political claims of much academic theory, and about the relationships between academic knowledge and lived experience. The Media, Education and Culture series will develop these themes and approaches, providing lively and accessible examples of original research and debate at the interface between Education and Media/Cultural Studies.

As one of the first volumes in the series, *Wired-Up* explores several of these issues in new and challenging ways. The book sets out to change the agenda of debate about young people's relationships with the electronic media. For far too long, many of the authors argue, discussion about the role of the media in modern society has been dominated by the 'effects' paradigm. Television in particular has been widely seen as harmful and destructive to children; and there are signs that these anxieties are now being transferred wholesale to the new digital media. By exploring the actual uses that young people make of these media, the research collected here moves beyond the limitations of this tradition. With evidence gleaned from empirical studies ranging from pre-schoolers to young adults, the contributors take as their starting point the fact that young people 'read' and use the media in very diverse and often thoughtful ways. At the same time, they do not espouse the cheerful form of consumer sovereignty which some have seen as characteristic of contemporary Cultural Studies. They do not regard young people as wholly autonomous makers of meaning. On the contrary, they show how their uses and interpretations of the media are defined by the social and interpersonal contexts in which they occur. These studies thus take us beyond the simplistic either/or debates which typically characterize public debate on these issues – the notion that the media are either harmless or harmful, and that young people are either powerless or powerful in resisting their influence.

Building on what is now a burgeoning tradition in Cultural Studies, these researchers are moving on to investigate audiences and media forms overlooked in earlier research. Among the new research topics covered here, for example, are preschoolers' television viewing, young boys' engagement with video games and adolescents' uses of the telephone. At the same time, these researchers are perhaps more sensitive to methodological issues and dilemmas than their predecessors. There is a considerable degree of eclecticism in the different research environments and the differing roles the researchers have played in the lives of their research subjects; but there is also a strong sense that what we can know about children is inevitably constrained by the methods we use to study them, and the circumstances in which we do so.

This volume is also sensitive to the educational implications of such research. If the media play such significant and diverse roles in young people's lives, what does this mean for traditional forms of pedagogy and curriculum? Some of the pieces here explore these issues directly – for example, by considering what feminism means for young readers of women's magazines or discussing the issues entailed in educating children reared on digital technologies. Yet most of the pieces imply that the media have now effectively become the new curriculum – albeit one which, like the old curriculum, is not simply imposed upon passive minds. Thus, a number of studies here draw attention to what young people are learning or understanding from their consumption of the media. Implicitly, they set a radical new agenda for curriculum development. The research reported here into young people's interpretations of television or their creative uses of video imply that schools and teachers need to take these phenomena as starting points for the curriculum, rather than seeing them as necessarily 'anti-educational' – as has been the case among conservative policy-makers in the UK in recent years. Schools need to recognize the diverse range of contemporary media cultures if they are to connect with – and to build upon – young people's everyday experiences.

Indeed, it is this attention to the heterogeneity of the modern media environment which particularly distinguishes this book. Television, video, computers, telephones, camcorders and so on are brought together to demonstrate a distinctive kind of 'mediated childhood'. Although most of the studies focus on only one of the technologies listed above, as a whole they indicate the need for a multi-focused, interdisciplinary perspective. Questions about young people's productive uses of media technologies are considered alongside investigations of how such technologies are consumed. In the process, the boundaries between 'production' and 'consumption' are crossed and blurred: studies investigating young people's use of camcorders are positioned next to analyses of the 'creative consumption' of horror videos or computer games. This juxtaposition implicitly raises questions about how knowledge might transfer across these complementary domains.

For us, writing several thousand miles away from the countries in which this research was conducted, there is much that is instantly recognizable. The fact that the work all derives from Australia and New Zealand should not be taken to imply that its interest is merely parochial. On the contrary, these studies would seem to confirm the existence of a kind of globalized media childhood, in first world countries at least. It is no surprise that the media technologies and texts discussed here are, for the most part, well known internationally. What is more striking is how the intellectual and political concerns of the book – its reformulation of questions about media 'effects', or its discussions of pedagogy – are shared by many in the UK, Europe and North America. At the same time, there are important local inflections in several of these studies – inflections which derive not just from local media, but from their interaction with indigenous cultures and traditions. In this respect, the book makes an important contribution to our understanding of how local childhoods are lived amid global media cultures.

David Buckingham
Julian Sefton-Green
London, June 1997

Preface

In September 1994, the Australian Teachers of Media (ATOM) association held its biennial conference in Adelaide, South Australia and it was in this forum that the research, on which several chapters of this volume are based, first saw the light of day. What became very apparent at this conference was that interesting empirical research was being conducted across Australia and New Zealand into questions concerning children and young people and their involvements with all kinds of media. Whether it was in relation to watching *Bananas in Pyjamas* or *Nightmare on Elm Street*, playing *Doom* or using a video camera, the image that emerged from these presentations was one of children and young people managing diverse media forms, enjoying them, thinking about them and integrating them, seemingly effortlessly, into their lives. This optimistic image, however, is not shared by others. Six months after the ATOM conference, a major international forum on children and television held in Melbourne had sessions entitled 'The Death of Childhood', 'Kids as Consumers', 'Television as Moral Guardian', 'The Violence Discussion' (no longer a 'debate' because the jury, the audience was told, is 'in' on this question) – all of which clearly demonstrated continuing anxiety about children's exposure to electronic media.

The construction of the 'child' that lies behind these anxieties is essentially an idealized and romantic one – the 'child' is naive, innocent, vulnerable, in need of protection; the media, on the other hand, are often demonized – they are rapacious, corrupting, exploitative and in need of regulation. Ironically, by uncritically reporting claims that some form of electronic entertainment is to blame whenever children prove less than perfect, the media themselves are largely responsible for perpetuating these constructions.

For many years now, studies which have rejected the old notion of a direct causal link between the media and children's subsequent attitudes, beliefs and behaviours have been generating fascinating insights into *real* children's *actual* interactions with all kinds of media forms. Research findings like these do not, of course, make such interesting headlines as the 'shock horror' claims and many excellent studies that might have challenged the general propensity to go for the easy answers have languished in scholarly journals only to preach to the converted. Research, in a form that is accessible to both the lay reader as well as those with a scholarly or professional interest in the field is vital if informed understanding is to prevail about how children and young people really *do* use, interact with and appropriate for their own purposes, electronic media of all kinds. The studies that are presented here are the result of recent scholarly research, and, I believe, are equally accessible to those who live and/or work with children and young people as well as students and scholars in the field.

This collection comprises separate studies covering a wide range of electronic media forms including: television, video, video/computer games and the telephone. In addition, the age-range encompassed by the studies includes preschoolers, primary school-aged children, adolescents and young adults. Boys' and girls' interests also receive separate attention. Of particular interest to scholars and students will be the diversity of the methods and theoretical contexts represented. The authors' backgrounds in cultural studies, media and journalism, psychology, sociology, education, anthropology and the humanities are all reflected in the theoretical frameworks they adopt. The methods, which are broadly qualitative, include analysis of linguistic and visual texts, data collection through surveys, interviews, discussion groups and participant observation and longitudinal and 'snap-shot' research designs. All the studies involve participants who represent the rich cultural diversity of Australian and New Zealand societies.

The chapters are ordered according to the age of the participants and so the collection begins with Geoff Lealand's study of New Zealand preschoolers watching television; it then ranges through research concerning primary school-aged children including Bill Green, Jo-Anne Reid and Chris Bigum's piece about children dealing with the complexities of playing video games; Mark Laidler on children's love of the 'disapproved' video *Nightmare on Elm Street* and my own chapter on how the (often despised) entertainment programming favoured by children, can actually make them think. Linda Sheldon's chapter is the result of a large quantitative and qualitative study and highlights what children find boring and 'cool' on TV. With Chapter 6 we move into adolescence with Nola Alloway and Pam Gilbert's piece on teenage boys and video/arcade game-playing. Their rather pessimistic account of boys 'doing gender' makes a striking contrast with Gerry Bloustien's more optimistic analysis (in Chapter 7) of teenage girls using the video camera to construct their gendered identities. Patricia Gillard, Amanda Bow and Karen Wale have contributed a chapter on an electronic means of communication that is now taken for granted – the telephone; here they show how important the phone still is to teenagers in the age of the Internet. In the final chapter, Sue Turnbull offers a thoughtful analysis of some of the problems in teaching about media at tertiary level, which illustrates some of the continuing 'generation gaps' this book is attempting to address.

A volume like this only comes together with a lot of assistance and encouragement. Thanks are due, in the first instance, to David Buckingham for suggesting that the ATOM papers, represented here, might best be preserved in some more permanent form. The University of South Australia also deserves thanks for awarding a small grant to assist with the costs of coordinating an enterprise that stretched from Perth to Waikato and from Townsville to Adelaide (more distance than I can calculate). I must also record my very great thanks to all the contributors to this volume who made the editing process such a pleasure – such an exercise in cooperation and collegiality. Some of us are so far apart that we can only know each other through e-mail; nevertheless, this new electronic form allows us to communicate in ways that permit warmth and 'virtual' friendship. Locally, thanks to Judy Gill for her generous scholarly support and to Drummond Jewitt, without whom I would have starved, languished and never survived the stresses that undertaking such an enterprise inevitably entails. Finally, this book is dedicated to my father who introduced me to television when he bought our family's first set when I was just a little girl. It was as a result of his teasing that I first learned about representation on television – he suggested that when the TV broke down, it was because it was clogged up with tiny dead cowboys and Indians. When I watched the repair man at work, I was shocked to discover that the set contained nothing more interesting than valves and wires. Like all children, however, I took this in my stride and moved on.

Sue Howard
Adelaide 1996

Chapter One

Where do snails watch television?
Preschool television and New Zealand children

Geoff Lealand

A little New Zealand girl called Monique (4 years old) and her mother are watching *Sesame Street*. An image of a snail appears on screen:

Monique:	That's not a snail!
Mother:	Yes it is. It was inside its shell. They live in their shell; it's their house. When they go for a walk and they get tired they just suck their slimy body inside their shell and have a sleep.
Monique:	Is there a TV inside their house?
Mother:	No, they don't need stereos and televisions in their house. There's just enough room for them.
Monique:	Oh, I thought there was a TV and stereo in there! [*Mother and daughter laugh*]

Ratings are the common currency of television in most countries, irrespective of whether the broadcasting system is commercial, licence-fee or taxation funded, or a mixed system. But in New Zealand, as in other countries, the very youngest viewers of television are not part of this currency exchange; children under the age of five years do not exist in the world of television ratings.

Lacking even such one-dimensional measurement, the audience for the special kind of programming called 'early childhood' lacks both coherence and visibility. There are, however, signs that some regard it as an important genre. In Australia, for example, the Australian content rules administered by the Australian Broadcasting Authority enforce a locally-produced P (preschool) strand in the daily schedules of the Australian commercial networks. In Australia too, a short-lived political row developed in 1996 over a scheduling clash between the competing attractions of broadcasts of Question Time in the House of Representatives, and afternoon screenings of *Sesame Street*. *Sesame Street* won.

In New Zealand, preschool programmes continue to be made locally or purchased from overseas sources, and screened in specific, advertising-free segments of the schedules of the three broadcast networks (Television New Zealand-owned ONE and Channel 2, and the private network TV3). In March 1996, there were three hours Monday to Friday (15 hours weekly) of preschool programming across all three broadcast channels, with a further 25 minutes of *The Magic Box* on TV3 on Sunday morning. Ten of TVNZ's 15 non-commercial hours broadcast each week are provided specifically for preschoolers (24 per cent of all TVNZ children's programming), while TV3's non-commercial preschool programming constitutes 20 per cent of children's programming.

These programmes, which are not interrupted by advertising (except for programme and station promotions as a form of self-advertising between programmes), are effectively subsidized by the high level of advertising (between 12–15 minutes per hour) which surrounds most other programming across all channels. This might be considered a lingering presence of the public service objectives of television in New Zealand, before the deregulation and free market ideology of the late 1980s swept aside the previous funding mix of a broadcasting fee and advertising revenue. Viewers are still taxed with an annual broadcasting fee ($NZ 110) but instead of this going directly to the broadcasters, it now goes to a quango called New Zealand On Air (NZOA), set up under the 1988 Broadcasting Act.

NZOA has the responsibility to collect and distribute the $NZ 85 million collected from 1.05 million fee-payers in New Zealand. In 1995/6, $NZ 45 million (53 per cent) of this went to funding television programming. It also has a cultural agenda, to fund and promote programming which will reflect the bi-cultural nature of contemporary New Zealand society. This means, quite specifically, that NZOA-funded initiatives in preschool programming must acknowledge that there are two official languages in New Zealand (English and Maori) and that children must be provided with a range of perspectives on culture and values.

In 1995, NZOA funded, in full or part, 476 hours of children's programming out of the 773 hours of such programming screened in that year. Children's programming was the third largest locally-produced genre on New Zealand television after sport and current affairs. Although this may seem like a sizeable block of programming, it has to be set within the context of the total 5018 hours of locally-produced television in 1995, which contributed only 19.7 per cent of total programming. Just over one-third (35.4 per cent) of prime-time programming was New Zealand-produced (NZOA 1996).

The *Statement of Intent* which governed NZOA's funding decisions in 1996/97 granted up to $NZ 7.7 million for 374 hours of children's programming but with no further funding for animation projects. Targeted funding of $NZ 1 million had been provided in the April 1996 funding round for the animated series *The Adventures of Cumie the Cloud*. Although there is acknowledgment of the popularity of animation for young viewers, the production expense limits more being made.

NZOA also played a part in the early stages of the research described here. In 1990–91, it funded the development stage of a TVNZ-produced early childhood series, *Our House*, which was designed to replace the New Zealand version of *Play*

School, a long-running programme based on its British counterpart. Part of this development stage involved multifaceted research designed to inform the shape of the new series, and part of this research involved observation studies of 35 young children (15 boys and 20 girls) watching television. The *Our House* series went no further than the production of five pilot programmes, falling victim to competitive bidding between TVNZ and TV3 for funding from NZOA. In late 1991, $NZ 6 million was awarded to the production house Kids TV, enabling them to put to air a daily early childhood programme, *You and Me*, on the private channel TV3 in July 1992.

The research done for *Our House* eventually informed a TVNZ in-house funded and produced early childhood series *Chatterbox* (1993–95) and, according to Kids TV producer Julie Weatherall, also influenced the format and content of *You and Me*. But it also became more of academic interest, rather than serving the original objectives of directly shaping new preschool programming. Nevertheless, the richness of the data obtained from the observation phase of the research for *Our House* prompted a desire to replicate and extend this style of child-centred research. It seemed a good idea to extend the detail and complexity of the original project, beyond the 'snap-shot' constraints of small-scale research (the constraint of one observation period per child) by proposing a longitudinal study, evolving across time and with a larger, more diverse group of children. It was proposed that more could be discovered with repeated visits to more children.

Field research began in September 1992 and continued until December 1993. The results of this research were published in 1995 as *Television and New Zealand Preschoolers: A Longitudinal Study*. This report set its findings within a wide discussion about the nature of the relationship between young viewers and television and canvassed the following aspects of the relationship.

Television and Early Childhood: The Research Literature

Given the almost total absence of New Zealand-based studies, research from Japan, the USA, Europe and Australia provided the theoretical base for this study. Some caution, however, was necessary in transposing cultural considerations onto the New Zealand setting. In Japan, for example, television is commonly used as an entertainment/education tool in formal preschool settings (the nursery school); this happens very rarely in New Zealand formal preschooling. Likewise, in the United States, figures suggest that young children watch more television and a greater range of programming (particularly in cable homes), than their New Zealand counterparts.

In much of the research on children and television, the first component (children) is often ill-defined or underinterrogated. There is often an assumption, for example, that childhood coincides with the beginnings of formal education (in New Zealand, at age 5), or later. In two important Australian studies of children and television, for example, childhood begins at 8 years (Palmer 1986) and 5 years (Cupit 1987) respectively. This means that amongst the thousands of research studies and policy statements on children and television, viewers under 5 years old are usually underrepresented and often ignored.

This would appear to be a major anomaly, given the general belief that very young children are living through their most formative years, subject to influences and expectations which will shape them personally and socially. These years, it is generally believed, are when children are in greatest need of guidance, supervision and protection. This is particularly marked in the Western dominant discourse about childhood as an extended period of innocence, dependency and vulnerability, as the following suggests:

> Examining the impact of television exposure on the moral development of young children is important for two significant reasons. The years two to seven are the most critical for a child's moral development. Also known is that children in this same time span are in their peak viewing years, watching more television per day than any other time in their childhood. The presence of television in the lives of young children is undeniable.
>
> (Albright 1994: 2)

There are reasons why very young viewers continue to be neglected by re-searchers. They comprise a specialist audience, their programmes comprise a minor part of production output and, as has already been pointed out, they are absent in ratings, the common currency of commercial television. Very young children are also difficult research subjects, seldom able to articulate, conceptualize or under-stand much beyond their own immediate experiences. As Fitch, Huston and Wright (1993) suggest, probably all children initially believe all television is 'real' and do not start to identify formal features such as animation until age 3 or 4. As a result, research on very young children and television is customarily mediated and filtered through adult perceptions, with a corresponding dependency on second-level data.

Another strand of research uses technology to intrude into the viewing situ-ation and record attention levels such as eye-contact and listening to television content. Such research informed the development and production of the American preschool series *Sesame Street*, but even though it can indicate interest levels and visible response to content, like most other research, it cannot give us much informa-tion on what is going on in the child's head. Given the silence from the children themselves, such observations tend to form the core of much research and are associated with the research methods employed in this study.

Summarizing the present body of knowledge about very young children and television, research findings (Choat 1988; Collins 1991; Kodaira 1990; Meltzoff 1988; Plomin *et al.* 1990) suggest the following:

- babies begin to show limited, sporadic attention to the television set before they are 1 year old;
- children as young as 1 or 2 years begin to imitate television models;
- between 2 and 3 years, there is a dramatic rise in the amount of television watched and the attention paid to television content;

- between the ages of 3 and 5, the majority of children watch television in a quite attentive manner, with boys and only children watching more than girls or children with siblings.

In addition, although often fragmentary and culturally specific, research on television and very young children suggests that television use and understanding of its content is strongly linked to sequences of cognitive development and age-defined abilities, even though such understandings are not necessarily uniform across groups of similarly aged children. Children must build on skills mastered earlier, earlier-processed schemas and previous experiences (including mistakes and mis-interpretations). As in other areas of the child's experience, television can add to these accumulated experiences to influence physical behaviour, verbal communication and cognitive abilities.

In an important Australian study (Greenblat and Glezer 1993), mothers reported on their children's use of television. They indicated that most were watching television by age 2 and up to an hour a day was being watched by the start of formal schooling. By this time, most children were choosing their own programmes, but the mothers reported only one in five was totally absorbed in his/her viewing. These Australian mothers thought their children had learnt particular skills from television, such as the recognition of concepts and relationships, as well as songs and rhymes.

Even though such research informed the shape and objectives of the present study, it seldom informs the public discourse about television and children in New Zealand. Periodic attention to this area of children's lives regularly and uncritically calls on a mix of conjecture, anecdote and North American empirical research to substantiate its case – most particularly, when negative effects are alleged. There seems to be little desire, for example, to interrogate the cultural specificity of imported 'effects' research, nor much interest in replicating and testing such research against local conditions, despite the growing body of research on trans-national media (Liebes and Katz 1990) which argues for national differences in reception and impact.

The research community in New Zealand generally continues to ignore research on children and television, and when it does call on research, it often encourages a form of intellectual imperialism through its unreflexive use of overseas studies. This present study was, in part, an attempt to redress this neglect.

The Research Method

Use was made of local school and personal contacts to generate a research core of families with young children. Further families were added through the time-honoured process of snow-balling and through formal approaches to early childhood education groups. The interest created resulted in unexpected offers of assistance;

in one case, a charge nurse with a medical centre facilitated access to 12 families with young children.

By September 1992, thirty-nine 3 to 4-year-olds were ready for the first visit of the researchers (Cycle A), with a further thirty-three children beginning in October (Cycle B). These children came from a wide range of backgrounds, living in the cities of Hamilton or Taupo, and small Waikato towns and rural areas. There was a wide range of family circumstances, with a special effort being made to recruit children from Maori families. These latter families (which contributed 12 children to the panel) were the special responsibility of Anne, a researcher with Maori affiliations. The other children were primarily of Pakeha (European) background, except for one Chinese family.

The characteristic that all these children shared was that in most cases the primary caregiver (usually the biological mother) was home with the children for all or considerable parts of the day and because of this, they were more likely to have access to daytime television programming. Over a 14 month period, a total of 306 visits were made by three trained researchers (Anne, Bevin and Claire), averaging 22 visits per month or approximately seven visits per month per researcher.

In all, a maximum of 78 children participated in this study, from a grand total of 120 children in the participating families. Children under the age of 3 years or over 5 years were not directly involved in the observation periods, except when they interacted with the children being directly observed. Because the research ranged over an extended period, there were some anticipated losses from the panel (10 children turning 5 and starting school) but these departures were more than compensated for through the addition of another 14 children in early 1993. The 1993 research panel began with 38 boys and 40 girls and these numbers remained stable through to the end of the field studies in December.

The 14 months of field studies produced 344 hours of observation, with the average observation period being just over one hour – a period which enabled useful data to be collected without unduly disrupting family routines. In all cases, observations were conducted in a 'natural' environment, with no special instructions being given to the children in anticipation of the researcher's visit.

Observing the Children

As in previous research which employed systematic observations of television use in natural sites (Palmer 1986; Zwaga 1992), all possible factors in the relationship between young children and the television set were included in the equation. Such factors included:

- the number of television sets and their placement in the home;
- the viewing environment, including the layout of the domestic setting. An open-plan setting produced different viewing dynamics from that which occurred in dedicated viewing rooms;

- the systems of control over the television set. This included parents/ caregivers controlling the on–off switches and remote controls, or if children were allowed or chose to use such technology;
- the weather on the day of each visit. This often determined how much use was made of television;
- the presence or absence of other children (younger and/or older), caregivers (mothers, grandparents, aunts) and other possible participants (visitors, pets);
- the customary structure or rhythm of the day for each child: when they customarily took daytime naps, ate or watched television. Obviously, visits were timed to coincide with the last activity. At other times, children were more likely to be doing other things or attending kindergarten or play centres;
- the presence of the researcher.

Anticipating the possible effects of having a relative stranger regularly visiting, deliberate strategies were adopted to neutralize the role of the researcher through simple techniques of distancing or deflection. For example, researchers promised to read a story 'after we have finished watching television'. In virtually all cases, however, significant or visible effects of the researchers' presence rapidly diminished with return visits to homes, echoing what Palmer (1986: 24) found in her research:

As participant observer, the researcher is part of the social situation of television viewing. Confidence in the results of this stage as reflecting children's usual viewing behaviour rests in the observer's ability to fit in with family patterns and to maintain a low-key but friendly presence. The observation record alerts the researcher to those occasions when the social situation was consciously adapted to the observer's presence.

Caregivers generally supported the judgment that the normal behaviour of their children did not significantly change, either during the researchers' visits or over the period of the field research. Commentaries by the three field researchers also argued for minimal researcher effects.

The behaviour of the children was recorded in two ways:

1 Through a record of each child's attention to television content, using a general code for every 10 minute segment which indicated the level of attention being paid;
2 a commentary and record of all events and conversation which took place within each observation period.

The information obtained approximates the combination of *running records* (qualitative measurements) and *rating scales* (quantitative measurements) flowing from such procedures, described by Wellhousen (1994).

Children Watching Television

The objective of this research was not to seek the unusual or exceptional; its purpose was to recognize, record and categorize *general* or *unexceptional* manifestations of behaviour. The assumption was that while watching television, children in general – and the children in the observation panel in particular – performed a range of activities within the framework of 'watching television'. Recent research (Clancey 1994; Morley 1986; Zwaga 1992) confirms that this is the case with adult viewers; television viewing is typically a 'distracted' or multifaceted activity, forming one of numerous parallel or competing activities. Such behaviour, the research argues, is particularly evident amongst female and young viewers.

As Palmer (1986: 62) points out, the range of behaviour and activities reported in observational studies characteristically occurs in the family context of children's television viewing. Many of these activities linger into adulthood – such as snoozing in front of the small screen – but there are also activities particular to young viewers, and to very young viewers specifically. Some of these are associated with the very tactile relationship young viewers have with the television set, often sitting as close as possible to the screen or touching it. Children from a very young age often create a personal space immediately in front of the set, for the acting out of rituals associated with viewing.

Interestingly, the distance between the set and children is at its closest with young children; as we grow into adolescence and adulthood, the distance increases. In the adult years, the distance is at its maximum – a distancing that is more than is required for good viewing, with such behaviour having more symbolic value than real value (keeping the television at more than arm's length). If further confirmation is needed, it can be observed in the practice of parents (also observed in this study) who move children back from the television set, or admonish them for 'sitting too close'.

Activity Around the TV Set

In addition to physical 'bonding' with the television set, the children in this study displayed the following range of activities:

eating and drinking (morning and afternoon snacks);
sleeping;
reading;
playing with toys;
playing with brothers and/or sisters;
drawing with pens, crayons or chalk;
talking with parents/caregivers, siblings, visitors, to themselves, to the TV;

singing television-associated or other songs and rhymes;
dancing, running and jumping;
tussling with siblings or family pets.

Other more static forms of behaviour included:

lying immobile on the floor;
intense viewing, thumb in mouth;
'viewing', but with hands over eyes.

The most frequent activity observed was talk, which included dialogue between the children and parents/caregivers, the researchers and siblings/friends; monologues directed to no apparent listener or unresponsive pets or toys and forms of interchange with television presenters or characters. Other very common activities included playing with toys, singing and eating.

Observation of children's attention to television yielded some interesting insights. These included evidence that fewer children watched the animated short programmes than the longer daily screenings of *Play School* and *Sesame Street* in the mornings. In addition, around half of the children who watched these 'lead-in' programmes did so with their full attention, while the other half were inattentive. Generally, across all observation periods in the morning, only half of the children were fully attentive to the television set, with just as many dividing their attention between the screen and other activities, or paying little or no interest. The primary viewing times were between 9–10 a.m. and 2.30–3.30 p.m. Attention to the morning screenings of the New Zealand-produced programmes *Play School* and *You and Me* remained fairly stable across the 20 minutes of programme duration. However, attention to the longer *Sesame Street* was uneven, possibly encouraged by the fragmented narrative style of this American series. The level of full attention to afternoon screenings of *Play School* and *You and Me* was higher, possibly due to the post-lunch/pre-nap role that such viewing often served. Viewing by preschoolers steadily decreased from mid-afternoon, with only one-quarter of the children who were watching television at the peak time of 2.50 p.m. still viewing one hour later.

These generalized measurements of attention were supplemented by running commentaries which provided richer and more complex details of behaviour. The information was processed and structured using the typology of television–child interactions developed by Palmer (1986: 69), whereby:

the relationship between child behaviour and television content is observed as it occurs in close proximity in time and place, or where TV content is expressed in the child's behaviour.

Use was made of Palmer's categories of *Expressive Interaction*, which included *Parasocial Interaction, Performance, Comment, Discussion, Self-talk, Monitoring* and *Remake* to describe and illustrate examples where television content was expressed, visibly and/or verbally in manifest behaviour (e.g. children repeating words or phrases first heard on television).

Palmer defines *Parasocial Interaction* as 'the conversational give and take' between viewer and television content (Palmer 1986: 71). Such interaction is encouraged in children's television where the common mode of address is direct, with children continually being invited to engage in a dialogue with presenters and/or characters. Such behaviour occurred at least once in every observation period, often with great frequency due to the abundance of opportunities in programmes such as *Play School*. Both boys and girls interacted in this way but girls were more likely to respond to invitations to 'talk back' to the television, as 4-year-old Louise, watching *Play School* with her mother, does here:

Louise: He's not a duck . . . he's got slippers on his feet. But it's a duck's face. I know what's going to be underneath . . . oh no, it's eggs! But they're geese, not ducks! [To song 'There's Nobody Like You'] Yes there is!

The category of *Performance* describes the 'acting-out, saying or singing of television content simultaneous with its occurrence on television' (Palmer 1986: 72). In the observations, girls were again more likely to engage in such behaviour, especially if singing and dancing were involved, or if familiar songs, stories or poems featured. Frequently, such direct imitation took the form of familiar rituals, such as singing to the opening theme of programmes (for example, 'Here's a house, here's a door . . .'). Here, Louise (4) and Alan (4) demonstrate such behaviour:

Louise mimics hand motion for ducks on *Play School* and copies 'quack, quack'. Counts '1, 2, 3, 4, 5 ducks' along with presenter.

Alan counts '3, 4, 5, 6, 7, 8, 9, 10, 12, 12' to *Sesame Street* count of 1 to 14.

Palmer uses *Comment* to indicate short pronouncements about what is being viewed in the form of asides and critical or amused commentaries. Such interaction is a characteristic of older children and adult viewers and, for the purposes of this study, was subsumed under the more inclusive category of *Performance*.

Discussion describes extended talk which is generated by television content. In this study, it occurred most usually between children and mothers/caregivers explaining something both had seen on television. In the case of the Maori children, efforts were often made to relate the content of television to the children's experiences, with an emphasis on translating English words and concepts into Maori. Television content often provided the foundation for long, quite complex conversations between children and mothers/caregivers, such as in the following example of Joshua (3) and his mother watching *Play School*.

Mother: Do you remember this?
Joshua: No.

Mother:	Do cats have glasses?
Joshua:	No.
Mother:	Which door would you fit through?
Joshua:	Through the yellow one.
Mother:	Who's got a long neck?
Joshua:	A giraffe . . . or a mouse.
Mother:	I think a giraffe is a little bigger than a mouse!
Joshua:	Cats have sharp nails.
Mother:	They're called claws.
Joshua:	Claws!

Joshua and his mother follow *The Hungry Dog* story on *Play School*, reading from their copy of the story in Maori. Mother reads English translation out loud, paralleling television narration.

The most interesting aspect of this conversation is that Joshua is a Pakeha (European) boy, being introduced here, by his mother, to the use of the Maori language in an everyday setting. Maori has equal status to English as one of the two official languages of New Zealand. Such emphases are also part of New Zealand preschool programmes such as *You and Me* and *Chatterbox*, as well as being part of the learning programmes of daycare centres and kindergartens in New Zealand.

A form of *Discussion* is *Self-talk*. This is where children explicitly link television content to their own experiences or world knowledge, using such content to prompt or recall recent or long-term experiences. This occurred most frequently with children who displayed well-developed verbal skills, as in the following example of Cody (3) and his mother:

Cody:	[points to character on TV] She's lovely. Is that my grandma?
Mother:	No, darling. Your grandma is dead.
Cody:	This is rubbish. It makes me laugh.
Mother:	Laughing is good for you.

Another example was Jordan (4) watching a TV commercial for nappies with his mother:

Jordan:	Oh yuck, the mother is kissing the baby's bottom. He'll probably poo in her face!

Monitoring encompasses a range of interactions, with the common element being a switching between attention to the screen, and away from it. It usually involved regular visual and/or audio checks being made of content, indicating at least some minimal level of engagement with stories or events. Such behaviour was more displayed in segmented programmes such as *Sesame Street*, where attention was to some narrative fragments and not to others.

Palmer (1986: 77) describes the activity of *Remake* as:

A small reference or event [derived from television] within an otherwise conventional game or play sequence. At the other extreme, it could describe a long episode in which children attempt deliberately to reconstruct what they remember seeing on TV.

Given the nature of this research, where concurrent forms of interaction were the focus, such 'residual' effects were not usually observed. Such information was primarily gathered from reports provided by parents/caregivers, during entry and exit interviews, or through occasional opportunistic observations, as in the following episode. The stimulus was a *Play School* programme about monsters, using the story *Where the Wild Things Are*. Four children were observed at play some time after the story had finished:

Sally and Raewyn are pretending to be trees whilst Anna and Tane are pretending to be ghosts and 'wild things' gobbling up the other children's feet. Tane hides under a blanket and emerges roaring at Sally. Sally retaliates by pulling his hair. They repeat this several times. Tane then covers the family cat with the blanket and he and Sally poke it through the fabric, attempting to produce a 'wild' response.

Tane: He's a wild thing in the forest!
Sally: I'm a wild buffalo!
Tane: He's a wild thing!

The examples above show that it was possible to isolate and categorize patterns of interaction amongst the children during each observation period. But, as might be expected, most children displayed a variety of such activities while they were watching television – activities which were determined and shaped by the factors already described (e.g. programming, gender, the physical setting). Much less common were extended periods of intent viewing: times of individual, silent attention to television, with children in relaxed postures and showing very little movement.

Such a style of viewing was observed on a number of occasions – most particularly when favourite programmes were screening – but it would be misleading to regard such viewing as the norm for all children on all occasions. Such viewing exhibited no discernible patterns of predictability or frequency amongst this large group of young viewers. Nevertheless, such a style of viewing – the stationary, transfixed and solitary child – informs many dominant models of the child–television relationship, such as the caricatures offered in influential books like Winn's (1977) *The Plug-in Drug*, and much of the public discourse about the 'effects' of television on children.

What Can This Research Tell Us?

All kinds of claims are made daily about the 'effects' of television on children, most usually deleterious effects. Many writings call on 'research evidence' to declare, variously, that watching television makes children fat, strains their eyes, or stops them reading. At best, research gives us half-truths, or generalized approximations of what happens in children's lives, particularly those elements of children's lives which remain elusive and possibly unmeasurable.

Recent criticism of the 'effects tradition', which still remains the dominant paradigm for investigating relationships between children and media use, has pointed to the decontextualizing characteristics of much of this research (see Buckingham 1993). A similar dissatisfaction with the belief that it is possible to take children to laboratories or other public settings, away from the natural sites of television viewing, in order to test for 'effects', determined the different emphasis of this research project. The children remained in as 'natural' an environment as possible and there was little disruption of their normal routines.

Unlike other claims, however, this research does not claim to speak for all children, nor for all experiences. It is research about special television programmes for a special audience: a mixture of locally-made and imported television series specifically constructed for very young viewers. These young viewers live in a small western democracy in the South Pacific and in a culture that is moving towards a sense of nationhood which acknowledges both its British heritage and bicultural origins.

As a result, it may not have much to say about young children elsewhere. But then again it just might, particularly if being a child is more important than culture, as Davies (1995) suggests:

> In terms of identity, being a child is possibly a more important fact about you than what culture you belong to. Development has many cross-cultural characteristics and is a powerful engine for change. I would suggest there is such a thing as a universal culture of childhood which cuts across other cultural differences, and is in many ways a counter-culture.

If one accepts this proposition, then it is possible that a 4-year-old watching *Sesame Street* in New Zealand and an American child watching the same programme share much in common. But what they may not share is a common culture with their older siblings when they reach an age when programming choices become more conscious, or a matter of taste orientations.

Certainly this research is about the relationship between children and television in their earliest or formative years, and has little to say about what an 8-year-old or a 10-year-old might do. As a result it tries to avoid generalizations about 'television and children', framed within totalizing notions of *children*. Indeed, it calls for more vigorous acknowledgment of difference within the general life-stage of *childhood*; and argues instead that 'childhood is not only a life phase but a cultural, economic, and social construction' (Frones 1994: 145) determined by age-stage, cultural background, parenting, social influences, and developmental and personality factors. More simply, every child shares something called 'childhood' but every child's experience of it is in some way unique. This study argues against the idea of the *typical child*, celebrating instead the ideal of plurality.

Despite these cautions, it is still possible to draw some conclusions from this research. To this end, the evidence produced is set against 'a litany of strategies germane to television screening and young children' provided by Eastman in a 1995 article in *Canadian Children*. These 'strategies' are typical of many so-called common-sense ideas which circulate not only in Canadian society but also in New Zealand, and the purpose of placing them here is to interrogate and contest them.

Claim 1: When your child is watching television, watch with him or her ... being proactive affords parents the opportunity to develop television literacy.

This study of New Zealand children suggests that this is already common practice when both parents and children come together to watch television, with positive outcomes in terms of understanding and parent–child relationships. It provides opportunities for both learning and pleasure, with no apparent conflict between the two, with both children and their caregivers benefiting from the regular experience of watching television together. As with other shared experiences, such as reading out loud, television viewing provides opportunities for parents to guide their children through life, expand their understanding of external realities, and to share moments of pleasure and laughter.

Claim 2: Parents should limit the amount of time their preschoolers watch television.

This is both a reasonable assertion and a meaningless one. In respect of very young viewers, the amount and times they watch television is already determined by the schedule or by the constraints of daily routines. Opinions vary greatly on what constitutes an acceptable amount of television viewing and, as this research shows, viewing does not preclude other activities.

Claim 3: Television should not be the sole source of recreational time in a household.

It seldom is, if the behaviour observed in this study is typical of what happens in other New Zealand homes. Preschool programming occupies only a small portion of the daily routines of young New Zealanders and is only one component in their developing understanding of their world. This study also suggests that we should think again about the common practice of commenting negatively ('They let their children watch too much television') on how other people accommodate television in their lives.

Claim 4: Parents should be careful about indiscriminate viewing of news programmes.

Preschoolers, as in this study, are extremely unlikely to be watching nor interested in watching television news. They are usually occupied elsewhere at times such programming screens.

Claim 5: Parents can plan special viewing times with their children.

This already occurs with preschool programming but it is possible – and often desirable – for parents to watch other, non age-specific programming with their young children. Use of the VCR for time-shifting or editing out inappropriate content makes this easier.

Claim 6: Parents can get their preschoolers to think about what they are viewing.

This research indicates that this also occurs with the children demonstrating, through their conversations and actions, a clear correlation between the content of preschool programmes, and cognitive and emotional development. In numerous cases, this was actively assisted through the mediation of adults.

Claim 7: Conversations are much more effective than lectures with young children.

Conversation is the usual mode of address in preschool programming, with presenters talking directly to children in a simulation of face-to-face conversation. In addition, understanding increases if such conversations are related to events in children's lives, through appeals to memory and through analogy.

Claim 8: Parents should be cognizant of the TV being left on for background noise . . . the avoidance of television as a babysitter.

Eastman argues that 'allowing the TV to be on constantly sets a pattern of TV dependence', but this study argues there is no real evidence to back this assertion. In many cases, the television did provide 'background noise' but only as one noise-maker in the chaos that is children's play. It provided no more distraction than a radio might. In addition, it is fair to argue that preschool programming can effectively serve as a safe 'baby-sitter', with mothers/caregivers feeling confident about leaving their children watching while they attended to other pressing tasks. Such opportunities are often needed when there are children of differing ages in the household.

Claim 9: Talk with your child about what is real and not real on television.

As anyone versed in media theory will know, the idea of the 'real' on television is a problem rather than a given. Nevertheless, parents must constantly remind themselves that children's 'reality' is still rudimentary and embryonic, and mistakes will always be made. In this study, such 'misreadings' were often corrected through the mediation of parents.

Claim 10: Parents need to create a setting where their children feel safe.

On the evidence of this study, current preschool programming on New Zealand television provides such a place. For this reason it must remain and continue to be funded and produced, providing a special kind of programming for a special audience at a special time of their life. It is up to readers in other parts of the world to decide whether the experiences of young New Zealanders speak to the experiences of young children in other places. Nevertheless, television programmes for very young viewers can achieve a global goal, to paraphrase British media educator Cary Bazalgette, by providing 'a way of giving them high expectations of television, of all media, and of themselves' (1991: 58).

References

ALBRIGHT, A. R. (1994) 'Effects of television viewing in early childhood on the moral development of children', paper to the International Communication Association Conference, Sydney, Australia, July.

BAZALGETTE, C. (1991) *Media Education*, London: Hodder & Stoughton.

BUCKINGHAM, D. (1993) *Children Talking Television: The Making of Television Literacy*, London: Falmer Press.

CHOAT, E. (1988) 'Children, television and learning in nursery and infants' schools', *Educational Studies*, **14**(1): 9–21.

CLANCEY, M. (1994) 'The television audience examined', special insert, *Journal of Advertising Research*, **34**(4) July/August.

COLLINS, P. A. (1991) 'The impact of television on preschoolers' perseverance, impulsivity and restlessness', paper presented at the biennial meeting of the Society for Research in Child Development, Seattle, WA, April.

CUPIT, C. G. (1987) *The Child Audience: A Guide to the Developing Child for Television Writers and Producers*, Canberra: Australian Broadcasting Tribunal.

DAVIES, M. M. (1995) 'The role of education and media literacy' joint session, World Summit on Television and Children, Melbourne, 12–17 March, taped address.

EASTMAN, W. (1995) 'Crisis, what crisis? Making television work for young children', Canadian Children, **20**(2) Fall: 41–44.

FITCH, A., HUSTON, A. C. and WRIGHT, J. C. (1993) 'From television forms to genre schemata: Children's perceptions of television reality', in G. L. BERRY, and J. K. ASAMEN (eds) *Children and Television: Images in a Changing Sociocultural World*, Newbury Park, CA: Sage.

FRONES, I. (1994) 'Dimensions of childhood', in J. QVORTRUP, M. BARDY, G. SGRITTA, and H. WINTERSBERGER (eds) *Childhood Matters: Social Theory, Practice and Politics*, Aldershot: Avebury.

GREENBLAT, E. and GLEZER, H. (1993) 'Reading with children and television viewing in the first five years', *Family Matters* (Australian Institute of Family Studies) no. 36, December: 16–18.

KODAIRA, S. (1990) *The Development of Programmes for Young People in Japan: A Report for NHK*: Tokyo, NHK [Japanese Broadcasting Company].

LEALAND, G. (1995) *Television and New Zealand Preschoolers: A Longitudinal Study*, Hamilton, NZ: Department of Film and Television Studies, University of Waikato.

LIEBES, T. and KATZ, E. (1990) *The Export of Meaning: Cross-Cultural Readings of Dallas*, Oxford: Oxford University Press.

MELTZOFF, A. N. (1988) 'Imitation of televised models by infants', *Child Development*, **15**: 1221–29.

MORLEY, D. (1986) *Family Television: Cultural Power and Domestic Leisure*, London: Comedia.

NEW ZEALAND ON AIR (NZOA) (1996) *Statement of Intent 1996/7*, Wellington: NZOA.

PALMER, P. (1986) *The Lively Audience: A Study of Children Around the TV Set*, Sydney: Allen and Unwin.

PLOMIN, R., CORLEY, R., DeFRIES, J. C. and FULKER, D. W. (1990) 'Individual differences in television viewing in early childhood: Nature as well as nurture', *Psychological Science*, **1**(6) November: 371–77.

WELLHOUSEN, K. (1994) 'Assessment of early childhood social development', *Dimensions of Early Childhood*, **23**(1) Fall: 32–35.

WINN, M. (1977) *The Plug-in Drug: Television, Children and the Family*, New York: Viking.

ZWAGA, W. E. R. (1992) *Families in Front of the Screen: Everyday Contexts of Television Use*, DPhil thesis, Massey University: Palmerston North, New Zealand.

Chapter Two

Teaching the Nintendo generation?
Children, computer culture and
popular technologies

Bill Green, Jo-Anne Reid and Chris Bigum

We've got to talk about the next generation. The Nintendo generation.
Rupert Murdoch[1]

There are no aliens yet but there will be.
Natalie (age 5)

Two hundred years ago, children were not expected to live very long, and so much childhood education in the affluent middle-class home concentrated on teaching them to endure pain and prepare for early death (Musgrave 1966). As we enter the twenty-first century, things have not changed very much for most of the children in the world. Affluent children, however, are expected to live long and almost pain-free lives, and their home education therefore concentrates on teaching them about ways to fill their time. Yet in many living rooms, playrooms and bedrooms around Australia, these children today are still experiencing early death. They are losing their lives and dying over and over again – not in reality, of course, and not with any physical pain to endure. Rather, these are electronic deaths, occurring vicari-ously, on the screens of their Nintendo machines.

As the children of the wealthy (white) First World become increasingly afflu-ent, the emergence of a mass-market computer and video game culture is a marked and increasingly significant feature of contemporary everyday life. So significant, that reference is often made to 'aliens', 'New Kids' and 'the Nintendo generation' to describe and evoke a new generation of children. This, of course, has important implications and challenges for educational theory and practice, some of which we want to address in this chapter. What does such a shift portend for the construction of childhood, and relatedly, for its associated institutional practices, such as state-sponsored, compulsory primary schooling?

In this chapter we seek to do two things. First, we undertake an analysis of the very notion of a distinctive new Nintendo generation of children by way of a critical reading of a selection of recent academic and popular texts in the area. Second, we initiate a series of introductory investigations, on and among school-aged children, in specific relation to computer and video games. These were undertaken in the spirit of a reconnaissance study, partly to explore the extent to which such children might appropriately be seen, and see themselves, as different and distinctive, in ways consistent with this rhetoric of the so-called Nintendo generation and what the implications might be, accordingly, for teachers, teacher educators and educational researchers.

The Children's Machine?

In the preface to his book, suggestively entitled *The Children's Machine: Rethinking School in the Age of the Computer*, Seymour Papert (1993) writes optimistically of 'the potential synergy of two trends in the world' – indeed, two revolutions as he sees it; one is technological in nature while the other is epistemological. He links both of these revolutions to children and hence to young people more generally who are, from his perspective, one of the classically disenfranchised groups in society. As he writes:

> Across the world children have entered a passionate and enduring love affair with the computer. What they do with computers is as varied as their activities. The greatest amount of time is devoted to playing games, with the result that names like Nintendo have become household words. They use computers to write, to draw, to communicate, to obtain information. Some use computers as a means to establish social ties, while others use them to isolate themselves. In many cases their zeal has such force that it brings the word *addiction* to the minds of concerned parents.
>
> (Papert 1993: ix)

As he notes, this is more than simply a matter of doing things with computers, or of exercising a particular form of mastery. There are real stakes to do with ownership and identity at issue here: the identification of a generation with new technologies, as an intrinsic element in their constitution and their destinies.

> Large numbers of children see the computer as 'theirs' – as something that belongs to them, to their generation. Many have observed that they are more comfortable with the machines than their parents and teachers are. They learn to use them more easily and naturally. For the moment some of us old fogeys may somehow have acquired the special knowledge that makes one a master of the computer but children know that it is just a matter of time before they inherit the machines. They are the computer generation.
>
> (Papert 1993: x)

And he concludes in this fashion: 'What lies behind the love affair? Where is it going? Can it be guided by the older generation into forms constructive or destructive? Or is its evolution already out of our hands?'

This is fast becoming a matter of public debate and a perceived social problem – indeed, the kind of moral panic increasingly endemic to mass-mediated societies (MacRobbie and Thornton 1996). In Australia, as elsewhere, there has been a spate of articles in newspapers and other media outlets, increasingly addressed to the problem of what is variously described as 'the lost generation' and 'techno-kids', along with teenage suicide and video culture. Among the issues that cause serious anxiety are what Turkle (1984: 20) calls the 'holding power' of video games, their fascination and their ambivalence:

> Video games are a window onto a new kind of intimacy with machines that is characteristic of the nascent computer culture. The special relationship that players form with video games has elements that are common to interactions with other kinds of computers. The holding power of video games, their almost hypnotic fascination, is computer holding power.
>
> (Turkle 1984: 66; see also Turkle 1996: 66–73)

The question is this: What are the implications of such developments and scenarios for educators and teachers and all those who work with the young, in the context of a burgeoning media culture? In Turkle's words, computers and computer games 'have already become *a part of how a new generation is growing up*' (our emphasis). She continues thus:

> For adults and for children who play computer games, who use the computer for manipulating words, information, visual images, and especially for those who learn to program, computers enter into the development of personality, of identity, and even of sexuality.
>
> (Turkle 1984: 15)

What then might it mean to be teaching (in) media culture today and tomorrow, and to be living and learning, and growing up, in a social context increasingly characterized by profound technocultural transformations and a new social order significantly organized around information and the image? More specifically, what is the significance of video-computer games and what we shall describe here as Nintendo culture, in relation to education and primary schooling and, more generally, children's experience and the discourse of childhood?

Talking about the Nintendo Generation

A key problem in initiating and prosecuting this sort of investigation is understanding just what is at issue in the very formulation we are working with here: 'the

Nintendo generation'. Part of the problem lies in the increasingly evident trend for journalism, popular debate and academic research and scholarship to be almost indistinguishable in this regard, as indeed they are in other aspects of cultural studies. Certainly the boundaries between them have become blurred. Hence a media baron-cum-self-styled technocultural visionary such as Rupert Murdoch can use the phrase, quite comfortably and even convincingly, in pointing to the need to take account of emerging synergies among cultural formations and practices, new technological initiatives, and emerging populations and markets.

For McKenzie Wark, an important scholar in the area of new forms of techno-logical practice and change and also a regular commentator on popular cultural and media issues in newspapers and magazines, 'there is indeed already a "Nintendo generation"', one 'which grew up following the development curve from Atari's crude games' of two decades ago 'to the latest CD-based systems' (Wark 1994: 22). For Sheff (1993: 7), 'the signs of the first Nintendo generation appeared as early as 1989 and 1990'. He writes of American culture in this relatively early period: 'Kids already spent more time in electronic environments (TV, radio, records) than they did in school or talking with friends or parents. Some of them spent an additional two hours a day on Nintendo'. Moreover, even when they weren't actually game-playing, 'they were being showered with the culture of Nintendo' (Sheff 1993: 7) in various intertextual, mixed-media forms. In particular, the move-ment from the arcade to the home as the principal site for game-playing, both representing and inaugurating new intensities in popular media-cultural practice, is a significant factor here, enabling different constituencies to enter into the 'game' – younger children, girls, and so on. Importantly, this is little more than a decade ago now, coincident with the emergence and subsequent consolidation of Nintendo as an industry trendsetter and pacemaker.

For Kinder (1991), what needs to be properly appreciated is that electronic games of the kind in question here, understood in the context of media culture and the digital–electronic apparatus more generally, are likely to have a decisive and particular significance for children's identity formation. Arguing that 'the wide-spread introduction of television into the home since the 1950s has affected the process of subject formation' (Kinder 1991: 36), she asks, apropos of her own child's early immersion in media culture, about 'the impact of seeing an imaginary world so full of rich visual signifiers before having encountered their referents or acquired verbal language' (Kinder 1991: 35). Such arguments and observations are immensely suggestive. They point to the likelihood of a major transformation underway in the Symbolic Order, and hence in the processes and problematics of subjectivity and textuality – hence, the significance of video games; as Wark (1994: 22) writes, 'the first digital technology socialising a generation on a mass scale, world-wide – the vast majority of game players are aged 12–17'.

In our own work, we have explored this broad area of hypothesis and specu-lation with specific reference to the concept of postmodern subjectivity. Our concern has been with 'the emergence of what we are calling the postmodern student–subject', that is, seeking to understand 'contemporary school populations within the terms of reference of conceptualising youth as the exemplary subject of postmodernism' (Green and Bigum 1993: 119). Drawing from the work of Katherine Hayles (1990) and others, we have postulated, as she does, that there is a profound difference (and even a disjunction) between those who *theorize* and otherwise seek to understand postmodernism and those who 'simply' *live* it. As she put it (in 1990!), the age of 16 might well be seen as the cut-off point here. Pointed and urgent questions can be asked, however, about 6-year-olds – those born in the 1990s and now entering school for the first time. These are children, by and large, thoroughly immersed in the flow of electronic images and the play of popular image-technologies. Technoculture is effectively naturalized for such children of the Second Media Age (Poster 1995); it is simply part of, and inextricable from, their lifeworld more generally – both a context and a resource for their living and their learning, their being and their becoming. Hence:

> The generation of kids in classrooms today have grown up in a semiotic and intertextual universe of endless media and commodity symbolism, of contradictory and mixed messages. Their universe is substantially differ-ent in kind from that accompanied by the print and media narratives with which the last 'modern' generation of the 1950s and 1960s grew up.
>
> (Luke and Roe 1993: 118)

Among other things, what this suggests is that the relationship between teachers and students, adults and children, needs to be carefully rethought in terms of the changing mediascapes and information dynamics of the postmodern world. As Kinder indicates, stressing the importance of transmedia intertextuality and its impact on children's identity formation, postmodern subjectivity is now inextricable from the logics and politics of new regimes of consumption, commodification and technological development:

> This process of reproducing the postmodernist subject and its dynamic of commercial empowerment is now being intensified and accelerated in home video games, in commercial transmedia supersystems . . . and in multi-national corporate mergers.
>
> (Kinder 1991: 38)

Audiences, Markets, Constituencies

A distinctive 'Nintendo generation' must be understood as both an *audience* of a particular kind and a *market*. Notwithstanding the fact that the cultural–industrial phenomenon of video games is larger than that associated with Nintendo as a specific corporate player, the term seems to have caught on, no doubt in due acknowledgment of Nintendo's extraordinary success in the trade to date. For our purposes here, we employ it deliberately and with a certain calculated sense of irony. In the first instance, it is not incidental that Nintendo is a brand name, a marketing label, and thus to refer to a generation of young people in tandem with Nintendo is a register of the power of advertising in popular culture, as well as evoking the corporate contexts in and through which such a formulation comes into common usage. It is important to take account of the fact that the video and computer games phenomenon represents Big Business, and is not simply a matter of children's culture.[2] Rather, it is a social construction with decisive and definite economic implications and consequences.

Viewing children as 'audiences' and 'markets' is not enough, however; or rather, it may well be necessary but not sufficient. In the case of video-computer gaming, to work at all with the notion of 'audience' is clearly problematic unless it is carefully redefined. What needs also to be considered is the proposition that children might well be usefully regarded in terms of *constituency* – as an ensemble of constituencies. There are two aspects to highlight here. One is that any notion of a distinctive Nintendo generation must take account of the fact that the children are also the constituency of (primary) schooling. As such, they are subjected to the communicational regimes and discursive practices of the school as well as to media and popular culture (although arguably the balance is shifting steadily and inexorably from the former to the latter). The second aspect postulates children as, at least potentially, a political constituency (Said 1983), in the sense that they represent a social presence in the world and one which might well be capable of generating a significant sense of agency in their own right and in their own interests. Children, and young people generally, are increasingly visible and active in economic and cultural contexts and new technocultural resources and practices may well have generational implications for politics as well.

Wark (1994), in proposing that a Nintendo generation already exists, points to the 'extraordinary semiotic skills of young game-players', and suggests that 'such competencies and their associated mindsets contribute towards a distinctive "culture"'. 'Culture' here is to be understood partly in the anthropological sense of a whole way of life, a way of being in the world, of living in accordance with a certain structure of feeling and valuing and partly in the more (post)structuralist sense of a complex, dynamic field of subjectivity, embracing specific forms of identity and agency, and therefore specific assemblages of skills and capacities, knowledges, and attitudes or dispositions. Importantly, in this instance, it involves the construction of *body-subjects* – reference is made constantly to matters such as hand–eye coordination, as well as to the physical concentration of players hunched over consoles or poised in front of monitors, acting at a distance with their attention simultaneously addressed to, and split between, hand-held control and the screen. It is, of course, a particular form of embodied subjectivity that is at issue here, a matter of game-players being and becoming *abstracted* body-subjects, congruent with new practices, formations and intersections of culture and economy, in a social world increasingly realized in and through images and information vectors.

What is immediately striking about the formulation 'the Nintendo generation', then, is its seemingly effortless yoking together of young people and a particular computer technology. Moreover, it is a particular orientation to computing – not work, but play; not education, but entertainment; not information so much as experience and pleasure. What is involved here is a new view of and orientation to *learning* (including computer learning). This view is one which puts the stress firmly and clearly on pleasure and activity, on having fun and overcoming or bypassing boredom. It sees entertainment and the education of desire as paramount considerations in developing and maintaining a constituency, subjected to a new holding power that extends into the larger worlds of work, play and learning more generally.

A Generation Facing Early Death?

Jamie let his body slump in an expression of despair. If Kevin and Ronnie were playing *Mortal Kombat*, they'd be at it all afternoon. Mom thought that when you died it was like the power went off or something, like it was something real, but on the video you could die over and over again, as many times as you wanted. It was so frustrating! There was so much parents didn't understand! They should make them take a test or something.

(Dibdin 1995: 4)

For the purposes of this study, three small investigations were carried out over 1995–96. In 1995, audiotape recordings were made of two brothers, Jack and Andreas (aged 12 and 9 respectively) talking about Nintendo at home, on separate weekends, when each had a friend to stay. Andreas's friend, Zach, did not own or play Nintendo at home, although he had played many times at the Smith's house. Jack's friend, Louis, had a Nintendo set at home and was a more experienced player than Jack, even though the boys acquired their games at the same time. In each case, the children were interviewed about their interests and opinions about playing Nintendo. The first interview was conducted in the living room, with the younger boys (Andreas and Zach) answering questions in turn. As the following extract illustrates, there was a stiffness and distance in the boys' talk about their computer game-playing, and about their social interactions related to Nintendo:

Interviewer:	How do you hear about new games?
Andreas:	Ads and kids talking about them at school.
Interviewer:	Who are the friends that talk about them to you?
Andreas:	Lance and Harry.
Interviewer:	And do you talk about them with Lance and Harry often at school? Anybody else?
Andreas:	No, only us.
Interviewer:	Not many other people have Nintendo?
Andreas:	No.

Such an interview, if taken on face value, might indicate that there may well be a mismatch of perceptions of the prevalence and nature of a Nintendo generation. A situation where Lance, Harry and Andreas are the only three children in their age cohort of a large, affluent, sea-side primary school, differs markedly from the literature suggesting the growing prevalence of hordes of children fixed to television screens, frantically pressing buttons A, B, X and Y to the plastic rhythm of the Nintendo soundtrack. It might also bring into question recent large studies, like that conducted by the British Film Institute and the British Library, which claimed that the 'increasing sophistication of domestic entertainment technology and its effects on the cognitive development of the child user, need to be reconsidered' (Whittaker 1995: 35).

Interviewing these Australian children, admittedly in the limited circumstances of our study, provided no evidence of especially sophisticated cognition. Yet even a casual observation of the rich language use surrounding the boys when they were actually operating the Nintendo set, indicated to us that this sort of 'interview about Nintendo' was inadequate to our purposes. Clearly we would need to find a different sort of methodological approach for our investigation of how this new generation of children see themselves as users of electronic game technology.

For these reasons, a different approach to this preliminary investigation was undertaken in the first part of 1996. Three 'snap-shots' of children's interaction with electronic games were planned. First, we recorded the boys at play. Second, we used a children's picture book about a Nintendo-type game (Rodda 1994) with a Grade One class, as the basis for a discussion about the children's own feelings and experiences playing electronic games at home. Finally, we asked a group of newly-graduated teachers to investigate the place of electronic games in relation to other leisure activities, particularly reading, in the lives of the children they were teaching. These are reported in the following sections.

Playing Nintendo

Instead of being interviewed, Jack and Louis were asked if they would mind being taped while they were actually playing a game and they eagerly took up this offer. Immediately, however, they began to draw upon the form of the earlier interview, conscious of the tape-recorder and assuming not-very-fixed American accents. The transcript which follows represents only 10 minutes of the game *Super Ghouls and Ghosts*, and may serve to put at rest the minds of many who fear the ill-effects of Nintendo on the educational progress and literacy development of their children. The boys demonstrate their ability to distance themselves from the game while enjoying its pleasures. Their conversation also demonstrates that the literacy demands of proficient Nintendo playing are considerable. As this conversation begins, the boys are alone in the living room of Jack's home, seated together on the floor in front of the television screen. Jack has the Nintendo controls, and Louis sits beside him with the microphone attached to the arm of a nearby chair. As Sefton-Green (1995: 33) says, 'computer games do not exist as texts in the same way as other media forms do (assuming we discount their coded or disc-based forms), but only come into existence when played.'

The text transcribed below is of continuous verbal production, with no omissions or breaks in the boys' talk. However we have broken this transcription into chunks for our analysis:

Louis: What is the game play about? What are you actually doing here?

Jack: Well, you're . . . what you do is you go around shooting zombies with weapons like daggers, arrows . . .

Louis: Like medieval-time weapons?

Jack: Yes.

Louis: Yeah, OK – What is your favourite level that you have encountered?

Jack: My favourite level has to be the first level . . .

Louis: The first level . . . Easy?

Jack: Yes, it's fairly easy.

Louis: Now, do you like playing the game normally, or do you like having it with codes inputted?

Jack: I like playing it with . . . both.

Louis: Oh, OK . . . What kind of codes would you put in for the action replay, which we have at this moment, Da Dah!!!!

Jack: I would, I would put . . . 'continuous jumping', which means you can just jump, and jump, and just keep jumping . . .

Louis: . . . and jump, and jump, and jump, and jump . . . What else? Infinite energy. Is that a code?

Jack: I'd make it immune. I'd make myself immune to my enemies. That means no enemies could rip me.

Louis: Oh, that's all right. I like how that goes.

As this first minute or so unfolds, the progress of the game is represented in their talk. What is noteworthy here is the nature and even the quality of their engagement, which is at least inconsistent with the all-too-common assumptions of deficiency or deviance in this regard:

it is often assumed in popular descriptions of game-playing that a facile process of identification occurs. It is this assumption which underlies many of the pathological descriptions of fixated 'video kids'. . . . given that one appears to play many games in the first person and that one is 'rewarded' by maintaining the 'life' of this character, it is all too easy to assume an identification between player and role, but characters in computer games are rarely complicated personae.

(Sefton-Green 1995: 34)

Certainly in the conversation between the two 12-year-olds, there is a clear sense that they understand they are playing a role in the game, and are clearly able to separate reference to themselves and their characters, whom they can control:

Jack: Like, how about . . . I wish I was Knight Arthur. Could you please explain who Knight Arthur is?

Louis: He is the character you play in this story. I wish I could be Knight Arthur with my little pro-action replay plugged in . . . and then I would turn on, I'd turn on the action again. I'd put in, let's see, 70027602 in the code importer, and you would get, you'd be immune to enemy attacks if . . . I can walk around it going through flames and lava and big demons like hydras and things.

They are also aware of the textual conventions of the characters they play, and of their 'enemies' and other characters in the game. 'Big cruel homicidal maniacs', for instance, are '20 times bigger than you are', comparatively, when you are in the role of the game character. Drawing both on their knowledge of other games and of the medieval setting of this particular game, the boys are able to make sense of the 'story' of the game as they play:

Louis: Which is the most wicked boss that you've had?

Jack: Um, that would have to be, oh, what was that? That would be . . .

Louis: Zardus, the fiend Zardus.

Jack: Yes, that is correct.

Louis: I'll just tell you about Zardus for a minute, then.

Jack: Good idea.

Louis: Well, he's captured you a girl. I don't know whether she's a princess. I'm not really sure about that. He's captured you a girl so you have to go through eight, no seven, seven levels of perplexing mazes and things like werewolves and zombies and big cruel homicidal maniacs and big zombies and all that facing a big . . . at the end normally consisting of the eighth level. But being Zardus, what he does, he's huge. He's about 20 times bigger that you are. Huge, he is absolutely big. He is so big that, let's see, um, three storeys. No, round two and a half storeys.

Louis's ability to make sense of, or read, the game here is demonstrated in his description of the role of the girl. She has been captured for you, the player, to provide a reason for playing. She is not important as a girl, and certainly not as an individual – the player is 'only playing' that this is a real quest for something that is desired by the player. The real desire, and the aim, is simply to engage with the game play and defeat the enemies. For the boys, in fact, the princess-trophy seems to be just an interruption in the process of self-congratulation for having finished the game:

Louis: While you are standing on the things you shoot an array of lasers out of his normal mouth, the mouth that's on his face. You actually hit his head with the power bracelet. That is how you kill Zardus. Then you go on and your little maiden, your little princess, comes down the bubble, then you ride home on a horse and then you see all the names of the bad guys. I'll tell you about the bosses and the levels in order. First – Level 1. You start up the thing with zombies.

For these boys, at least, seeing 'the names of all the bad guys' is the culmination of the game-play, not the release of the princess-maiden, nor even the 'ride home on a horse'.

Also evident from this transcript is the way in which the boys interchange between text and non-text information on the screen and on printed pages, as they manipulate the objects and codes of the game to increase or decrease their powers and enhance the pleasures they can obtain from the play:

Louis: You need some page flicking, you go through the handbook looking for the thing. What code are you putting in right now, Jack?
Jack: 'Immune to enemy attacks'.
Louis: Immune to enemy attacks. The first one. That's the third code in the book but the first one he's putting in. As I told you before, the code is 70027602. Normally all the codes in the action replay, they all start off with 70 'cos that is the most popular starting.

As the pace of the game accelerates here, interrupting his explanation, Louis's commentary continues thus:

Louis: Now, if we listen to this closely, Jack will keep repeatedly jumping. He's jumping a terrible jump here. Come on! A turbo-jump! There he is shooting. He's got the bow and arrow, the cross-bow, shooting a zombie here carrying a pipe. He's getting a bonus, but *not* getting the bonus. Very bad. Not getting the bonus. Got two lives. And the werewolf. I forgot . . . Shoot it! He's entering the fire demon cave. Shoots that very easy. This is the first part of the level I was telling you. The second part consists of weeds and flaming skull carts and a treasure chest, a secret treasure chest there. And the third part is of a boss. I'm not going to tell you what it is yet so ha, ha, ha. Hmmm. There's another treasure chest up the top there. Going up a ladder there's a werewolf, he's gonna shoot it. There's something very bad about the arrow weapon. When you fire with code armour . . . Could we please have that power up there? Listen to it. Hear that. That noise was the power being used.

At this point, he noticeably shifts key. His commentary ceases, and he moves into a more reflective mood, even though Jack continues to play, moving forward through the game. Louis takes time out to make explicit verbal sense of a problem that Jack's ongoing play has begun to solve for him as he watches:

Louis: There's something bad about the arrows. He's using double jump now. There's something bad about them. What is that cross-bow fires three arrows of fireball at fire? You just fire one which sends three balls across the screen. You cannot fire another bullet until all the trace of the other bullet from the last turn is . . . it's not there . . . it disappears. So you've got to wait until all the things, oh, what do you call them? All the fire balls and the shot of your last fire disappeared before he can fire again.

What is intriguing in this commentary is the engagement of the 'non-active' player in overt reflection about the game-play. It is through practice and in company that Louis is able to further his understanding of the game. At this point, both boys are now well-positioned to develop a meta-knowledge of the programming principle of this particular game. In this way, they are actively involved in computer learning, at home, in a way very different from their learning in school.

Reading A Book about Nintendo with Grade 1

How do young school children see and understand the presence of electronic games and computer technology in their homes? In order to obtain a perspective on this question, we moved out of the home situation to a class of Grade 1 children (aged between 5 and 6) in a large sea-side primary school. Anxious not to find ourselves facing a similar inability to distance and reflect on their practices around the technology, as had characterized our interviews with the 9-year-olds, we chose to work from a representation of a Nintendo-type game in the home, in the children's picture book *Power and Glory* by Emily Rodda (1994). The book reading was selected as a familiar and comfortable classroom experience for the children. It was hoped that the story of a young child's frustration at being constantly interrupted by the repetitive and mundane real life demands of his family as he moves through the heightening levels of danger and excitement of his computer game would provoke discussion about the children's own Nintendo experience.

The children and their teacher sat together on the mat area of the classroom where one of the research team recorded the discussion that occurred around a shared reading of the picture book. Some of the children's families, it transpired from incidental talk, have two or three computers around the house, while others have none at all. As we had found for Andreas and his friends, though, the social networks around Nintendo and electronic entertainment were narrowly defined:

Researcher:	How come not many girls play *Doom*? Do girls play *Doom*? No. It looks to me as if there are some games that girls play and there are some games that boys play. Do you think that's true? Have a think to yourself. Do you think that there are any games that both boys and girls like to play?
Thomas:	My favourite game is . . . if I'm shooting all the robots with all different weapons and . . . the reactor and when you blow the reactor up, you have to end it and get out of it. And, there's shields. They help you . . . you're gone . . . First, if the robot shoots you, it can't . . . the shield . . . then smart missiles. When you shoot the smart missiles, lots of swords come out.
Researcher:	Do they? What's that game called?
Thomas:	*Defence.*
Researcher:	*Defence.* Who else has got *Defence*? [counts] Quite a few people have got that game. Do you talk to your friends about all the games you play? And how you've nearly played them all? What do you talk about? . . . What's your name? Madeline! What do you talk about?
Madeline:	I've got – I've got lots of games . . . Sometimes I collect Barbies.
Researcher:	I didn't know Barbie dolls were on computer games . . . Or do you mean the dolls? You talk about your dolls? There might be quite a few other games that you little girls play? Do little boys play Barbies?
Students:	Yuk/No way!/*Doom*! *Doom*!
Stephen:	My uncle's got one. We got this game . . . you've got a knife and you've got to try and stab . . . to get your gun back.
Researcher:	So you've got to earn your weapons back all the time? That sounds pretty violent to me. Doesn't it sound violent to you?
Students:	No. No.
Teacher:	Can I ask you something? Are there any games that are not killing people or shooting people? Don't forget those listening rules. Roxanne, you put your hand up.
Roxanne:	I like the *Safari* game where you go into the jungle.
Teacher:	. . . and what happens then?
Roxanne:	When you press this little . . .
Teacher:	What do the animals do? Do they just come out and have a look at you?
Roxanne:	Yes, yes, they just stop and stand still. You can have a rattlesnake.

It is clear that the teacher is keen to shift the focus of this discussion away from the unacceptable violence of killing and shooting people. These are not safe topics for a Grade 1 classroom. Little children in school need to be steered towards more wholesome fare if the explicit work of the curriculum is to be done. Yet there can be little real hope that the sanitized *Safari*, where wild animals just 'stop and stand still', and where there is no potential for the thrilling fear of an unexpected early death by rhinoceros or rattlesnake, can have any of the impact on its players that the visceral excitement that *Doom* creates. The teacher, quite understandably, is not confident to take the risk of following the researcher's track here – if the children (the boys here) really do not see these games as violent, then they are indeed quite alien, and beyond her ken. She has no resources to deal with this power, which, if released, may well threaten her security as a teacher of the older generation, with many years' experience, and a firm belief in her own knowledge of children and child behaviour.

Reflecting with New Teachers about Nintendo

If the older generation of teachers is understandably threatened by the dangerous difference we see in our 'game children', what about the new generation of teachers? Our third investigation was designed to include this group in its wider context, with specific focus on teacher education. Twenty-eight graduate teachers were all taking a Children's Literature elective unit towards the completion of a double degree in Arts/Education. They were asked to conduct a small study in the primary school classrooms to which they were attached, by comparing the amounts of time children spend engaging with electronic media (television, video, Nintendo/Sega systems, computer games) and engaging with print media (books, magazines, newspapers, comics). All had completed their initial teacher training for registration, and were already working part-time as classroom teachers while they finished their final year. Few own or regularly play computer games – Sega or Nintendo – although all are aware of their growing popularity among children.

Dale Spender writes that she is 'constantly shocked at the level of ferocity and hostility that surfaces among some teachers when the introduction of computers is discussed'. She continues thus:

> Future generations of teachers will need no convincing of the new world that electronic information opens up. Perhaps we will just have to wait until they take up their positions. We cannot rely on all of today's teachers (in schools or colleges) making the necessary transition. There is much powerful and painful resistance within the profession.
>
> (Spender 1995: 114)

Our findings show that this resistance is likely to be evident, interestingly enough, even among the current batch of student-teachers, already more or less successfully socialized into the culture of teaching (and print). This is indicated in comments such as the following, from a final-year graduate student, responding to Marsha Kinder's (1991) account of children and Nintendo:

Firstly this article was based in America and although children will be children, I still believe that Australian children aren't the same as American. I believe using computer and games on the computer are educational to an extent. But Gameboy and Nintendos are evil. They kill – and all the children do is compete with everyone or brag to say, I've got 'x' and you don't.

(FM 1996)

Whittaker similarly notes that teachers are often reluctant or unable to engage with these aspects of children's popular culture and experience:

Teachers' ignorance of the capabilities of the technology leads to an inability to solve basic problems and the promotion of too narrow a range of applications, such as machines being used more as typewriters than as word processors . . . The pedagogical strategy of using pupil consultants in IT goes awry when teachers cannot assess their knowledge and capabilities.

(Whittaker 1995: 36)

That people only a decade older than the so-called Nintendo generation (and with similar interest and involvement in cultural matters such as *The X Files*) speak with the same sort of disquiet and concern about this new phenomenon as their parents, indicates the rapidity with which the Nintendo generation has become different and therefore perceived as problematic. Also, in response to Kinder (1991), a 21-year-old graduate teacher raised the following questions in her journal reflections:

The preps [in my class] also discuss the computer games they have played, what level they got up to and what score they got. Everyone in the class except for three children had a computer at home and I was surprised to find out that the girls played on the computer just as much as the boys.

(CT 1996)

Broad and common access to computer games was found among the whole age range of primary school children, where the teacher of one Grade 6 class, for instance, said that there were only four children in her class of 20 who did not own or play computer games. These were a boy and three girls. The most popular games among this class of children were divided on gender lines, with *Aladdin* and *The Lion King* most popular among the girls, and *Super Mario* and *Donkey Kong* among the boys. While one or two of these 10 to 11-year-old boys mentioned enjoying games such as *Mortal Kombat* and *Streetfighter* ('because they've got good graphics'), one girl preferred *Moldy Mouse* 'because I just love what he dose (burps, farts, throughts snot) [*sic*].' This teacher found that both her male and female pupils mainly reported talking to their fathers about computers.

In another class of 9 to 10-year-olds, though, several children, boys and girls, reported that they talk to their mothers about computer games and Nintendo. 'I ask her how to get out of things,' one 9-year-old girl said. One boy said that he often talks to his mother about 'how hard [the games] are, so I tell Mum to see if she can do it'. Their teacher also reflected on her reading of Kinder (1991) thus:

The interesting topics this article raises for me are:

- the lack of female images/role models in the computer games available;
- would girls be more tempted, or likely to play these games if there were more female 'characters'?
- why haven't the big companies tried to tap into the possible female market by making female-centred games?

Her professional resolution was as follows:

- encourage girls to get involved with, and play computer games, if they have access to them;
- gain a background knowledge of the games that my students will be playing, so that I don't seem so 'out of touch' with their world;
- encourage parents to play with their children, if they don't already, as a means of shared play.

(CT 1996)

– something which seems relevant to teachers generally.

While admitting that her own aversion to many computer and video games may well be due to her unfamiliarity with this form of entertainment ('I did not grow up with computer games'), another teacher wrote:

My father lives with his partner who has four sons. Two of the sons are what I call 'Computer Holics'. When their mother was out, and my father, they could be found calling Sierra in California to assist them in the next stage of a computer game. Needless to say the phone bill was gigantic! As well as this, the teachers at high school found it difficult to get homework out of the boys.

While teaching at a primary school in Melbourne for a one-week round (placed at [a western suburbs school]), many children came to school with Game Boys that they would constantly play in and out of the class. Teachers had given up, and one commented that 'at least they're not disturbing the remainder of the class'!

(CO 1996)

Another commented on what she saw as the isolating effects of game-playing, but went on to imagine possible ways in which the children's computer game culture could be built on in the classroom:

Socialisation skills? Almost every time I have watched children play video games, there is little conversation that takes place – one child plays, the other watches in silence so as not to ruin the concentration of the other. However it is terrific to see children discuss their strategies and use their language skills to find solutions – reading through tip books, instructions, magazines – interpreting the information and relaying this to the other player/s. Children should be encouraged to share their interests with others – peers, parents, teachers.

Teachers can draw on children's experience with video games, as with any other game (i.e. board, card). They have developed the skills to follow instructions and therefore they could write instructions for others, invent their own games and rules, use characters or events in games to use as a basis for imaginative writing and roleplay.

(SB 1996)

In another school, one teacher attempted to investigate the relationship of time that members of his Grade 5/6 class spent engaged in different activities out of school hours. He discovered that 'the children spend more out-of-school time participating in recreational activities other than formalised reading of literature' (BR 1996). However, these 'recreational' activities also included a high proportion of time involved with electronic types of literature, such as television, computers, video movies and video games. In fact, as Table 2.1 indicates, no members of his class spent 'most time' reading, while 50 per cent of the class spent most time using electronic literature. Although most of the children participated in all of the activities listed below, half the class spent most of their leisure time engaged in use of electronic forms of literature.

Table 2.1   Percentage of time spent on out-of-school activities

Majority of time spent on:	Percentage of Gr 5/6 class
Electronic literature	50
Reading	–
Sport	12.5
General play	37.5

What then, are we to make of these findings? Several members of the new generation of teachers represented here seem to be thinking and talking about Nintendo in ways that are more like their parents than their little brothers and sisters. They are concerned to make a link between computer game play and antisocial, aggressive, 'non-literate' behaviour. On this basis, it would seem that teacher education has a long way to go, though we acknowledge the limits of our sample here.

These are 'snap-shots' only, however, as we indicated at the outset. They are included here so as to provide a somewhat more concrete account of educational experience, albeit all too briefly, and to provoke some observations on research. There is nothing startlingly new in this material – but then again, there is little in the way of informed, systematic empirical research available currently anywhere, in our view. Buckingham (1993) notes, with regard to much work on popular culture and associated textualities, that despite considerable theoretical 'heat', 'the empirical basis for the arguments is often extremely limited'. He calls for more 'detailed analysis of empirical data', and better articulations with 'cultural and educational practice' (Buckingham 1993: 22). We concur wholeheartedly on this point, but cannot keep from suggesting that it is easier said than done.[3] Indeed, our view is that working in this space throws up a number of important and quite fascinating research dilemmas and problems.

A central issue among these is the politics and ethics of *representation*. Research like this is always as much about 'us' as about 'them', and the question then becomes: Who is 'us', and what are our agendas and investments in this regard? Why do research of this kind and in this area? Why not wait a few years until the Nintendo generation grows up and can do its own research on these questions, tell its own stories? To what extent is research of this sort inevitably positioned to operate only from the outside, looking in, forever at a remove from what is increasingly 'alien' experience? Is there not already a certain measure of fantasy and anxiety, of voyeurism mingled with horrified fascination in such work? Linked to these questions clearly are issues of power, knowledge and desire, and their interrelations. One response would be to argue the need for and value of initiating such inquiry *in the present*. We need to sensitize current stakeholders to what is really at stake in generational and cultural tensions in a world rapidly being reorganized in accordance with global logics of information and the interrelation of image, risk and complexity. If we are to continue to take risks, however, the obligation to engage in radical acts of the imagination – to keep re-imag(in)ing the future – remains primary. More often than not, this will mean working for and with difference, in ways that will be profoundly unsettling for many of us of the old school, trained and formed in accordance with other social logics and visions. In some respects, we are already well and truly outside the game altogether. As Jenkins (1993: 69) writes:

> We need to become more attentive to the experience of playing the games rather than simply interpreting their surface features. We need to situate them more precisely within their social and educational contexts, to understand them more fully within their place in children's lives.

Yet what is important is 'playing the games' *from the standpoint of the child*. As many commentators indicate, this is not just difficult in itself, but also likely to be significantly changing (and estranging). The task becomes well nigh impossible and certainly daunting. That is, unless we recognize our own 'will to Truth', and reset our sights, becoming more humble and realistic about what is possible and what is desirable in this regard.

What is the research that is likely to be 'really useful knowledge' at this time? In our view, it involves attending more carefully to and looking more actively out for the signs of difference, in textual and cultural practice, in classroom exchanges and student productions, and in the transactions between home and school, work and play. It means dealing critically in the classroom with the uncomfortable questions of violence and sexism and racism that children may otherwise only deal with alone, in front of the screen. Among other things, this requires collaborative and negotiated activity with young people as researchers and informants. Certainly, there is much more reassurance to be found in the transcript of the tape made by Jack and Louis than in any of the official interviews between researchers and children. These boys were able to use, and play with, the form of 'the interview' as they played with the Nintendo machine. In this way, the 'Nintendo generation gap' may well be bridged not by the power of adult research knowledge but by the powerful models that our research projects can provide of ways (outside the parameters of the game) of taking risks in the search for important understandings that cannot, any longer, be instantly replayed in order for us to get it right – safely, slowly – before we move on to the next level.

Conclusion(s) Pending: Teaching the Nintendo Generation

In the preceding sections, we have attempted to lay out two distinct, albeit supplementary, accounts of children, computer culture and popular technologies, with reference specifically to video-computer games and gaming, the entertainment industry, and primary schooling. Our concern, in the end, is above all else *educational*. What are the implications and challenges in such phenomena for education and schooling, curriculum and literacy? How might teachers and teacher-educators respond to, and participate in, the changing forms and relations of education and media that are so markedly a feature of the now no longer new, postmodern scene? How to understand and engage, *and* work with, the different constituencies that are moving into our classrooms and schools, and increasingly our lecture theatres and seminar rooms?

Importantly, it involves taking popular culture seriously, and recognizing and accepting that this is increasingly and even overwhelmingly technologically textured in significant ways. As we have suggested, children's changing culture and experience are necessary reference-points in this regard, as are their investments (however these might be mediated by Significant Others). Video games and the like are central in this regard. As Papert writes (referring to parents, although the point applies equally forcefully to teachers): 'video games, being the first example of computer technology applied to toy making, have nonetheless been the entryway for children into the world of computers' (1993: 4).

Others also acknowledge the dark side of video-computer games and note their risks, pointing in particular to the game culture's more militaristic and masculinist orientations – evident, for instance, in the exchanges between Jack and Louis.

> This tendency in the evolution of interactive environments present an urgent
> need to co-opt them into the educational system in ways that promote their

potential as a learning tool and diminish their attraction as a gaming environment for the testing of the skills of war.

(Lazlo and Castro 1995: 11)

It may well be that life and learning in the context of what we have called the
digital-electronic apparatus is noticeably faster, and that indeed cognition is changing as a consequence of being formed in quite different technocultural conditions.
There may well be a mismatch, in this regard, between the imag(in)ed subjects of
mainstream schooling and those of postmodern media culture. Enquiring into these
difference-relations is currently a first-order research imperative. At the same time,
moral panic in its various forms is unhelpful, to say the least, and points as much
as anything to the anxieties prevailing among the more established generations,
increasingly excluded, as it would seem, from a possibly different future.

What also needs to be considered is the production and realization of increasingly finer and finer distinctions not simply *between* generations but *within* them.
At issue here is competition between different companies and producers, linked to
which is extensive (and expensive) work by each industry player to construct
specific constituencies in their respective images. Wark, for example, suggests that
while there may well be a Nintendo generation, in his terms, there is also a recognizable Sega generation 'following hard on their heels'. As he writes:

For a long time now, media cultures have taken us on roller-coaster rides
that start out with the surprise of the new, rapidly roll over into familiarity
and just as quickly plunge into boredom with the form.

(Wark 1993: 12)

This pattern and momentum of consumer satisfaction and dissatisfaction, this
rhythm of affect and (dis)engagement, is important because it evidences the way in
which, and also the extent to which, commercial and technological imperatives and
processes are thoroughly implicated in media cultural phenomena such as this. Of
course it is by no means the case that consumption is automatically or necessarily
negative, or indeed socially and culturally counter-productive. As commentators
such as Collins (1995), MacRobbie (1994) and Jenkins (1993) argue, 'users' may
well find spaces for creative work and play *within* the technocultures of
commodification and consumption, and hence develop new resources thereby for
being and becoming. Opportunities for 'discrimination' continually present themselves. Yet while there may well be significant distinctions to be observed between
Nintendo and Sega generations, what remains the case is that, at another level of
abstraction, they share a commitment to and investment in computer culture and its
associated industries. It is in this sense that what is at issue here is, more precisely
and distinctively, a computer generation – and, even more to the point, a generational
break, in this instance between television and computing.[4]

The key to this break is the shift to *interactivity*: the fact that, increasingly,
children are able literally to interact with media texts and media products, and to
play with them in ways that are qualitatively different from those associated with

reading books and watching broadcast television. The key to interactivity in its heightened, technologically enhanced forms is the digital revolution – what commentators such as Negroponte (1995: 5) see as promoting an 'exponential' leap in sociotechnical practice and human possibility. Current moves towards relatively accessible virtual reality technologies suggest that what the future holds, in this regard, is new potent combinations of interactivity and immersion (Smith 1996). At the moment it would seem that interactivity has priority over immersion as a market imperative – the market consisting predominantly of children, as a particular kind of audience, in all their assumed whiz-bang hyperactive enthusiasm. The point remains, however, that digital media represent a breakthrough in interactive opportunities and semiotic experience, and a major shift in both orientation and sensibility. Further, video-computer games represent an important and extremely effective *entrée* into this newly emergent, rapidly consolidating culture. Educators ignore or slight the Nintendo generation, or indeed demonize them, at their peril.

Notes

1 Cited in Wyndham (1992).
2 The best single account of this is Sheff (1993). See also Shuker (1996) and media coverage such as the following: *The Age* (1995) and *The Australian* (1996) along with features such as McGregor (1993), Elmer-Dewitt (1993).
3 Important work is beginning to emerge in this regard. See Haddon (1992), Buckingham (1996), Bazalgette and Buckingham (1995). For Australian research on this topic see Smith *et al.* (1995), Nixon (in press), Downes and Reddacliff (1996) and Beavis (in press).
4 Note however that 'television' and 'computing' are themselves converging, as media technologies and as culture-industries, with televisions and computers becoming increasingly interchangeable. See Gilding (1992) and Negroponte (1995). This is something increasingly picked up in popular media coverage, e.g. *The Weekend Australian* (1996).

References

The Age (1995) 'Games at the Crossroads', 16 May: 40.
The Australian (1996) 'Economics of doom: The way of the future', 28 May: 53.
BAZALGETTE, C. and BUCKINGHAM, D. (eds) (1995) *In Front of the Children: Screen Entertainment and Young Audiences*, London: British Film Institute.
BEAVIS, C. (in press) 'Computer games, culture and curriculum', in I. SNYDER (ed.) *Taking Literacy into the Electronic Age*, Sydney: Allen and Unwin.
BUCKINGHAM, D. (1993) *Changing Literacies: Media Education and Modern Culture*, London: Tufnell Press.

BUCKINGHAM, D. (1996) *Moving Images: Understanding Children's Emotional Responses to Television*, Manchester: Manchester University Press.

COLLINS, J. (1995) *Architectures of Excess: Cultural Life in the Information Age*, New York: Routledge.

DIBDIN, M. (1995) *Dark Spectre*, London: Faber and Faber.

DOWNES, T. and REDDACLIFF, C. (1996) 'Young children talking about computers in their homes', http://www.spirit.com.au/ACEC96/papers/downe.htm.

ELMER-DEWITT, P. (1993) 'The amazing video game boom', *Time*, **8**(39) 27 September: 54–59.

GILDING, G. (1992) *Life After Television: The Coming Transformation of Media and American Life*, New York: W. W. Norton and Co.

GREEN, B. and BIGUM, C. (1993) 'Aliens in the classroom', *Australian Journal of Education*, **37**(2): 119–41.

HADDON, L. (1992) 'Explaining ICT consumption: The case of the home computer', in R. SILVERSTONE and E. HIRSCH (eds) *Consuming Technologies: Media and Information in Domestic Spaces*, London: Routledge.

HAYLES, N. K. (1990) *Chaos Bound: Orderly Disorder in Contemporary Literature and Science*, Ithaca, NY: Cornell University Press.

JENKINS, H. (1993) '"x Logic": Repositioning Nintendo in children's lives', *Quarterly Review of Film and Video*, **14**: 55–70.

KINDER, M. (1991) *Playing with Power in Movies, Television and Video Games*, Berkeley, CA: University of California Press.

LAZLO, A. and CASTRO, K. (1995) 'Technology and values: Interactive learning environments for future generations,' *Educational Technology*, **35**(2): 7–13.

LUKE, C. and ROE, K. (1993) 'Introduction to special issue: Media and popular cultural studies in the classroom', *Australian Journal of Education*, **37**(2): 115–118.

McGREGOR, A. (1993) 'Nintendo rules, OK!' *Good Weekend*, 16 October: 28–33.

MACROBBIE, A. (1994) *Postmodernism and Popular Culture*, London: Routledge.

MACROBBIE, A. and THORNTON, S. L. (1996) 'Rethinking "moral panic" for multi-mediated social worlds', *British Journal of Sociology*, **46**(4): 559–74.

MUSGRAVE, F. (1966) *The Family, Education and Society*, London: Routledge and Kegan Paul.

NEGROPONTE, N. (1995) *Being Digital*, Sydney: Hodder and Stoughton.

NIXON, H. (in press) 'Fun and games are serious business', in J. SEFTON-GREEN (ed.) *Digital Diversions: Youth Culture in the Age of Multimedia*, London: Taylor and Francis.

PAPERT, S. (1993) *The Children's Machine: Rethinking School in the Age of the Computer*, New York: Basic Books.

POSTER, M. (1995) *The Second Media Age*, Cambridge: Polity Press.

RODDA, E. (1994) *Power and Glory*, St Leonards, NSW: Allen and Unwin.

SAID, E. (1983) 'Opponents, audiences, constituencies and community', in H. FOSTER (ed.) *The Anti-Aesthetic: Essays on Postmodern Culture*, Seattle, WA: Bay Press, pp. 135–59.

SEFTON-GREEN, J. (1995) 'Computer games and media education', *20:20*, Issue 3, Autumn: 32–34.

SHEFF, D. (1993) *Game Over: Nintendo's Battle to Dominate an Industry*, London: Hodder and Stoughton.

SHUKER, R. (1996) 'Video games: Serious fun', *Continuum*, **9**(2): 125–45.

SMITH, A. (1996) *Software for the Self: Culture and Technology*, London: Faber and Faber.

SMITH, R., CURTIN, P. and NEWMAN, L. (1995) 'Kids in the kitchen: The social implications for schooling in the age of advanced computer technology', paper presented at the Australian Association for Research in Education Conference, Hobart, November.

SPENDER, D. (1995) *Nattering on the Net: Women, Power and Cyberspace*, North Melbourne: Spinifex Press.

TURKLE, S. (1984) *The Second Self: Computers and the Human Spirit*, New York: Simon and Schuster.

TURKLE, S. (1996) *Life on the Screen: Identity in the Age of the Internet*, London: Weidenfeld and Nicolson.

WARK, M. (1993) 'Game, set and match to the teens', *The Australian*, 22 December: 12.

WARK, M. (1994) 'The video games as an emergent media form', *Media Information Australia*, No 71: 21–29.

The Weekend Australian (1996) 'TV's destination has arrived', 21–22 September: 2 [Syte supplement].

WHITTAKER, R. (1995) 'Adult-free zones: Children and entertainment technology', *20:20*, Issue 3, Autumn, 35–37.

WYNDAM, S. (1992) 'Hollywood's new player', *The Australian Magazine*, 22–23 August: 18–25.

Chapter Three

Zapping Freddy Krueger:
Children's use of disapproved video texts

Mark Laidler

Joey drifts into sleep with his dog Jason by his side only to wake moments later in the boot of a junked car in a scrap yard. The dog starts pawing at the ground, lifts its leg and ejects a stream of fire. The ground opens, and below we see a pile of human bones which begin to move. They reassemble and the skeleton becomes covered in flesh. A hand picks up a hat. Freddy Krueger is back to invade dreams and seek murderous revenge, using the latest in special effects.

Thus, another episode of *A Nightmare on Elm Street* swings into action.[1] This series of films in the 'teens-in-peril' subgenre of horror plays out the same basic story. Freddy Krueger, accused of a series of brutal child murders, was freed on a legal technicality but was subsequently hunted down by a group of suburban mothers who incinerated him in his Elm Street home. Freddy, however, is a modern vampire in that he becomes an 'undead' and returns for revenge by invading the dreams of teenage children. They, in turn, are drawn into each other's dreams but if Freddy kills them in their dream then they die in reality. The last teen standing kills Freddy but we know that he'll be back in the next installment. This is *A Nightmare on Elm Street*, a very popular series of films with young viewers; they are fun to watch and they don't take themselves too seriously. Most adults, however, don't see it this way – but then most adults don't bother to view the films; it's easier to disapprove, and assume these films are harmful to children.

Central to the debate regarding children and television has been the issue of violence and anti-social influences. This discourse reaches back to pre-television days when, in the early 1920s, serious academic debate began in response to surveys which indicated that children were spending a significant amount of time at the movies. Such issues as the moral well-being and the passivity of the child viewer, their exposure to acts of crime, theft and dishonesty were all cause for concern much as they are today (see Luke 1990 for a comprehensive genealogy of this phenomenon).

The participants for this project were a group of children under my classroom care at an inner-urban primary school in Melbourne, Australia. This school had a pupil enrolment of 238 in July 1990, with 27 different language backgrounds represented and with approximately 40 per cent of the children coming from Muslim families. The children came from diverse economic backgrounds but irrespective of family income, one of their pastimes and popular pleasures was an avid video consumption which often involved viewing films generally disapproved of by many adults.

The project reported in this chapter examines, in some detail, 11 children's responses to the viewing of an independently viewed 'disapproved' video text: the 1988 production of *A Nightmare on Elm Street 4: The Dream Master* (directed by Renny Harlin). The analysis was arranged to investigate three main themes: horror narrative: structure and responses; comprehension and consequences; and popular pleasure and narrative control. The names of the children have been changed to preserve anonymity.

Horror Narrative

Generally, when adults view a narrative film we take it as a task to construct meaning from the information presented. Our ability to do so will depend on our experiences of the medium, structural schema and story components as well as the sensory input being experienced. Thus narrational activity is a complex task. Bordwell states:

> To make sense of a narrative film, the viewer must do more than perceive movement, construe images and sounds as presenting a three-dimensional world, and understand oral or written language. The viewer must take as a central cognitive goal the construction of a more or less intelligible story.
>
> (Bordwell 1985: 32–33)

This cognitive goal is clear for the adult viewer who expects that there is, indeed, a story to unfold. However, when considering the less experienced viewer, it is necessary to consider other goals. When children are asked to retell the story of an episode of *A Nightmare on Elm Street*, there is quite clearly some narrative confusion, as the following extract from Sanna, an 11-year-old girl, illustrates:

ML: Tell me what the film is about.
Sanna: It's about a guy turning into Freddy Krueger, and this girl keeps dreaming about him, and then she goes into the nightmare hospital and this guy jumps off a cliff and um, and then, they all call their friends. They've got this thing, I don't know what it's called, everybody picks a wish and everybody can do what they like. The girl does a flip, and then kicks them, and then and at the end of the movie Freddy Krueger makes himself as her father

and she hugs him. And then he puts his fingers right into his stomach and then he dies. Then her friend starts crying, all those kids she was helping.

Although Sanna appears confused about the story of the film, she has a clear grasp of key components which are horror-genre specific. It may be that, at her age, discussing the development of a narrative is a cognitively difficult or impossible task. We need, therefore, to look further at the nature of narrative to understand more about the child viewer. Bordwell's use of the concepts of *fabula*, *syuzhet* and *style* provides a possible explanation for the success of such films with children and, at the same time, gives an insight into the reasons for their disapproval by adults (Bordwell 1985).

The presentation of visual and aural information both cues and constrains the viewer's construction of the story – this construction is termed the fabula:

> The fabula is thus a pattern which perceivers of narratives create through assumptions and inferences. It is the developing result of picking up narrative cues, applying schemata, framing and testing hypotheses . . . The viewer builds the fabula on the basis of prototype schemata (identifiable types of persons, actions, locales, etc.), template schemata (principally the "canonic" story), and procedural schemata (a search for appropriate motivations and relations of causality, time, and space).[2]
>
> (Bordwell 1985: 49)

Thus the film's fabula is never present as a material object but is, rather, the construction the perceiver makes of the presented information – presentations which can assist or retard our ability to build the fabula. This system of presentation and arrangement is the syuzhet, or the plot structure. The syuzhet is presented in a filmic medium which uses devices and techniques in systematic ways and this system is referred to as the style. Thus style 'is the film's systematic use of cinematic devices' (Bordwell 1985:35). The difference between style and syuzhet can be understood by treating the syuzhet as the dramatic content of the film, perhaps the scriptwriter's input, while style concerns the technical aspects, perhaps the director's and crew's input. These two aspects act together in the film medium in a mutually dependent manner. The child viewer, then, is expected to perform a complex task: applying schemata and inferring the fabula from the syuzhet – a task for which he or she may be inadequately prepared.

This then begs the question as to why, if the understanding of the fabula is only partial, the horror film is so popular. Some reasons for this popularity, it is suggested, lie in the nature of the horror plot structure, the nature of the feelings (and thoughts) it engenders and the spectacular nature of the film's excess.

Following Hodge and Tripp's work, it is instructive to analyze *A Nightmare on Elm Street* from its paratactic structure only (Hodge and Tripp 1986: 35–40). That is, to identify the 'and then . . . ' nature of the narrative. We can simplify this

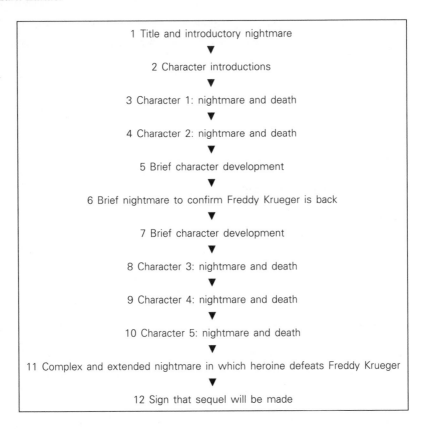

1 Title and introductory nightmare
▼
2 Character introductions
▼
3 Character 1: nightmare and death
▼
4 Character 2: nightmare and death
▼
5 Brief character development
▼
6 Brief nightmare to confirm Freddy Krueger is back
▼
7 Brief character development
▼
8 Character 3: nightmare and death
▼
9 Character 4: nightmare and death
▼
10 Character 5: nightmare and death
▼
11 Complex and extended nightmare in which heroine defeats Freddy Krueger
▼
12 Sign that sequel will be made

Figure 3.1 The paratactic structure of *A Nightmare on Elm Street*

narrative schematically as in Figure 3.1. From this, it is clear that the film can be simplified to a series of 'and then' events; there is one nightmare event followed by a character development, followed by four nightmare events, then follows a further character development and another four nightmare events. The paratactic nature of the narrative is therefore very apparent.

If one wishes to make a case for a hypotactic structure it can be done, how-ever, it is argued here that the paratactic accessibility of this film is one of the factors which accounts for its enormous popularity. Although there is an overarching narrative with motivated and consequential events, the film makes available a view-ing experience in which this narrative is not required for enjoyment. Like a 'Tom and Jerry' cartoon, it provides this series of 'and then' events which can be viewed in any order and without reference to each other. Films like this require little interpretation or inference for enjoyment and, it is argued, such an alternative read-ing (or perhaps non-reading) is ideally suited to the abilities of the young viewer. Fiske suggests that such a paratactic reading provides for a plurality of readings as well as a plurality of modes of reading:

Episodic viewing is a way of resisting or at least evading the social meanings structured into the text . . . Such childish, undisciplined ways of reading are also popular ways. They treat the text with profound disrespect: it
is not a superior object created by a superior producer-artist . . . but a
cultural resource to be raided or poached. Its value lies in the uses it can
be put to, the relevances it can offer, not in its essence or aesthetics.
Popular text must offer not just a plurality of meanings, but a plurality of
ways of reading, or modes of consumption.

(Fiske 1989: 144)

Art Horror

The difference between real-life horror and fiction-induced horror is demonstrated
by the concept of 'art horror', developed by Noel Carroll (1990). In general, this
concept deals with the effects of thought on emotional and physical reactions to a
fiction. Carroll (1990: 79–80) argues that just entertaining a thought is enough to
provoke our emotional responses and involvement. Thus, what viewers experience
with art horror are genuinely experienced emotions. They may feel repulsion, fright
and fear in the cognitive dimension, they may feel nausea or they may scream,
recoil and so on in the physical dimension. Art horror has both a physical and a
cognitive dimension (Carroll 1990: 24–7). Specifically, Carroll argues that the
responses of the characters in a film seem to cue the emotional responses of the
audience and that this is the key element of the horror genre. When the characters
in the film are surprised, frightened or horrified, then this is the expected emotional
state of the audience; art-horror causes emotional and physical agitation because it
relies on the coexistence of a state in the viewer which is parallel to the state of
the fictional character.

Back then to *A Nightmare on Elm Street* and Freddy Krueger. The ontological
problem is that we know that Freddy Krueger does not exist in real time or space
– he is a fiction – so the question arises, what is the viewer reacting to? The answer,
according to Carroll (1990), is that the viewer is reacting to the thought of Freddy.
Here Carroll's idea of objective and formal realities is useful; the concept of
objective reality is one where we can entertain the idea of something's reality without recourse to a formal commitment to it (that is, a reality based on material
existence). In this way, we can entertain the *idea* of Freddy Krueger without a commitment to his *formal reality*. Thus our emotional responses to fictional protagonists,
like our emotional responses to fictional monsters, are genuine because they are
directed at objects whose ontological status, while not being formal, have nevertheless a reality in our minds (Carroll 1990: 89).

Viewers do not have to identify with the character to share these emotional
responses; it is better to argue that as audience members we assimilate the character's situation. However, as viewers, we do not just see the situation from the
character's perspective, we also see it from the viewpoint of a knowledgeable outsider; we not only share the protagonist's fear, we also feel additional apprehension

47

because we are more aware of other dangers, unknown to the protagonist. Our thoughts involve us in a greater range of emotions than those specified by the character. The emotion of shock or surprise, however, is the one emotion generally shared at the same initial level between character and audience.

The act of enduring the emotional responses produced by art horror videos can be approached by some young viewers as a test of courage, as the following extracts show. The first is from Ekrem, a 12-year-old boy:

ML: What does it feel like when you are about to watch a horror film?

Ekrem: Normal.

ML: Do you expect to be scared?

Ekrem: Sometimes.

ML: What does it feel like when the film is over?

Ekrem: You feel like a hero.

ML: What do you mean by that?

Ekrem: If you're scared to go through the lane, and after you watch the film when Freddy gets bashed you won't be scared to go through there. You'll feel confident.

The following is from two boys, Oktay (6) and Jimmy (7):

ML: What's the scariest film you've watched?

Oktay: *Terminator*, and also Freddy Krueger.

ML: You just said earlier that Freddy Krueger wasn't scary.

Oktay: It is scary but I didn't get scared.

ML: How do you stop yourself from getting scared?

Oktay: You just sit there and watch it.

Jimmy: I just sit in the chair and relax. I just watch it, and if it's a scary part I just keep myself there, so I show them I'm not scared.

ML: Is it like a test to get through and not be scared?

Jimmy: Yes.

It is suggested that it is this feeling of trial, coupled with the vicarious thrills experienced during the emotion of art horror which explains, in part, the fascination this genre holds for children. As well as the immediate pleasure in new experiences, it is clear from Ekrem, Oktay and Jimmy's responses that some children use these films as personal tests of maturity or bravery.

Excess

A 'fellow-traveller' with the narrative is identified by Roland Barthes (1977: 52–68) as the film's third meaning. Barthes describes the first meaning as communication and the second meaning as signification. His third meaning consists of a transition from denotation and connotation to a symbolism which exists, but whose meaning is obscure. This third meaning is difficult to grasp because it is not necessary for the narrative or the intentional symbolism of the film-maker. Kristin Thompson (1981: 287–95), referring to the same concept, defines it as the film's 'excess' – elements of a film which are non-narrational in function. In this sense she argues that the word 'meaning' is misleading, 'since these elements of the work . . . do not participate in the creation of narrative or symbolic meaning' (Thompson 1981: 288).

A closer examination of one of *A Nightmare on Elm Street*'s dream sequences will help to demonstrate this concept of excess although, without the experience of the colour, framing and sound used, this can only be partial. The sequence in question concerns where Kristin falls victim to Freddy Krueger and the following summary will show the 'excessive' nature of the scene:

1   Kristin wakes on a peaceful tropical beach and sees a little girl called Alice building an elaborate sandcastle.
2   The water foams and Freddy Krueger's hand appears like a shark's fin. It speeds through the water, with a glint of flame, up through the sand to the sandcastle which explodes to reveal Freddy Krueger.
3   Kristin runs and falls in the soft sand. Freddy Krueger catches up and with his foot pushes her beneath the sand. He cackles as we see her head disappear.
4   Kristin appears through a hole in the ceiling of an old house. She crawls across the ceiling to the sounds of thunder and a baby crying. She crawls through a door and resumes normal gravity.
5   Kristin runs down stairs to a basement filled with large heating ducts; there are splashes of green light and clouds of steam.
6   Freddy Krueger appears and indicates Kristin is about to die. They circle each other. The furnace door explodes and we see close-ups of steam escaping from valves and pipes. We, and they see Alice asleep in her bed, tossing and turning.
7   A wall explodes and Alice enters the dream. Freddy Krueger remarks, 'How sweet, fresh meat'. Kristin tries to send Alice back out of the dream. Kristin is then thrown into the furnace. Freddy Krueger lifts his striped shirt to reveal his torso which is made up of the screaming, agonized heads of his victims.
8   Alice wakes up in her room to find a postcard from Freddy which then catches fire.

For many viewers, this sequence, like many others in the film, may seem entirely excessive and gratuitous. It really adds little to the overall narrative, or to the development of the characters, and in fact includes some elements that have absolutely no relevance to either. For example, the sound effect of the crying baby (there is no baby in the story) and the screaming heads which make up Freddy Krueger's chest are entirely gratuitous and yet both add much to the impact of the sequence. While such devices are excessive for the experienced viewer, they may indeed be significant points of involvement for the young.

What is being argued is that the excess of the horror film may be partly responsible for the disapproval felt by many (older) viewers and, equally, may be responsible for the pleasure felt by others (the younger ones). Furthermore, the possible connotative meanings of this excess may be just as obtuse for both sets of viewers.

Popular Pleasure

An observer of children at play in a school playground will notice that amongst the seeming chaos there are constant episodes of freedom and conflict enacted. Children will alternate between periods of happy play and periods of conflict and argument; they are constantly in a flux between acquiescence to the rules of the game, no matter how ad hoc, and conflict about interpretation and subversion. It is through this play that children develop experiences and concepts of social control and order. As Fiske (1987: 234) states:

> The essence of play is that it is voluntary and therefore free and that it creates order. The order that it creates is in the control of the players or, at least, is one voluntarily accepted by them, but the orderliness is never total, for it has built into it chanciness, the impossibility of knowing what will happen. The main structuring principle of play is the tension between social order and the 'freedom' of anarchy and chance.

As can be seen from the earlier discussions about the narrative of *A Nightmare on Elm Street*, these videos can be seen as the interplay of anarchy and order. The basic plot hook, i.e. the action of the vigilantes in killing Freddy Krueger, initiates this tension. The stories thereafter are a series of episodes in which the characters fight for a sense of rational control over destructive chaos. It is postulated that from the relative safety of the video, the children are able to experience a vicarious level of high tension which translates into the experience of fun. That is, the children are involved in 'play'. The following statements from the children explain their feelings of pleasure and fun.

Ekrem (male; age 12)
ML: Why do you watch the Freddy Krueger films?
Ekrem: He's a good guy, he's scary . . . you enjoy it.
ML: What's enjoyable about watching it?
Ekrem: It makes people scared, sometimes, that's in the movies.

Sanna (female; age 11)
ML: Sanna, why do you like watching horror movies?
Sanna: Because it's fun.

Maxi (female; age 9)
ML: Why do you watch them if you get frights?
Maxi: 'Cos they're funny, they're horror and that's why I like them, they
        get you scared and all that. It's funny, it's fun.

Elizabeth (female; age 7)
ML: Do you like watching scary movies?
Elizabeth: Yes.
ML: Can you tell me why?
Elizabeth: No.
ML: Why do you both like watching movies that make you feel
            worse?
Elizabeth: Because I like the tingle.

The one inescapable conclusion which must be drawn from the interviews with the children is that horror videos are a source of pleasure. All of these children are regular viewers of *A Nightmare on Elm Street* and similar films. As can be seen, when asked why they watched these films a range of expressions to express pleasure are used, including 'enjoy', 'good', 'gets people's attention', 'fun', 'funny', liking 'the tingle', and 'best'. There are no equivocal statements.

Children appear to gain genuine pleasure from watching these kinds of movies in spite of general adverse opinion from the adult community regarding the suitability of videos like *A Nightmare on Elm Street*. A closer reading of the transcripts, however, indicates that most of these children have viewed these films with their parents or at least with their approval. One child started watching horror films at the age of 5 when her brother hired them; a group of girls relate a sleepover where they watched four videos while the grandparents stayed in another room. One girl talks of watching horror videos with her mum while others report regularly viewing with cousins or parents. Each of the children has viewed these films in a social setting or for a purpose which exceeds the mere private fun of the films. The social setting in which the films are viewed may be a very important element in the fun experienced from watching them.

Narrative Control

The most important factors in the use of video when compared with film are time, choice and cost. Each of these factors creates considerable independence and power for the consumer. The viewer is no longer tied to the scheduling of the cinemas when viewing a video. The choice is not only of time of day, it is also which day and what length of viewing session. Further, the viewer is now able to review scenes, slow-motion sections, fast-forward and freeze frames. These all constitute a power over time which is not available in the cinema. The video now provides a freedom of use which was previously only available in print, or to a lesser extent in sound recordings.

This use of video functions for a close examination of video texts, while not always undertaken, is certainly reported in some of the interviews. Here Ekrem (12) discusses his use of this strategy:

ML: How many times would you stop a Freddy Krueger film to slow-motion or replay it?

Ekrem: Ten or 15 times.

ML: Do you ever look at something more than twice in a film?

Ekrem: Yes. In this frightening movie. This guy comes and chops this baby's head off in the pram. I watched that a couple of times to see how it happened.

ML: Were you worried the first time you saw it that they really had a baby?

Ekrem: Yes.

ML: So you were upset and watched it again?

Ekrem: And found out how it really happened.

ML: How did they do it?

Ekrem: They stopped the movie and changed the baby and put a doll and chopped its head off.

ML: Then a video is much better than a film?

Ekrem: Yes.

ML: If you went to the movies it would be scary. You wouldn't know how the tricks were done.

Ekrem: Yes.

ML: Do you ever watch films where you can't work out the trick?

Ekrem: Yes. In *Death Wish*. The guy shoots in the middle of his eyes and he's bleeding and he's talking, and there's a hole there.

ML: You stopped it and had a look, but couldn't work it out?

Ekrem: Yes, three times.

ML: But you knew it was a trick?

Ekrem: Yes.

Maxi (9) explains how she works out 'video tricks':

ML: Do you ever use the pause button to go over bits?

Maxi: Yes. Disgusting bits and scary bits.

ML: Why do you look at the disgusting bits?

Maxi: Because they're funny.

ML: What about the scary bits?

Maxi: Because they're spooky.

ML: Do you do it to find out how they trick you? Do you look very carefully to see what the trick is?

Maxi: Yes, sometimes it's just like a concert. If they're miming you can tell, like Kylie Minogue. She had the music on and she was miming and then she called Jason Donovan and the rest of the song was going on while she was calling Jason Donovan. It's just like that.

ML: Are the people in the film miming?

Maxi: Well, you can tell that they're not really killing them 'cos you like . . . something I brought home from Greek school. It's a real knife with a head band and there's a handle there [gestures front of head] and a knife there [gestures back of head] and that's the way they stick a knife through you.

ML: So it's like tricks?

Maxi: Yes.

These children are clearly using the video player's control of time to make sense of the film. By controlling the passage of time, as can be done with a book, they are able to read the presented text more carefully. This not only allows for greater understanding of the narrative, it leads to reassurance about the fate of characters/actors and it facilitates the repetition of particularly interesting or pleasurable episodes. These children, when confronted with a disturbing episode, appear to be willing to pause and seek information about the event. By using the slow-motion and freeze-frame attributes of the VCR they search for understanding and reassurance. This would indicate that children are exercising far more control over their viewing than might be supposed by adults. Further, it is suggested that this use of the VCR is more likely to happen with children than with adult viewers. It is presumed that experienced viewers are able to accept that film-trickery is being used and are not interested in the detail of how it is done. On the other hand, children, while accepting that events are being faked, still need to be reassured that this is the case and, they want to know *how* it is being done.

It would seem that the technology is as important as the text for the child, both as a means to develop understanding about TV/video as a constructed medium and for pleasure.

Comprehension

Common questions asked of children during media-based activities are, 'Is Batman real?' or 'Are Tom and Jerry real?' and so on. Children of all ages in the primary school will answer yes or no depending on their perception of what the question means. The problem is that both answers are right. Tom and Jerry are real. The children can go home and see them on TV – cartoon characters have an artistic reality. Batman is real. He is not a cartoon. A person is playing the character – Batman has substantial reality.

Some children, however, will understand the 'correct' answer being sought. They will understand that the question is based on extant reality. They will appreciate that Tom and Jerry are cartoons and that Batman is a character depicted by an actor. Therefore the difficulty is one of communication with the child. If the question is open to diverse interpretation then perhaps the question becomes an unsuitable tool for investigation with young children. The following discussion with two girls, Laila (8) and Ilknur (6), illustrates these points.

ML: Is Freddy Krueger a real person?

Laila: I don't know.

ML: Is he real or is it someone dressed up to look like that?

Laila: In this movie, they just showed you in the film that you watched, they wanted to take Freddy Krueger like off but he never got off, I think he's really true.

ML: Do you think that someone really looks like that?

Laila: Yes.

ML: Does that scare you a bit?

Laila: This man looks like him.

ML: Does he really get into people's dreams?

Laila: He gets into people's dreams.

ML: In real life or in the movies?

Laila: Well sometimes when I watch Freddy Krueger and scary movies I have a dream like when. When I don't want a bad dream it comes a bad dream. I don't really mind. When I wanted a good dream it came true.

ML: Ilknur, do you think that Freddy Krueger films are true or are they stories?

Ilknur: They are stories because they always just dress up.

ML: Is he a real person or a person dressed up?

Ilknur: Well, they're just masks on him, they put nails on him, he's not real.

ML: Laila, do you think he's real still?

Laila: I think he's got a mask, I think they just painted him like crooked. The camera maybe, it's just a story, not true. The camera, like lots of movies, the camera makes them look real. The camera makes Freddy Krueger when his nails get sharp.

ML: How did you find out about the camera and how movies are made?

Ilknur: It's not true so how did they make Freddy Krueger? He must be dressed up or painted faces.

ML: You worked that out?

Ilknur: Yes.

ML: What do you think?

Laila: I just think that won't be true, like some movies, that won't really be true that they do things like that. I reckon that some movies are really true. Every movie should, when I watch a movie and it's scary, they tell us if it's true or not true. But that will be the main thing they have to tell you. That will be better and to not scare no one.

The obvious point to note in this transcript is that the younger child has a greater understanding of the question than does the older. Even though Ilknur has less to say, there is a maturity in her responses which possibly indicates that she has discussed the point with an older person. Laila, on the other hand, exhibits considerable confusion about what is meant by the term 'real'. Her first answer suggests that she does not completely grasp the concept of fictional characters, and when asked if Freddy Krueger can really get into dreams she answers logically. That is, he can get into *her* dreams.

Most interestingly, after Ilknur's input, we can observe a transformation in Laila's thinking. She is now much clearer on the notion of staged reality in film. She is now asserting that the camera is somehow involved in making characters look real. Her final statement that films should have a message stating whether they are true or not, relates to an earlier part of the interview when she was talking about a docudrama.

Conclusions

Although this study deals with a small sample from a community which many would not consider mainstream, it is possible, I believe, to make some useful generalizations which, at the very least, enable us to think through the often intuitive statements which surround the topic of children and their viewing of certain videos.

Children, even at a young age, are eager to encounter new and powerful emotional experiences. In order to do this they are utilizing the horror video as a predictable stimulus. For some children, these heightened states of fear and shock are used as an ordeal of courage, while others simply enjoy the involuntary reactions generated. Children use or 'read' the text in ways which reflect their age, experiences and capabilities. Often this viewing may occur in the safety of an extended social setting such as a sleepover, or with other members of their family.

The viewing of a video is different in important ways from cinema viewing. The technology of presentation affords the child control over the narrative flow, as does the setting. Children can pause, re-view and fast-forward as well as leave the room, play and talk comfortably – activities not approved of in commercial cinemas. It is because of these attributes, specific to videos, that children can watch disapproved films as a form of play – a play that involves the anarchy and order, challenge and trial which feature in a good deal of children's activity.

Certainly there will be children for whom the watching of horror videos will be an unpleasant and frightening experience; however, as this study indicates, many children will find delight and pleasure from the vicarious thrills available. As in all cases with children, it is the responsibility of parents and carers to make informed judgments and to supervise children's viewing activities. It is also our responsibility to question our intuitive responses and to recognize that our beliefs about what children ought and ought not to watch may be based on false assumptions.

By examining one aspect of popular culture and by listening to a small group of students from one school, some insights into their cognitive and social processes have been gained. Further, this process has also enabled a better understanding of a misunderstood text – the horror video.

Notes

1   The *Nightmare on Elm Street* series includes:

> *A Nightmare on Elm Street* (1984) Director: Wes Craven;
> *A Nightmare on Elm Street Part 2: Freddy's Revenge* (1985)
>   Director: Jack Sholder;
> *A Nightmare on Elm Street 3: The Dream Master* (1988)
>   Director: Renny Harlin;
> *A Nightmare on Elm Street 4: The Dream Child* (1989)
>   Director: Stephen Hopkins.

2   Canonical story format: introduction of setting and characters – explanation of a state of affairs – complicating action – ensuing events – outcome – ending.

References

BARTHES, R. (1977) *Image–Music–Text* (ed. and trans. S. Heath) Glasgow: Fontana/Collins.

BORDWELL, D. (1985) *Narration in the Fiction Film*, Madison, WI: University of Wisconsin Press.

CARROLL, N. (1990) *The Philosophy of Horror*, New York: Routledge.

FISKE, J. (1987) *Television Culture*, London: Routledge.

FISKE, J. (1989) *Reading the Popular*, London: Unwin Hyman.

HODGE, B. and TRIPP, D. (1986) *Children and Television*, Cambridge: Polity Press.

LUKE, C. (1990) *Constructing the Child Viewer: A History of the American Discourse on Television and Children, 1950–1980*, New York: Praeger.

THOMPSON, K. (1981) *Eisenstein's Ivan the Terrible*, Princeton, NJ: Princeton University Press.

Chapter Four

Unbalanced minds?
Children thinking about television

Sue Howard

No one, it seems, thinks that much good comes from children and young people watching television. As I riffle through my file of newspaper and magazine clippings collected over the last few years, television, it appears, has been responsible for making children fat, lazy, murderous, violent, greedy, disrespectful of their elders, illiterate and suicidal. These claims are contained in reports of research, in pitches by lobbyists and in the opinions of leaders as disparate as Prince Charles, Paul Keating (ex-Prime Minister of Australia), Pope John Paul II and Bob Dole, Republican candidate in the 1996 US Presidential election.[1] With press like this, it is not hard to see why television has such a bad reputation in the public mind.

And yet, if my students' perceptions are any guide, people make a distinction between 'good' and 'bad' television. Each year, the student-teachers in my classes claim that 'educational' television is good for children – 'educational' here generally describes non-fiction programmes that deal with wild-life, geography, history, science, news, current affairs and so on. Having assumed a pedagogic mind-set, my students can approve of these kinds of programmes because 'they help children learn about the world around them'; 'they teach valuable things'; 'they make kids think about important issues' – these are the functions of 'good' television. Although these same students will cite a wide variety of soaps, family shows, dramas and situation comedies that they themselves enjoyed as children, they now claim that entertainment programming is worthless – if not downright dangerous – for the children they are about to teach. It 'destroys their imagination', 'shows them that violence is a good way to solve problems' and 'teaches them bad morals'. As Adele (19 years) put it: '[these kinds of programme] are a bit like chewing gum – they're readily available, they give you something to do when you're bored and they have no "nutritional value" whatsoever!'. This, then, is 'bad' television.

On the verge of teaching careers where they will be regarded as 'responsible people' in society and where they will have a great deal to do with children's minds, my students' revisionism can be seen as a taking up of the popular discourse about television's negative effects. Within this discourse, probably second only in

57

importance to the argument that television teaches children to be violent, is the claim that it destroys not only their ability to think but also their capacity for creativity and imagination.[2]

The argument that television has a deadening, stultifying effect on children's minds has a long history and one of its most prominent figures has been Marie Winn. In her influential book, *The Plug-in Drug*, first published in the United States in 1977, she cites parents' and teachers' anecdotal evidence, as well as selected scientific claims, that children's minds are affected during and as a result of television watching. The growth and effective functioning of children's brains, their cognitive and linguistic development are all, it is claimed, impaired by TV watching in much the same way that taking harmful drugs might do. Since the publication of Winn's book, the television-as-drug metaphor has been persistent, with children often being described as 'TV addicts' or 'hooked on television' in public discussion. A more recent book entitled *Kick the TV Habit* continues this same idea in its content as well as its title (Bennett and Bennett 1994).

This chapter aims to challenge the pervasive belief in the 'system shut-down' effect of watching entertainment programming on television. While no great claims will be made for television in this regard, I shall be arguing that children use whatever is available to think *with* and *about* and this includes their favourite television programmes. One might assume that non-fiction programmes would be best suited to this activity. These shows, however, while presenting intriguing problems at the outset, also usually provide the solutions before the programme finishes. David Attenborough, for example, may ask how animals survive in the freezing conditions of the Arctic but then he goes on to explain how they do; the presenters of *The Curiosity Show* may ask how telephones work or how it might be possible to make a cunning tractor out of a cotton reel, a rubber band and a couple of matchsticks but then they go on and show you.[3] Generally, people do not expect programmes like *The Simpsons* or *Bananas in Pyjamas* or *The Bill* actually to engage children's minds but, as the data presented in this chapter will show, children find things in these programmes that both entertain them and make them think.[4]

A Model of Thinking and Learning

Like television, cognitive developmental theory has also been held in low regard in recent times. Poststructuralist scholars (see, for example, James and Prout 1990; Urwin 1985; Walkerdine 1984, 1985) have attacked the work of theorists like Piaget for a number of reasons, most of which concern the essential structuralism of the theory and its inadequate recognition of 'the social' in determining what and how children think and learn. Many cognitive psychologists would now agree that while Piaget provides us with a highly compelling model of individual thinking and learning in his theory of 'equilibration', his characterization of the child as the 'lone scientist' privately acting on the world, forming and testing hypotheses and arriving at conclusions that form 'logical structures' is no longer adequate. Vygotskyan theory has had a major impact here in showing how the culture's ways of knowing, thinking and solving problems are passed on to children by more competent others through social transmission, social experience and communicative talk (see Meadows 1993; Vygotsky 1978; Wood 1988). In Vygotsky's (1978: 163) terms:

> Any function in the child's cultural development appears twice, or on two planes. First, it appears on the social plane, and then on the psychological plane. First it appears between two people as an interpsychological category, and then within the child as an intrapsychological category.

This notion of internalization or interiorization is crucial in Vygotskyan theory, because it is this process of inner reconstruction – preserving some of the external properties but changing others – that transforms the social into the psychological (see Marti 1996 and Wertsch 1985 for a fuller discussion of this). The problem is, however, that Vygotsky did not explain this reconstruction process in a precise way. Unlike Piaget, he provides no explicit model of individual functioning; no explanation of how individuals create new meanings; no indication how a child might go about transforming the socially transmitted material, and so on. The fundamental question of how experience is incorporated, represented, constructed and reconstructed in the mind is left largely unanswered.

Clearly, thinking and learning can best be explained as outcomes of the interaction of both internal cognitive processes and external social processes. Acknowledging the social origins of thought does not preclude the necessity for understanding what enables individuals to take up cognitively, make sense of, elaborate, reflect upon and consolidate the socially transmitted information in more or less useful and constructive ways. A model of thinking and learning that can account for both social and individual perspectives is thus probably one that combines aspects of both Piagetian and Vygotskian theory – Piaget's theory of equilibration and Vygotsky's theory of the 'zone of proximal development'.

Piaget's theory of equilibration offers a still widely accepted means of conceptualizing the thinking/learning process (see for example Meadows 1993; Sigel and Cocking 1977; Wood 1988 for fuller discussions of this topic). Papert (in the introduction to Piaget 1975/1985: xi–xii), for example, says:

> if through I do not know what misfortune, this [equilibration] theory should prove erroneous, what would the next step be? I really think that I can anticipate the answer. It would be to establish a new theory that would also be a theory of equilibration.

What is equilibration? Essentially it is a drive for order. Piaget (1954) claimed there seems to be an instinctive or innate need in people to find order, structure and predictability in their existence. Equilibration involves the testing of our understanding against the real world. When our understanding explains the events we observe, the world makes sense and we have equilibrium. When we can't explain what we see, based on what we already understand, disequilibrium (or cognitive conflict) occurs and the search for new and better understanding begins.

According to Piaget, in order to make sense of experience we organize it into cognitive schemes which then become basic building blocks for thinking. The twin processes for creating, adding to and modifying these schemes are called assimilation and accommodation. Disequilibrium, or cognitive conflict, is the process for activating the two. Assimilation occurs when people use their existing schemes to understand experiences or events in their world. It involves trying to understand something new by fitting it into a scheme representing what is already known (e.g. 'This is a TV game show. I've seen lots of game shows. This is another'). Sometimes the new information may have to be distorted to fit it into the existing scheme and this may lead to overassimilation (e.g. 'All TV characters who talk are real; Bugs Bunny talks, therefore he's real'). In both cases, assimilation can be seen to be conservative in that its primary function is to make the unfamiliar, familiar, to reduce the new to the old (Piaget 1954).

Sometimes schemes have to be adapted, modified or new ones created and this is a result of the other process: accommodation (e.g. 'These other men I've been calling "Daddy" protest when I call them this, don't live with us, don't take me to childcare, don't read me a bedtime story; maybe I need a new name for these people'). If an experience cannot be fitted into any existing schemes then a new, more useful one must be created or an old one modified. Thinking is adjusted to fit the new experience rather than the new experience being adjusted to fit existing ways of thinking: 'accommodation is the source of changes and bends the organism to the successive constraints of the environmen' (Piaget 1954: 352). Disequilibrium occurs when assimilation no longer works. This produces intellectual discomfort, curiosity or confusion and motivates the search for a more satisfying solution through accommodation. In this way, thinking changes and becomes more complex. Piaget, however, never showed much interest in the phase of disequilibrium – its significance for him was as a stepping stone to accommodation and cognitive progress.

Vygotsky's 'zone of proximal development' can be seen as a companion state to Piaget's disequilibrium in so far as it describes the space within which disequilibrium occurs. It also shows how accommodation may be achieved through social support or what Bruner (1986) called 'scaffolding'. The zone of proximal development is defined as the distance between the actual developmental level of a child as determined by independent problem-solving and the level of potential as determined through problem-solving under adult guidance or in collaboration with more capable peers (Vygotsky 1978: 86). In other words, Vygotsky saw children as being constantly on the verge of acquiring new learning in that crucial gap between existing knowledge and skills and the potential level of development beyond this. For Vygotsky, this process is collaborative with social interaction hastening development by providing both content (what to go for) and provisional support (how to get there).

Thus, Piaget's equilibration provides an explanation for the internal aspects of cognitive development and concept formation that Vygotsky's interiorization leaves unelaborated. Vygotsky's zone of proximal development, on the other hand, shows how cognitive advancement is, principally, socially mediated rather than the product of logical structures developed in isolation, and, moreover, how serious cognitive activity can occur in the phase that precedes accommodation.

The Study

The work to be discussed here provides a good example of what Willis (1992: 90) describes as being 'surprised' by one's data, 'of reaching knowledge not prefigured in one's starting paradigm'. I had set out to explore children's perceptions of the reality of television and, to this end, had small groups of boys and girls, of different ages, discuss how 'real' they thought different programmes were. Their discussions were tape-recorded, transcribed and subsequently analyzed using NUD•IST, the computer programme for managing and asking questions about qualitative data (Qualitative Solutions and Research 1990). This software tool enabled me to organize the text of the children's discussions in a category system which was rudimentary at first but which became more complex and refined as I worked and reworked the data.

Each time I revisited the text of the discussions, I found there were certain sections that were too intriguing to ignore, but which either did not fit comfortably into the analysis that I had developed to understand the children's responses about television reality, or I had a hunch that something more than I was recognizing was going on there. These sections of text were indexed as a separate 'problem' category. Quite late in the project, the contents of this category were re-examined (for what I expected to be the last time) and suddenly their significance began to become clearer. The episodes where children seemed to be confused, lost for words or where they engage in what I term 'distraction technique' (i.e. deliberately drawing attention to things that were not 'relevant' to the topic; changing the subject) suddenly made sense when seen as examples of cognitive conflict or disequilibrium. This led me back to reconsider other text, particularly that which dealt with speculation about how certain television effects are achieved.

The programmes that were unsettling these children's cognitive comfort and which seemed to be making them think were not documentaries or news programmes but cartoons like *The Simpsons* and *The Bugs Bunny Show*, preschool programmes like *Sesame Street* and *Bananas in Pyjamas*, dramas like *The Bill* and *Children's Ward*, game shows like *Vidiot* and family shows like *The Cosby Show*.

The 3 and 4-Year-Olds

The youngest children in the study were preschoolers. They were given coloured pictures of some familiar TV characters and were simply asked 'How real is [the character]?' and 'How do you know?' In the following passages, it becomes clear that for Jimmy (4) and Tim (4) 'talking through a moving mouth' is an important signifier of the 'real TV character' scheme or concept. Here they are discussing whether the two outsize Bananas from *Bananas in Pyjamas* are real or whether they are people 'dressed up':

SH: OK. Are they real bananas?

Tim: Naaah!

SH: Why aren't they real bananas? What's the difference?

Jimmy: Because I wrote them but they couldn't talk, can't even . . . bananas can't talk.

SH: Bananas can't talk?

Jimmy: No.

SH: Are you sure about this?

Jimmy: Only there's, there's only a man inside there but the man's talking . . . inside the banana.

SH: Sorry, what's inside there? What's inside there? Did you say?

Jimmy: A man.

SH: A man inside there.

Jimmy: Yeah but, but, but the man just tells all them, them that, but not the them, only the men tells them story, all them.

SH: I see. So there's a man inside the banana.

Jimmy: Yeah and all the others.

SH: And all the others. And, and how does he talk then?

Jimmy: He's a man.

SH: He's a man inside the banana and he talks. Is that right?

Jimmy: Yeah.

Jimmy and Tim's scheme for 'bananas' does not include talking – as Jimmy says, 'bananas can't talk' – so there must be another explanation for the fact that these two bananas do. Either they have worked out for themselves, or someone has told them, that these characters are 'not real' but people dressed up in banana suits, so the talking comes from the 'man inside there'. But this scheme does not appear to work equally well for Big Bird from *Sesame Street*. Here, this huge yellow bird is judged real. Jimmy, it's true, momentarily doubts this judgment and hesitates, but then he returns to the 'talking' signifier. No one is inside Big Bird because, 'He can talk real.' As Tim says: 'Only real ones can talk, eh'.

SH: OK, OK. What about Big Bird? Is there a man inside Big Bird?

Jimmy: Nah. He, he can talk.

SH: He can talk.

Jimmy: He can talk real. But, but it's not real. He t . . . he talk . . .

Tim: He's a real one.

SH: He's real? Tim, you think he's real?

Jimmy: Yeah, 'cos he, 'cos he, 'cos he, because he can talk real, he can talk real not, there's no man inside.

SH: No man inside.

Tim: Only real ones can talk, eh.

SH:	Sorry, Tim? What did you say?
Tim:	Real ones can talk eh.
[. . .]	
Jimmy:	No, 'cos the man's not inside his body.
SH:	He's not inside the body. So how does Big Bird talk?
Jimmy:	With that there [gesturing beak] that mouth.
SH:	Through his beak.
Jimmy:	Mm?
SH:	Through his beak, like this, through here.
Jimmy:	Through your mouth there.
SH:	Through your mouth. So Big Bird can talk to the other people in Sesame Street.
Jimmy:	Yes.

The boys appear to be rather confused here. On the one hand, the Bananas are judged to be people dressed up in banana suits because bananas *can't* talk. On the other hand, a huge yellow bird is judged real because it *can* talk. One explanation for this contradiction is to be gained from Jimmy's focus on the mouths of the characters in question (and it is important to know here that the Bananas' fibreglass suits have unmoving mouths while Big Bird has a beak that moves up and down while it 'speaks'). For Jimmy and Tim, one of the signifiers for this scheme of 'real' TV characters appears to involve talking through a moving mouth. Further evidence comes from the boys' consideration of Bugs Bunny who, of course, is a cartoon not a costume character:

SH:	Is Bugs Bunny real?
Jimmy:	But he eats carrots.
SH:	What do you think? Do you think he is?
Jimmy:	Yes 'cos he can talk with that mouth there [points to Bugs's open mouth in the picture].
Tim:	'Cos there's, 'cos there's no man inside him.
Jimmy:	But not the man inside his body no.
SH:	No, no man inside this one.

So, the ability to talk through a moving mouth is an important signifier of 'realness' in the case of Big Bird and Bugs Bunny – it appears, however, to lead Jimmy and Tim into a difficult situation over the characters in *The Simpsons*:

SH:	Are the Simpsons real?
Jimmy:	No, they, they just show 'em on the TV, they, but they can talk, they can talk, they can talk.
SH:	They can talk, and they talk with their mouths, don't they? So, does that mean that they're real?
Jimmy:	No. [pointing to the characters in the picture] He can talk, she can talk . . . um she can talk and he can talk and he can talk and she can talk.

> SH: Sure, they can all talk. So does that make them real?
> Jimmy: Yep.

Jimmy is in trouble here. He wants to claim that the Simpsons are not real, but they talk with moving mouths. The problem is, his scheme for real characters includes moving mouths. The discussion that follows about these characters (not quoted here) is unusually desultory for Jimmy, who tends to engage in what can only be described as 'distraction technique' (e.g. pointing out interesting little details in the picture before him, commenting on my spectacles and so on). Cognitive disequilibrium is uncomfortable – even embarrassing – as the schemes that have worked well in making sense of the world up to now are suddenly exposed as flawed. This new experience cannot be assimilated into the old scheme. It clearly doesn't fit so all Jimmy can do is stall for time in order to try and figure out, in Piagetian terms, how to accommodate.

Three girls, Nancy, Sally and Kerry (all 4 years old), also experience the same difficulty as Jimmy. Part of the exaggerated cartoon style of *The Simpsons* involves a yellow skin colour which Nancy and Sally identify as evidence that these characters are not real:

> SH: How are [the Simpsons] different from real people?
> Nancy: 'Cos they've got different skin.
> SH: Different skin? What, what way is it different?
> Sally: That stuff's yellow. That why.

The theory that different coloured skin discriminates the real from the not real works again for these girls when considering the character called Book Worm from *The Book Place* (he's not real because 'he's brown') but it becomes problematic as a signifier when Bert and Ernie from *Sesame Street* are considered. These characters are judged real because one has yellow skin and the other has orange skin, but I then point out that they have already judged the Simpsons to be *unreal* because they have yellow skin. This causes cognitive disequilibrium for these girls and they deal with it in the same way that Jimmy did:

> SH: OK. Does that make them ... does that make them like the
>   Simpsons then, 'cos they've got yellow skin, haven't they?
> Nancy: Yeah.
> SH: But you said the Simpsons weren't very real.
>   [Four-second pause]
> Sally: They got all of what's lots of skin.
> SH: Say that again.
> Sally: What?
> SH: What did you say? They've got all ...
> Sally: They got all skin, all together.
> SH: Right. But they're, they're not real, you said, but these two are
>   real, is that right?

Sally:	Yes.
SH:	Why are these two real [Bert and Ernie] and these [the Simpsons] not real?
	[Two second pause]
Sally:	Look he's talking [pointing to picture of Bert with his mouth open 'talking' to Ernie], look.
SH:	He's talking? What about these [the Simpsons]?
Sally:	They're talking.
Kerry:	Yes they talking.
SH:	They talk too. OK. But you still think that the Simpsons are not real . . . and Bert and Ernie are real . . . yes?
Kerry:	[pointing to Bart] And he's got a slingshot.
SH:	He's got a slingshot, that's right.
Nancy:	Slingshot . . . I didn't recognize that.

Once the contradiction has been pointed out, Nancy and Kerry fall silent, leaving it to Sally (4) to try, unsuccessfully, to explain what appears to be an anomaly. With the two pictures in front of her, Sally maintains that the Simpson characters are not real but Bert and Ernie are. The 'talking' signifier is mentioned but that cannot help in assimilating Bert and Ernie into the *real* TV characters scheme because the Simpson characters also talk. Once again, the episode illustrates what happens when assimilation no longer works and disequilibrium takes over. The girls are caught in a contradiction as it is clear Bert and Ernie cannot be assimilated into the scheme of *real* TV characters using the same criterion they have used to disqualify others. When they are probed a bit more, the girls, like Jimmy, seem to engage in distraction technique, pointing out interesting features of the pictures that do not appear to be very relevant to the problem at hand – a perfectly understandable response to contradiction and disequilibrium.

These discussions between Nancy, Sally and Kerry regarding Bert and Ernie from *Sesame Street* and Tim and Jimmy about *The Simpsons* seem classic cases of discovering a concept to be no longer functional. The petering out of the discussion into a sharing of 'irrelevant' observations about the image before them seems a good example of the confusion and perhaps embarrassment that occurs when one's working theories (ones that have worked quite well up to now), are suddenly exposed as flawed. In Piagetian terms, the only way out of this confusion is to accommodate – rethink the original scheme, modify and adapt it or create a new one to make sense of the data.

The 5, 6 and 7-Year-Olds

Children in this age group speculated intensely about many aspects of television content. The children largely relied on schemes they had already developed to deal with television and real life experience and they tried either to fit the new experiences into an existing scheme or, if this did not work, to modify the scheme or develop a new one.

Most of these children have schemes that can assimilate characters like Big Bird – they are either puppets or 'a person dressed up'. Peter (7) declares 'There are people inside them and they're acting.' Ross (6) and Elizabeth (6) account for Big Bird's size by claiming there are two people in the outfit, one standing on the other's shoulders. Tom (6) says: 'I think um, he's a person dressed up um with a birdie on top and um he talks inside so the birdie could um say . . . but he talks to the people from inside the thing.' Using the same scheme of 'people dressed up' to assimilate Bert and Ernie, he accounts for their small size by claiming: 'They must be little childs.'

Some of the 'quaintness' or the 'errors' (from an adult point of view) in the children's explanations are often due to the ingenious ways they are approaching the necessity of accommodation. One group, for example, speculates that Skippy is a person dressed up but the problem then is to explain how this person jumps convincingly like a kangaroo.[5] They modify their 'person dressed up scheme' to accommodate Skippy by claiming that there are 'tools in there and, um, when it bounced they had a moving trampoline.' Katie (7), on the other hand, assimilates Skippy into a 'real kangaroo' scheme because she says she can't see the join where the head piece of a costume meets the body and thus she cannot fit Skippy into her 'people dressed up' scheme.

Overassimilation is often apparent, particularly in discussions about cartoons. In this study, very few 5 to 7-year-old children had any accurate idea about how cartoons are made, but each discussion group speculated widely about their nature. From their talk, it is clear these children know cartoons are contrived, however in their explanations the majority refer to 'people dressed up' and 'puppets' rather than the fact that cartoons are drawn. What seems to be happening is that without the crucial knowledge about how it's done, cartoon characters are assimilated into the pre-existing scheme which makes sense of other types of characters whom the children have already worked out are not real.

The question of zippers supports this explanation. Some children have the reasonable theory, based on real-life experience, that if a character is someone dressed up, then there is likely to be a zipper on the suit somewhere. Not only does this lead them to claim they can see zippers that aren't there on *Sesame Street* characters like Big Bird and Snuffy, some children also claim they can see zippers on cartoon characters. Belinda (6), for example, says: 'Bugs Bunny isn't real . . . and Daffy Duck. 'Cos they both wear suits 'cos when they turn round you can see the zip up the back' – a clear case of adjusting the new experience to fit the existing scheme, or in Piaget's terms, making the unfamiliar, familiar. In the absence of accurate information, the children's existing schemes are stretched to fit – they overassimilate all characters they believe to be unreal into the existing concept of 'people dressed up'. The children who claim cartoons are drawn, on the other hand, have accommodated. They have either worked out or been shown how cartoons are created and thus they have a new scheme to explain the phenomenon.

That the process of accommodation is difficult, however, is demonstrated in the discussion about *The Simpsons* which occurs between Sean (5), Seth (5), Blair (5) and Con (6). To follow it, it is necessary to know that Bart's stylized spiky haircut does look something like a crown, there are no hair details round the back or sides of Bart's head and what remains of Homer's hair is suggested by a few bent lines jutting out from the base of his scalp.

SH: What about *The Simpsons*, what pile would you put that on?

All: Unreal.

SH: Unreal? Why is it unreal?

Con: Because um, it's a cartoon . . . and um, and people don't look like cartoons.

Sean: It's a cartoon.

Blair: And they don't have spiky hair.

SH: They have spiky hair?

Con: Yeah, they're yellow.

Sean: No, they just put a crown on . . . the crown on.

SH: Ah ha. OK. Do you agree with this Seth – it should go on this pile?

Seth: Yes. Um, but, the . . . I don't see it as a crown on there because it . . . because that, um because, then they'll, they'll see it's on the sides but it's not on the sides.

Sean: Yeah well they could just have a special crown and they um make it . . .

Seth: They could stick it on.

Sean: Yeah, they stick it on here [points to top of head] and then so it doesn't come down here [points to base of scalp].

Seth: And I know 'cos it's a cartoon 'cos uh, that uh, 'cos they turn away and then they still haven't and, and, and you, they don't have hair. They don't have ordinary hair, it doesn't . . .

Blair: Only the mother has it . . . hair.

SH: Sorry?

Sean: No.

Blair: Only the mother has hair.

SH: Only the mother has hair.

Sean: The mother turns around and then you can just see a bit.

SH: Right. So what you're saying is when they turn around . . .

Con: No and the dad, and the dad he has a little bit of hair.

Sean: No that's just pretend . . . spikes.

Seth: Or it might just be drawn on.

Sean: No, no it might be spikes, um, like stuck on or sticks.

SH: OK.

Seth: No, they're bent though.

Everyone agrees that *The Simpsons* are unreal, however only Con, the oldest child, uses the term 'cartoon' with anything like confidence. Attention focuses on the stylized representation of human beings that is used to depict the Simpson characters, in particular, the way their hair is drawn. In their discussions, the younger boys try to assimilate the exaggerated and simplified hair of the cartoon characters to their existing scheme of 'people dressed up' and so Bart's hair is explained as a 'special crown'. When this does not seem a very satisfactory explanation, the observation that Bart has no visible hairline when he turns round is used by Seth in an attempt to accommodate – cartoon characters are different from others in that they do not have a hairline on the back of their heads. That doesn't work, however, because Sean and Con point out that you can see the back of both Marge's and Homer's hair. Even though Sean claims Homer's hair is 'pretend' and Seth suggests it may be drawn, they revert to the old scheme of 'people dressed up' to explain the way Homer's few wispy strands of hair are depicted – they are 'bent sticks' or 'spikes' that have been 'stuck on'.

For these boys, all the elements for a new scheme are there – the concept of drawn pictures, the awareness that the characters are not 'real people' and the knowledge that the term 'cartoon' somehow has an explanatory function. However, despite the obvious disequilibrium, attempts at accommodation are not satisfactory and while assimilation to an old scheme is still possible, it is a strategy that the boys continue to use.

Vidiot, a popular game show involving knowledge about pop music, television programmes and video, intrigues because it has special effects that make it appear as though impossible things are happening in a real place and to real people. Contestants materialize at the beginning of the show as though they have been beamed down (using the 'Beam me down, Scotty' effect from *Star Trek*). When a question is answered incorrectly a bomb sound effect goes off. In the following discussion Sean (5), Seth (5) Blair (5) and Con (6) speculate about the 'bomb' which upsets their schemes for understanding what is materially possible in a TV game show:

Con:	I think [*Vidiot*] is real.
Seth:	It's not real 'cos it has a bomb, a bomb it goes down except you can't see it.
SH:	A bomb?
Con:	No, it's this drum that goes [drum/bomb noise]
SH:	Right.
Con:	And this . . . um . . . and this, um . . .
Blair:	Con!
Con:	. . . thing.
Seth:	It's not a drum.
SH:	Not a drum?
Seth:	No.
SH:	What is it?
Seth:	It's um, I think . . . that . . .
Con:	When it comes down it's just a brick they throw down.
Sean:	Or it might be a drum that's thrown down on the ground.

While cartoons, programmes with costume characters and those with special effects like *Vidiot* lend themselves to this kind of speculation, some TV live action shows encourage it too. Here Nick (7), Theo (5) and Carol (5) worry about the American family programme *The Cosby Show*. Initially they agree that the Huxtables' house is a real one but then they modify their position:

Nick: But the background's not. It's just a big wall or something, the background.

SH: So, what are you saying here?

Nick: Er, it's in between as well 'cos the background should be . . . like a background. The background's different.

SH: OK. So, if it's not in a real house, where is it really?

Nick: In a real house but the background's um like . . .

Carol: The garden, the garden . . .

Nick: Like a big wall, just like a big wall.

Carol: You have a big piece of cardboard painted with the background.

Nick: It has to be thick cardboard.

SH: Thick cardboard with the background painted on it.

Nick: But it's not – it is strong cardboard.

[Some minutes later after discussion of another programme]

Nick: I think um, um *The Cosby Show*, you know why er, I don't, now I don't think they've got the background on a big piece of cardboard because um, if that was cardboard how would, how would it balance?

SH: So it would, it would fall over you think?

Nick: Mm.

SH: OK.

Theo: Yeah, because er, the background, there's stairs on the background and they couldn't climb up the stairs because it's a background.

SH: So there would be nowhere to go.

Theo: Yes, they'd just walk straight past it.

Where the Huxtables live in *The Cosby Show* does look convincingly like a comfortable home; we usually see the living room with the stairs ascending to the upstairs bedrooms; we often see the bedrooms of different characters and sometimes scenes take place in the kitchen. Nick's judgment that it is a real house, then, appears to be based on this sense of authenticity. Children of this age, however, are also developing a strong awareness that television is a constructed medium (see Buckingham 1993; Hawkins 1977; Hodge and Tripp 1986) and it is the clash of these two contradictory schemes (real house versus not real house) that leads Nick into this speculation about 'the background' in his attempt to restore equilibrium. Lacking crucial knowledge about TV studios and sets, he tries to figure out how this illusion of a comfortable family house is created and he comes up with the notion of a big sheet of (thick) cardboard with a background painted on it (drawn perhaps from knowledge about painted theatrical backdrops). For the time being, these anomalous aspects of *The Cosby Show* are accommodated in a scheme that combines real houses and painted backdrops – but it is an uneasy accommodation and Nick does not find it very satisfying. After the discussion has moved on to another topic, he returns to *The Cosby Show* – the accommodation won't work because cardboard wouldn't balance. Theo agrees, pointing out that cardboard would not do at all because there are stairs at the back of the Huxtables' living room and people cannot climb a painted staircase.

The 8, 9 and 10-Year-Olds

The Cosby Show as well as some live action dramas like *The Bill* and *Children's Ward* also produced disequilibrium for the older 8 to 10-year-old children in this study. As was the case for 7-year-old Nick above, the problems seem to arise because of a need to balance the programmes' authenticity against the awareness that their status is actually fictional. At this age, however, this is expressed as confusion about the status of characters as well as about locations. Some programmes appear to be so realistic that old schemes for making sense of real life situations are used either to assimilate or, after modification, to accommodate the television experience. Like the 5 to 7-year-olds, these older children were asked to sort a number of different programmes in a way that showed those that were more 'real' and 'true to life' and those that were less so. Here, the discussion between Garry (10), Mark (10) and Alex (9) had suggested that in *The Cosby Show* there was some belief that the Huxtables were a real family:

> *SH:* And are they a real family? In real life?
> *Garry:* Yes.
> *Mark:* No, the dad and the boy, not the boy, the dad and the girl is, but the rest isn't.
> *SH:* What are the rest?
> *Garry:* They're just friends I think.
> *Alex:* Yes.
> *Mark:* Acting friends, not like . . . They didn't know each other until then.

In the following extract, James (9) modifies his original claim (not reported here) that the cast of *The Bill* are real police officers and claims instead it consists of both actors and real police. Dipesh (10) agrees. Anton (10) initially does not agree but then he either changes his mind or defers to James and Dipesh:

> *SH:* Are they real policemen in the programme?
> *James:* Yes.

Anton:	No.
James:	Some are, some ain't.
SH:	How can you tell the difference between them?
James:	'Cos like they . . . the ones that er get like . . . the ones that like . . . when I watched it once . . . the ones that got beat up . . . like they were real because they could take it. But the other ones couldn't. So they don't punch them up, they punch the people that are policemens up. I think.
SH:	So, the people who are in the programme are actually policemen in real life.
Dipesh:	Some.
James:	Some.
Anton:	Yes.
Dipesh:	'Cos they can't get lots and lots and lots of police officers . . .
SH:	Who are the other ones then?
Dipesh:	Actors.
SH:	Just actors.
Anton:	Yep.

An example in relation to *Children's Ward* (a live action children's drama set in a hospital) shows James (9) and Dipesh (10) also trying to balance the programme's authenticity against its fictional status. James 'can't remember' whether he actually saw the fake needle but fake needles are consistent with fictional stories – on the other hand, some of the children on the ward are long-term residents and only really sick people are kept in hospital for long periods of time. Initially these boys had said that *Children's Ward* was 'real':

SH:	What about the kids in *Children's Ward* – are they really sick children?
Anton:	No. Just pretend . . .
Dipesh:	No, not all of them.
SH:	Just pretend?
Anton:	Most of them are pretend.
SH:	Just acting are they?
Anton:	Yes.
Dipesh:	Yes.
James:	Like 'cos like . . . that boy wanted an operation and he's got this invisible thing, a teddy bear or whatever it is, and he didn't really get an injection or something.
SH:	You don't think so?
James:	I think that was just pretend like. If they showed you – I can't remember whether they showed you or not – there was just a blunt needle and when they pushed it in, it didn't go in, it was a blunt needle and it went straight up into the thing again.
SH:	So you think this was just pretend.

> *James:*   When people are brought in, they're just pretend, but when like they've been in there since the beginning, I don't think it's pretend like, there's this girl's got a broken arm . . . and there's a girl that's got a broken neck . . .
>
> *Anton:*   . . . and they run away.
>
> *SH:*   And you think she's probably really sick?
>
> *Dipesh:*   Yes.
>
> *James:*   Yeah.

It would be unwise to think that the confusions illustrated above are evidence that 8 to 10-year-old children believe they are seeing life as it is actually happening for the people in these programmes or even that they are viewing a documentary. In the examples above, and elsewhere in their discussions, there is plenty of evidence to suggest that the children are well aware that they are watching a scripted, fictional story. The difficulty arises because live action drama on television often *looks* very real, it *looks* very authentic. The children have seen real police officers, they know they are trained to defend themselves, they have been inside hospitals and they know they have sick people in them. What they see on *The Bill* and *Children's Ward* is consistent with these real life experiences so the real life schemes for 'police' and 'hospitals' can be used to assimilate what they see on the television. They also know now, however, that TV is a constructed medium, that parts are taken by actors, that special props can create the illusion of, say, a real injection. The understanding that TV programmes are essentially fabricated, however, does not square with the very convincing visual authenticity that programmes like *The Bill* present. The children in the extracts above have reached an accommodation of sorts; they conclude that a mixture of actors and real people populate these programmes. Alex (9), who reasons that the characters in *Children's Ward* must be actors because you can't ask sick people to act, demonstrates both the competing schemes and the fragility of this accommodation.

Conclusion

The popular press loves to use images of wide-eyed children staring fixedly at television screens to illustrate stories or articles about children and television. Such pictures are usually interpreted to mean that any serious brain functioning is on hold – the child is mesmerized, hypnotized by the flickering screen. From the evidence presented here, however, it's more likely that the child viewer's 'bug-eyed' look comes from serious concentration and an intense scrutiny of the televisual image. How else would one know that Bart Simpson's hairline doesn't exist round the back of his head or that some TV characters talk through moving mouths like humans and others don't?

The young participants in this study have certainly been watching television closely and thinking about how its images relate to reality. With their emphases on talking mouths, natural skin colour, zippers on costumes and so on, these children are using real life experience as the original against which representations of the real are calibrated and they are developing 'rules of reality' which increase in sophistication as they grow older. The 8 to 10-year-old participants here, for example, are puzzling over the status of characters in TV realism whereas the younger children are still working out how to make sense of costumed characters like Big Bird.[6]

As a way of conceptualizing this thinking and learning process, Piaget's equilibration model is particularly valuable. Children are developing hypotheses and theories to explain television's representations of reality. All the while their viewing experiences can be explained in terms of familiar conceptual schemes (or through making only minor adjustments to them), there is cognitive balance or equilibrium. Sometimes, however, as can be seen from the children's talk, these schemes are stretched in order to squeeze in information that does not really fit. These nobbly, unwieldy schemes may suffice for the time being but disequilibrium cannot be held off for long and sooner or later these portmanteau schemes will have to be unpacked and the contents redistributed into new schemes that make better sense of the world. Cognitive disequilibrium brings feelings of uneasiness or embarrassment and it is this uncomfortable state that drives the search for a better way of making sense of things. Only through accommodation can cognitive confusion be transformed into equilibrium.

Both disequilibrium and equilibrium can be experienced through collaborative discussion. Throughout the transcripts presented here there are examples of children's theories being unsettled by their peers as well as examples of children 'scaffolding' one another, building on each other's ideas in order to accommodate discrepant television experiences. Many of these attempts to accommodate are ingenious and creative but sometimes 'scaffolding' is not productive if one's discussion partners cannot supply crucial information. If these children were told or shown how cartoons are made; how TV studio sets are created; how actors rehearse and have lives outside the TV series; how special effects are achieved, then they could move on and devote the impressive amount of mental energy being expended on these questions to other more interesting things. There is a clear need here for adults to do much more in the way of 'scaffolding' than they presently do.

One way in which this can be achieved is to watch television with children and provide a commentary about the kinds of things discussed in this chapter – indeed 'good parents' in our society are exhorted to do precisely this. In so far as adults have the time and/or the inclination to engage in this activity, it is reasonable advice, although such didacticism is likely to impair the pleasure children experience in watching their favourite programmes. A preferable strategy is to let teachers do it in a carefully developed media studies curriculum.

In the crowded timetable of the primary school it is hard to argue for the inclusion of yet another 'essential' subject, but this chapter shows that television has value for children other than as entertainment or a popular pastime. If the participants in this study are any guide, primary school-aged children pay close attention to their favourite television programmes and these have the capacity to stimulate even the very young into thinking about such philosophical issues as the nature of social reality and questions of representation. In the media studies class-room this spontaneous intellectual activity can be supported and extended in the true sense of 'scaffolding'. Collaborative discussion about television/reality schema can be encouraged and facilitated; important 'technical' information (e.g. how cartoons are made) can be introduced; issues can be raised and children can be allowed to explore them in ways that both acknowledge their pleasure and extend their understanding.

Contrary to popular opinion, this study shows that television can actually stimulate intellectual activity rather than prevent it – if Bill Cosby and Homer Simpson have a role to play here, then it's time these characters made an appear-ance in school!

Notes

1 Buckingham (1993: 3) cites an address by HRH The Prince of Wales on opening the Museum of the Moving Image in London in 1988. The Prince attacked what he saw as 'an incessant menu of gratuitous violence on both cinema and television.'

In 1992, Paul Keating, then Prime Minister of Australia, reported that one of his daughters had suffered nightmares after watching a violent film on television. At his insistence, TV stations changed the broadcast time for violent feature films from 8.30 to 9.00 p.m. in 1993.

In 1994, the Pope attacked 'graphic depictions of brutal violence' on television and told parents to switch off their sets.

Senator Bob Dole is reported as saying on the floor of the US Senate: 'Those who continue to deny that cultural messages can and do bore deep into the hearts and minds of our young people are deceiving themselves and ignoring reality' (*Rolling Stone* 22:2:1996).

2 Indeed, many of my own students claim that the children they have taught on teach-ing practice have had their imaginations and their creativity eroded by television because recycled television material frequently appears in their written work, drama and free play.

3 *The Curiosity Show* was an extremely popular children's science programme, produced (on a shoe-string budget) in Adelaide, which ended up being broadcast Australia-wide for many years. The enthusiastically avuncular presenters, Rob Morrison and Dean Hutton would demonstrate, each week, how such things as scientific phenomena and household items worked or they would show children how to make simple but effective devices.

4 *The Simpsons* is an animated comedy about an American family which, in many ways, is the antithesis of the idealized family featured in such shows as *The Brady Bunch* and *Family Ties*.

Bananas in Pyjamas is an extremely popular programme created by and presented on the public broadcasting network in Australia (The Australian Broadcasting Commis-sion). The two main characters (B1 and B2) are people dressed up in fibreglass suits that look like huge bananas – and, yes, they are wearing blue and white striped pyjamas. The other characters are teddy bears and they are also people in costumes.

The Bill is a British live action drama series set in and around a London police station. It is a programme intended for an adult audience but many 8 to 10-year-olds in this study reported watching and enjoying it.

5   *Skippy* is a much loved Australian children's drama, featuring a real kangaroo in the title role.

6   For a fuller discussion about the 'rules of reality' that children develop as they think about television, see Howard, S. M. (1993, 1994) as well as Hodge and Tripp (1986) and Buckingham (1993) cited above.

References

BENNETT, S. and BENNETT, R. (1994) *Kick the TV Habit*, Harmondsworth: Penguin.

BRUNER, J. (1986) *Actual Minds, Possible Worlds*, Cambridge, MA: Harvard University Press.

BUCKINGHAM, D. (1993) *Children Talking Television: The Making of Television Literacy*, London: Falmer Press.

DAVIDSON, J. (1996) 'Menace to society', *Rolling Stone*, 22 February.

HAWKINS, R. P. (1977) 'The dimensional structure of children's perceptions of television reality', *Communication Research*, **4**(3): 299–320.

HODGE, B. and TRIPP, D. (1986) *Children and Television: A Semiotic Approach*, Cambridge, Polity Press.

HOWARD, S. M. (1993) 'How real is television? The modality judgements of young children', *Media Information Australia*, **70**, November.

HOWARD, S. M. (1994) ' "Real bunnies don't stand on two legs": Five, six and seven year old children's perceptions of television reality', *Australian Journal of Early Childhood*, **19**: 35–43.

JAMES, A. and PROUT, A. (eds) (1990) *Constructing and Reconstructing Childhood: Contemporary Issues in the Sociological Study of Childhood*, London: Falmer Press.

MARTI, E. (1996) 'Individuals create culture: Comments on van der Veer's "The concept of culture in Vygotsky's thinking" ', *Culture and Psychology*, **2**(3): 265–72.

MEADOWS, S. (1993) *The Child as Thinker: The Development and Acquisition of Cognition in Childhood* London: Routledge.

PIAGET, J. (1954) *The Construction of Reality in the Child* (trans. Margaret Cook) Basic Books: New York.

PIAGET, J. (1975/1985) *The Equilibration of Cognitive Structures* (trans. Terrence Brown and Kishore Julian Thampy) Chicago, IL: University of Chicago Press.

QUALITATIVE SOLUTIONS AND RESEARCH (1990) *NUD•IST Software (v 3.0)* Melbourne: Latrobe University.

SIGEL, I. E. and COCKING, R. R. (1977) *Cognitive Development: From Childhood to Adolescence: A Constructivist Perspective*, New York: Holt, Rinehart and Winston.

URWIN, C. (1985) 'Constructing motherhood: The persuasion of normal development', in C. STEEDMAN, C. URWIN and V. WALKERDINE (eds) *Language, Gender, and Childhood*, London: Routledge and Kegan Paul.

VYGOTSKY, L. (1978) *Mind in Society: The Development of Higher Psychological Processes* (ed. M. Cole, V. John-Steiner, S. Scribner and E. Souberman) Cambridge, Mass.: Harvard University Press.

WALKERDINE, V. (1984) 'Developmental psychology and the child-centred pedagogy: the insertion of Piaget into early education' in J. HENRIQUES, W. HOLLOWAY, C. URWIN, C. VENN and V. WALKERDINE (eds) *Changing the Subject: Psychology, Social Regulation and Subjectivity*, London: Methuen.

WALKERDINE, V. (1985) *Psychology and Schooling: What's the Matter?* Bedford Way Papers No. 25, London: Institute of Education.

WERTSCH, J. V. (1985) *Vygotsky and the Social Formation of Mind*, Cambridge, MA: Harvard University Press.

WILLIS, P. (1992) 'Notes on method', in S. HALL, D. HOBSON, A. LOWE, and P. WILLIS (eds) *Culture, Media, Language*, London: Routledge.

WINN, M. (1977) *The Plug-in Drug: Children, Television and the Family*, New York: Viking Press.

WOOD, D. (1988) *How Children Think and Learn*, Oxford: Basil Blackwell.

Chapter Five

The middle years:
Children and television – cool or just plain boring?

Linda Sheldon

For some years, as part of its children's research programme, the Australian Broadcasting Authority (the ABA) has been talking to 5 to 12-year-old children about television.[1] The first stage of the present research project examined classification issues; these were defined by the ABA as those things that concern or bother children about television violence, kissing, nudity and swearing.[2] The second stage of the project examined what attracts children to certain programmes.[3] When it came to talking about television, the transcribed comments below indicate something of the enthusiasm and the diversity of opinion that the children who were the participants in these studies brought to the task:

> There's a bit of a line between what kids understand and adults can't
> – kids will go laughing and laughing and adults will just go ohhh! My
> parents think *The Simpsons* is so boring – and like, we're fully cracking up!
> (Stephen, Grade 6)[4]

> Stupid bad is when it's boring, but stupid good is when it's *so*, so stupid.
> (Kyle, Grade 3/4)

> If it was based on a true story you would feel really sick if someone died
> or if something really bad happened, you would feel really bad inside. But
> if it is just a movie and it isn't based on a true story and it is like a horror
> and you are scared or something you think, well it is not real, it doesn't
> really matter.
>
> (Amy, Grade 5/6)

Previous Research

Australian researchers have been investigating issues of violence on television for some years (e.g. Edgar 1977; McCann and Sheehan 1985; Sheehan 1980; Tulloch and Tulloch 1992). Generally, when it comes to questions of children's feelings about the violence depicted specifically on news and current affairs programmes, it is concerned adults who have spoken for and about children and only recently have children's views been heard. One piece of research that has solicited children's views, however, is the work of Gillard *et al.* (1993). Here, 8 to 12-year-olds were asked to discuss their recollections of the Gulf War. It was found that girls took the realism of the news presentations and the gravity of the subject very literally, which produced anxiety about and/or avoidance of further depictions of the conflict. Boys, on the other hand, watched more television coverage of the war and were generally more interested in the telecasts of it.

This research builds on earlier research (Noble and Freiberg 1985; Palmer 1986) which showed that news and current affairs were the types of programmes that were least popular with children. Both Palmer (1986) and Roberts (1989) have claimed that children are unlikely to freely choose to watch the news unless parents direct them to do so – a view supported by Burton (1991), who reports many 8 to 12-year-olds are scared by some things on the news but that parents insist they watch. Noble and Freiberg (1985) found that news programmes are unpopular with 6 to 12-year-olds because the 'fluttery feeling inside' (i.e. arousal or excitement that attracts children to watch certain shows) is least present for news programmes.

Qualitative work in Australia by Russell (1993), who worked with groups of 11 to 12-year-olds, showed most concern was about the violent content of news broadcasts. Any violence presented in these programmes was perceived to be real and to represent the world as it really is (in contrast with drama). Specific concerns mentioned by children included depictions of physical assault and intrusion into personal grief and suffering in news programmes.

Gender differences, similar to those discovered by Gillard *et al.* (1993) described above, have also been identified in other Australian research (e.g. Chung 1990; Russell 1993; Sheehan 1983). Russell reports that girls show more concern about news, current affairs and drama programmes depicting violence and 'scary' situations. Longitudinal research by Sheehan (1983) shows consistent sex differences; boys (especially those in Grades 3 to 5) watched their preferred programmes more, preferred more violent programmes, were judged as more aggressive by their classmates and day-dreamed in aggressive ways more than girls. There was no indication, however, that subsequent behaviour was causally linked to viewing. Edgar (1977) reported that males aged 12 to 14 years enjoyed watching violence on television more than females. Both males and females in this study reported being more upset by seeing animals hurt than they were by viewing gunfights.

Children's television preferences – what they enjoy and why they enjoy it – have also been studied.[5] While much of the research is from a quantitative perspective, there has been a recent shift in the methodology to more ethnographic or qualitative research models. Gunter, McAleer and Clifford (1991), for example, interviewed children and found they saw television as a convenient source of entertainment, a time filler, and a way to learn about things. Children spoke of gaining companionship from television characters and being exposed to places and aspects of life that might otherwise be unattainable to them. Television was also something that most children had in common and so it provided a shared interest and topic of conversation. Children claimed that television (particularly soaps like *Neighbours*) gave them information for dealing with 'personal problems' (Gunter and McAleer 1990; Gunter *et al.* 1991). *Neighbours* was also especially liked by British children for its cliffhanger endings and its realistic portrayal of characters – children felt that this programme got the balance between participation and escape just right. Quiz shows were liked for their intellectual challenge but children were critical of difficult language and they liked shows to have gimmicks, sound effects and/or computer graphics.

Rubins suggests children watch television for several reasons: they watch it to pass time and to relax; for arousal and companionship; to learn and to forget (Rubins 1977, cited in Signorielli 1991). Zohoori (1988) also found that children watch TV for companionship and for escape. Noble and Freiberg (1985), in an Australian study, found that the top two reasons for watching television were to pass the time when there was nothing else to do and to provide company when the child was lonely and had no one to play with; the third reason for watching was for entertainment because television was seen as exciting. Palmer (1986) found that children wanted to learn about the world, not in a narrow educational sense, but in ways that were enjoyable and involving.

Lyle and Hoffman's 1972 study (cited in Comstock and Paik 1991) found that, in terms of types of programme, first graders preferred comedies and cartoons, whereas sixth graders preferred situation comedies and action adventure programmes. Children also tended to find programmes produced for adults appealing. Luke (1990) suggests this is because adult programmes are supported by higher budgets and contain state of the art production techniques.

There were gender differences with television preferences just as there were for television concerns; Palmer (1986), for example, reported that once children reached the ages of 11 or 12, girls showed markedly different preferences to boys. Girls enjoyed serial dramas which they defined as 'realistic', whereas boys still enjoyed adventure stories with 'goodies' and 'baddies'.

The two ABA studies to be discussed in this chapter have sought to combine the qualitative and quantitative research methods that have been a feature of work on children and television over the last 10 years. The first study asked children what they found worrying in relation to television violence, swearing, kissing and nudity. The second study asked children to talk not only about their favourite programmes but also about those they disliked.

The Studies

The first study involved two stages: a qualitative stage that consisted of 18 exploratory focus group discussions with 5 to 12-year-olds in New South Wales (NSW) (a total of 108 children) and a quantitative stage that involved 54 primary schools in NSW which included a final sample of 1602 children in Grades 3 to 6; these children were 8 to 12-year-olds. The qualitative stage was conducted in April 1993 and the fieldwork for the quantitative stage in November 1993. The sample of 1602 primary school children was stratified by region and within regions according to the NSW Department of School Education statistics and the research was conducted in schools using individual questionnaires. Consent forms and letters of explanation to parents about the research were translated into 15 community languages and provided to schools on request. Parents' views were also considered in this research and a matched sample of 517 parents were interviewed. During the focus group discussions, segments from television programmes and videos were shown to children as stimulus material. All clips were either from C-rated programmes (children's classified programmes); G-rated programmes (programmes for general viewing) or PGR-rated programmes (programmes where parental guidance is recommended).[6]

In the second study there were 11 focus groups, including pairs of friends and five affinity groups (friendship groups recruited through schools). Discussions with children aged from 5 years (Grade 1) to 12 years (Grade 6) involved a sample of 117 children. These discussions were held in April, May and August 1995.

As the research design for this project was based on qualitative methods, results are not, of course, representative of all children aged 5 to 12 years in Australia; instead, they provide a descriptive account of current trends in these particular groups of children. It is also important to note that what children say or claim to watch in the unusual situation of the research discussion group is not necessarily an accurate reflection of what they really think or prefer – both boys and girls are probably influenced to some degree by social desirability factors and are using the situation to their own social advantage.

Children's Concerns about Television

Contextual data collected for the first study included information about how much television children actually watched and children's and parents' estimates were compared. Results from the survey of 1602 children showed that nearly two-thirds (62 per cent), claimed to watch television every day and there was strong agreement between parents and children over this reported frequency of viewing. Twenty-seven per cent of children said they watched television most days but not every day and 1 per cent didn't watch or only watched at other people's houses. Children's and parents' opinions differed in relation to the actual times of day children's viewing occurred. For example, parents were less likely than their children to report that television was watched before school (35 per cent of parents/53 per cent of children); during dinner on school days (34 per cent of parents/54 per cent of children) and in the afternoon after school (71 per cent of parents/87 per cent

Table 5.1   Household rules: Comparison of children's and parents' responses

	Child reporting (%)	Parent reporting (%)
When I've finished my homework*	61	71
I'm only allowed to watch certain programmes*	56	91
When I've finished special jobs or things like music practice*	41	63
I'm only allowed to watch a certain amount of television*	32	67
I can't watch television before breakfast*	32	42
I can only watch at certain times*	30	63
It has to be turned off at meal times*	24	41
I am not allowed to watch television at other people's houses†	6	4
No rules, can watch anything I like*	8	2

n=517 (matched pairs).
Multiple responses allowed.
* Significance at 0.01 level using Wilcoxon Matched-Pairs Signed-Rank Test. Reflects disagreement between parents and their children.
† Indicates agreement between parents and their children.

of children). Parents and children tended to agree about the incidence of viewing in the evening after dinner both on school days (84 per cent parents/79 per cent children) and at the weekend (88 per cent parents/82 per cent children); these latter results may be because co-viewing is more likely to happen at these times, whereas at other times parents are generally working or are occupied with other activities in the home.

Nearly all children (89 per cent) identified rules about watching television at home. Most rules related to the completion of tasks, such as homework, special jobs and music practice before TV watching was allowed. Most parents (98 per cent) reported the existence of rules, with the major ones concerning the regulation of certain programmes, restrictions on the overall time spent viewing and not allowing television watching until homework had been done. There were significant differences between parents and children in the reporting of household rules, but, overall both recognized the existence of a variety of rules relating to television (see Table 5.1).

'Finishing homework' was an important rule for both parents and children with 71 per cent of parents and 61 per cent of children citing this rule. However, 91 per cent of parents claimed to exercise control over the types of programmes they allowed their children to view, while only 56 per cent of children reported or were aware of such rules.

We ask him to go to bed at 8.30 p.m. so that he doesn't see the bad stuff.
(mother, 35–44 years)

> If a show was unsuitable I'd probably watch it with her and discuss it and
> if it was way out of line I'd switch it off.
>
> (father, 25–34 years)

On average, children reported approximately three television rules operating in their household, whereas parents were able to report an average of four and a half rules. Since parents were the main rule-makers about television viewing, not only were they able to report more rules, they were more aware of certain 'less specific rules', such as restricting children from watching certain programmes or only allowing a certain amount of television viewing. Children, on the other hand, may have interpreted these restrictions as regular household routines rather than recognizing their status as rules. It is also important to be aware that there are some social desirability factors in asking parents about television-watching rules. Australian society places importance on being a 'good', responsible parent and one way that this can be signalled to others is in claims about monitoring children's television viewing. The fact that 89 per cent of children indicated the presence of family rules about television viewing in their households, however, suggests that this was not just a matter of social window dressing and that such rules really do exist.

The responses of parents about what incidents, programmes or types of programmes upset their children were compared with their children's responses. The three categories of programme which attracted frequent responses from both parents and children were: violence, 'real life' depictions and specific movies and programmes. The types of incidents or programmes where agreement between parents and children was closest related to the portrayal of monsters/horror, death, accidents and advertisements. There was also strong agreement between particular parents (28 per cent) and their children (26 per cent) where it was claimed that nothing on television upset or concerned the child. Disagreements between parents' and children's judgments were found in categories concerning 'real life', violence, specific movies and programmes, sex, nudity and kidnaps.

Within each of the broad categories mentioned, a range of items were cited. The main types of incidents or programmes that parents considered had upset their children were categorized as: news/current affairs (34 per cent); movies (21 per cent); people being bashed/fighting/violence (15 per cent); animals being hurt or killed (14 per cent) and children being hurt/killed/murdered/abused (10 per cent). By comparison, the incidents or programmes nominated most often by children were categorized as: animals being hurt or killed (21 per cent); people/someone being killed (16 per cent); movies (11 per cent); news and current affairs (8 per cent); people being bashed and fighting (8 per cent) and people being murdered (8 per cent). Of the main themes or incidents mentioned by children, all but two related to violence. Parents were more likely to name the type of programme which gave rise to their child's concern. Thus news/current affairs and movies were cited ahead of violent incidents. While the emphasis is different between parents and children, both lists are, in fact, very similar.

> The news scenes, like the Somalia footage or children starving or if she sees
> guns on TV she'll cover her eyes – even documentaries with animals dying.
>
> (mother, 35–44 years)

Current affairs stuff worries her, when she sees kids being hurt or older people being bashed or robbed – basically any injustices. Most of the stuff that upsets her is seen on the news. Any factual real life stuff.

(father, 35–44 years)

There were strong gender differences in this research, with girls being more likely than boys to exhibit self-censorship. More than half the children surveyed (55 per cent) had stopped watching television by either leaving the room or changing channels because something had upset them. Girls (66 per cent) were more likely to report this behaviour than boys (44 per cent).

Most children indicated they watched the news (92 per cent). Reasons most commonly given were personal interest (36 per cent) and to find out what had happened that day (25 per cent). In relation to the news, children in Grades 1 to 4 specifically mentioned not liking to see blood as it made them feel sick, especially when they were eating their dinner.

We usually get our tea when the news is on and therefore I don't like watching it when all the blood and guts and that sort of stuff is on when you are eating.

(Carlo, Grade 3/4)

News items on television concerning things happening near where the children lived were particularly frightening for this group because this seemed 'very real'. As the news clip we used in the study did not deal with local news items, most of the age group were not particularly worried by it. They generally thought that the news should be on TV to let people know what was happening in the world.

They need to show it because that is what happened and they are just showing what happened.

(Alicia, Grade 5/6)

The type of violence a drama programme contained largely influenced the way the children reacted. The strongest negative reactions were evoked by programmes depicting violence where children and animals were the victims. Sixty-two per cent of children said they didn't like to watch programmes that showed children being hurt or 'whacked' and 60 per cent rejected programmes that made it look as if animals were being hurt or killed. Fifty-nine per cent of children also said they did not like to see programmes that showed parents arguing and hitting each other.

It just shows that when it goes just a bit too far on TV shows. It's all right to get smacked with a smack one time, but on shows they just go a bit too far and they do it about 10 times, and it really bothers you.

(Sean, Grade 5/6)

Positive reactions were evoked by programmes that were action-packed with fights, guns and car chases with 50 per cent of all children claiming they really liked to watch them and only 20 per cent claiming they didn't. Forty-nine per cent of children really liked to watch programmes about monsters and ghosts that were 'real'; they enjoyed, for example, programmes like *The Extraordinary* that discussed the supernatural as though it were a real phenomenon, blurring the lines between fantasy and reality. These were easily distinguished from programmes that were 'fake' horror. Programmes that showed real life crimes and talked about real criminals, however, were less popular, with only 34 per cent of children claiming that they really liked to watch these programmes. Specifically, children were talking about *Australia's Most Wanted*, a programme which re-enacts current crimes in order to encourage members of the community to provide information which will assist in solving them. There were mixed responses to programmes with people fighting and beating each other up, with 41 per cent of children claiming they didn't like to watch them compared to 25 per cent who did.

For some children, violence was one thing, but kissing and nudity were quite another.

I like violence because it's not like . . . I don't like much kissing. I just like machine guns and everything.

(Nicholas, Grade 1/2)

[About a kissing scene in *Beverly Hills 90210*] That bit at the end, I know it's not for kids but, well, I know it's not educational or anything, but some kids, they like to have a break in life. They can't keep on watching educational shows every day. They have to have a break and watch soaps or something.

(Maria, Grade 3/4)

Programmes with adults kissing 'a little bit' were acceptable to a large proportion of children but programmes in which adults were 'getting carried away' with their kissing were less popular:

If they are just going for a swim or anything my parents don't worry about it but if they are going to make love or anything, they make you go out of the room or something like that.

(Joe, Grade 3/4)

In regard to nudity, 58 per cent of children said they didn't like to watch programmes showing grown up men with 'hardly any clothes on', while 47 per cent of children said they didn't like to watch shows featuring women with 'hardly any clothes on'. As far as swearing was concerned, most children who participated in the focus groups weren't especially worried by it and some said they didn't actually notice much in the programmes they watched.

There is only about three or four words in there. If there's a whole movie and every second word is a swear word, then I wouldn't exactly watch

that, but if it was just three or four words every now and then just a word
every now and then, then it'd be OK to [watch].

(Sarah, Grade 5/6)

Children generally thought that their parents wouldn't mind them watching
shows with swearing in them as long as they didn't contain 'bad swear words' such
as the 'F-word'. Children were easily able to separate the bad swear words from
the ones more commonly used in everyday speech. Programmes with a little bit of
swearing were quite acceptable, with 35 per cent of children claiming they really
liked to watch these kinds of programmes while 14 per cent of children claimed
they didn't. Thirty-nine per cent of children, however, said they didn't like to watch
programmes with people using very rude words.

Across each of these classification areas there were strong gender differences
with girls being more likely to react negatively to most programme scenarios involving varying degrees of violence, action, horror, kissing and swearing.

What Children Like and Dislike on Television

The second stage of the children's research programme was conducted in 1995 and
focused on what children like to watch on television. The main reasons why children said they watched television were education, entertainment, escape, company
and 'something to do'.

Essentially, when children spoke about a programme being a favourite or
'good', the words they used included 'funny' or 'exciting and interesting' or it had
'action'. It was difficult for them to explain what they meant in greater detail as the
following extracts show:

Interviewer:	What makes programmes that you like 'good'?
Ashlee:	Different.
Angela:	Serial.
Elizabeth:	Fiction, they're not non-fiction.
Georgina:	Not depressing like things like Rwanda and stuff.

(Grades 4–7)

Exciting – like you want to know what's going to happen and you get all
excited.

(Amelia, Grade 6)

Children indicated that shows that become their favourites are pitched at a level
they can understand. These tend to be what they call 'family shows', often have
an adult orientation and are not overly complex in the plot or humour. Roy and
Franco (Grade 6 boys) are here discussing shows that are difficult for children to
understand:

Roy: Except for the *X Files*, other than that, some of the movies – if you don't really know how to understand it – if you watch the show – you don't like get the plot at all. You probably wouldn't know who's in movies . . . what the story is and things.

Franco: Sometimes if you see a movie and it's for adults you're asking your parents all the time, 'What – is that guy good or is he bad?' or something like that.

Essentially in this study comedy, variety, drama, cartoons and situation comedies were all children's favourites. Age tended to influence choice rather than gender. There was a tendency for Grade 1/2 children to be downward-looking in their selection of favourite programmes, still preferring some preschool programmes such as *Bananas in Pyjamas* and other children's programmes, such as *Blinky Bill*, which are scheduled in the afternoon after school. Grade 3/4 children were more upward-looking in their selection, preferring programmes, such as *The Brady Bunch* and *The Simpsons*, that were scheduled in the early evening timeslot. Grade 5/6 children preferred a diverse range of programmes. Adventure comedies, such as *Lois and Clark* were popular, soaps such as *Neighbours* and *Home and Away* were frequently mentioned as were animated programmes such as *The Simpsons*. Older children appeared to enjoy programmes that rated well with adults; most of the programmes these grades enjoyed were on in the 6.30 p.m. to 9.30 p.m. time slot.

Children's comments in the earlier discussions suggested that physically attractive characters in a programme heightened their enjoyment of the programme; this possibility was confirmed by producers, directors, writers, editors, child development experts and network representatives who were subsequently consulted. The latter indicated that children like to see attractive people, the latest fashions, stars, personalities and celebrities on television. Jonathan Taylor Thomas from *Home Improvement*, for example, was spontaneously mentioned by one group of girls as 'gorgeous' and clearly he was part of the reason for watching this show: 'that guy . . . ohhhhhhhhh!' A few older boys mentioned Pamela Anderson from *Bay Watch* as part of the reason they watched this show. It was found, however, that while good-looking characters were noted and enjoyed by children, acting ability and the right 'attitude' were considered much more important. It was a 'turn-off' if a good-looking character acted in an anti-social manner. *Beverly Hills 90210* was regarded as having cute guys but 'some drink too much alcohol. Luke Perry is really good-looking but he's acting really stupid'. Being cute but a hopeless actor or 'try hard' was not appealing. In discussing good-looking guys, girls said:

Not just because of that – I watch it for – watching them act.

(Rachel, Grade 4)

You do [notice if boys are cute], but you don't have a word for it.

(Brooke, Grade 6)

Discussing the 'cute guys' or 'spunks' was a source of embarrassment for this age group who giggled and looked at each other when the topic was discussed.

Boys in Grade 5/6 used a variety of words to describe good-looking girls such as 'chicks' or 'babes'. It wasn't the main reason for liking a show, but it helped.

Christopher: If there's too much like good-looking girls it gets a bit boring – if they throw one in here and there, then it's all right.
Mark: . . . Stuff like *Bay Watch*. That's a boys' show.
Liam: If you're a total dead-beat you watch it for the story-line
– but there is none.

Not all boys could discuss the concept of 'hunky' guys on television without a tinge of embarrassment or protestations of homophobic, macho denial. It was more important that male characters were funny, such as Jim Carrey. Here some Grade 6 boys discuss the matter of looks:

Interviewer: Are guys good-looking on TV programmes?
Alexander: I'm sure to some girls they probably would be.
Interviewer: Not to boys?
[Laughter]
Grant: Not unless you're G-A-Y.

Children were asked what age group they preferred their favourite television characters to belong to. Most children (i.e. both girls and boys and different age groups) reported they liked seeing characters their age, a few years older, teenagers and young adults. Their definition of young adults was 'people in their early 20s' as the following extract from some Grade 6 boys shows:

Interviewer: Do you like seeing kids your age on television or do you
like people who are older?
Matthew: Teenagers are sort of good I reckon.
Henry: Our age, you can kind of relate to what they're saying.
Oliver: Yeah, our age and teenagers and stuff. Don't like old people.
Interviewer: How old do you have to be to be old?
Matthew: Twenty and over.
Oliver: At least 40 and over.

Most of the older children, however, often had difficulty in articulating why they preferred certain ages. The reasons given for their preference for older char-acters were often that they 'acted better' and had 'better roles than kids have, usually doing more exciting things'.

Children recognized that children, adults and family dynamics portrayed in television programmes were not 'true to life'. Adults acted differently from their parents and were often much less strict. This was mentioned specifically in relation to some of their favourite characters such as Homer Simpson, who was much easier for Bart to handle than their parents were. It was clear that Bart's naughtiness appealed to children; he could get away with things in a way they couldn't at home or at school. The children also appeared to enjoy this programme because parents did not always approve of it.

Animation was immensely popular with all children. *The Simpsons* met with unconditional acceptance from the vast majority of children; they were aware it was not primarily aimed at children, but the more adult themes added to their enjoyment as they were presented in a way children could understand. Many children continue to enjoy repeats of this show as the following quotation from Jessica (Grade 4) shows:

> *Interviewer:* If you had to take one show to a desert island, if you were going to be stuck there for a very long time, which one would you take?
>
> *Jessica:* Endless Simpsons.

Comedy programmes were favourite shows and magazine and quiz/game shows were popular as long as they had good prizes, gimmicks and had questions that did not patronize children. Both boys and girls watched sport on television and it was not necessary for the child viewer to be a player of a sport to enjoy watching it. Televised basketball games were very popular with children; the reasons they gave for their enjoyment included the fast pace, the hype, good production standards, the atmosphere of deliberately stimulated excitement and enthusiasm, good music, special effects, big name stars and great action. Soaps which dealt with teenage social issues were also of great interest, particularly to Grade 5/6 children – many children felt they had 'grown up' with a particular soap opera:

> I've been watching it [*Neighbours*] for a very long time and I suppose I've just grown to like it and it's . . . well, it's a lot different to *Home Improvement*. Say, because most of the kids in *Neighbours* are a lot older. People in *Neighbours* actually grow. Within *Home Improvement* they just stay the same and you don't see their birthdays or anything. Like they go through year 12 and all this stuff.
>
> (Peter, Grade 6)

Programmes which explored an issue, such as adoption or racism, had to be interesting and entertaining for the programme to be attractive to children. Issues that younger children (i.e. Grades 1 to 4) claimed were of concern to them related to their domestic situation (e.g. death of a parent or pet, house robbery) or were school-based (e.g. concerns about not completing homework, getting a detention or not doing well at school); they worried about their pets out at night, their parents dying in a car crash while out for dinner or robbers coming to their house. Older children in Grade 5/6 tended to worry about such things as their interpersonal relationships, the onset of puberty and things they'd seen on television or read about, for example: 'once I read a book on war and families getting separated and everything – sort of sad'.

Children used the word 'boring' a good deal to refer to shows they did not like. Boring programmes were those without humour; without action and adventure; those they had outgrown such as preschool programmes; news programmes; programmes with 'grown-up' humour that children didn't understand; documentaries; political programmes and subtitled programmes. Here some Grade 5/6 children give examples:

Interviewer: When kids say boring – what do they mean?
Frances: Rather just turn the channel if there was nothing on.
Rachel: If no excitement.
Natalie: No action in it.

Gemma: Some stuff like they're just 'try hard' actors like when they cry, it's 'oh, oh, oh' . . . like *Neighbours*, just 'try hard' actors and have a laugh because they're so stupid.

Rebecca: Things you don't understand, no humour, ordinary life, usually love . . .
Sandy: . . . You've already lived through this day and now you are watching your day again [on television with shows like *Days of Our Lives, Home and Away*].

As the first stage of the research indicated, children did watch the news to be informed about the world but they also indicated they would prefer more child focused news with more humour: 'News doesn't always have to be so boring and serious' (Jenny, Grade 4).

The main way children discovered new programmes to watch was through programme promotions, which children called 'ads' or 'commercials', or else through the peer network which operated at school during recess. This was openly discussed in groups which included friends; here the children were candid about how prevalent television was as a topic in their school playground. Grade 5/6 children, especially, were confident communicators about their television preferences, holding to individual points of view and being able to argue their case without being dissuaded by friends. When one sixth grade boy admitted to watching *Neighbours*, his friends said, 'Get out of here!', but he ignored this and continued to explain what he liked about this programme. New programmes, soon to be on television, were discussed at school after children had seen 'promos'. In addition, good programmes and movies that were on the previous night were discussed at recess:

We'd either watch it on TV, like the commercials or we talk about it. We go like, 'Are you going to watch this today', like that.

(Phillip, Grade 6)

Both boys and girls talked about what were new shows at the time of the study, such as *Gladiators*, and old shows with interesting story-lines such as *The Simpsons*.

Like, did you see Bart do this and that – like we talk about the funny [things].

(Sam, Grade 4)

Girls were more likely to talk about programmes such as *Lois and Clark*, *The Simpsons* and *The Nanny*. Children reported asking each other, 'Did you see *The Nanny* last night?' Boys spoke about *The Simpsons*, *Gladiators* and sport. With sports such as rugby, it was considered to be important to know the score – even if you had only watched the sports news.

Interviewer:	Do you ever feel left out if you haven't watched *The Simpsons* or *Gladiators*?
Jonathan:	No.
Amanda:	You can feel like that – 'Oh, can I listen to the conversation' – they said get away from me and stuff because you don't know what they're talking about and you feel a bit left out.
Interviewer:	What about boys if you haven't watched the game?
Liam:	If you haven't watched the game they kick you away.
Charlie:	They just say did you see that – and you say 'yes' even if you didn't watch it.
Interviewer:	Do you lie and pretend you saw something on telly when you didn't really?
Charlie:	Yeah.
Liam:	Yeah.
John:	I'd rather tell a lie than get bashed up.
Sam:	I don't say what it was – I just say, 'Oh yeah, oh yeah', and I go 'What do you mean?' The other person will go: 'Blah, blah', and I go: 'Oh yeah, I remember that.'

(Grade 4 children)

Children want peer acceptance – to belong to the group – and television appears to be one way of making this possible even though one watches at home alone. Some children reported that they felt 'bad' and an outsider if they were unable to join in a television discussion.

Children used the TV guide to help them choose what to watch and, as stated before, they also found out about programmes through promotions. Some children thought that the 'ads' were a better way of finding out what would be on television than word of mouth.

Interviewer:	What got you into watching these programmes – how did you find out about them?
Amanda:	Telly.
Amber:	Yes.
Nina:	Clips on them looked exciting.

(Grades 4–7)

It was clear that some children achieved social status in their peer group by being knowledgeable about new programmes on television – knowledge which they could then impart to others:

> If one person watches it then they sort of tell someone about it and then
> it goes up through the school and you find out about it and you decide to
> watch it and see that it's really good and you keep on watching it.
>
> (Brian, Grade 5/6)

Conclusion

The major findings from the first stage of the research were that children were discriminating in their television viewing, made active choices about programmes and exercised self-censorship about things that concerned them. More than half the children surveyed had stopped watching television by either leaving the room or changing channels because something had upset them. Girls (55 per cent) were more likely to report this behaviour than boys (44 per cent). While violence was a major concern for children on television, boys were more interested in 'blood and guts' type programmes than girls. However, for both sexes, 'real life' television, as it is presented in news and current affairs programmes, was much more disturbing than fictional or fantasy violence. Ninety-two per cent of children indicated that they watch the news, primarily for personal interest and to find out what has been happening that day. This is in contrast to the work of Palmer (1986) and Russell (1993), but perhaps in the last 10 years children have wanted to be better informed and prepared for the world on their doorstep. Sex, nudity and swearing did not upset large numbers of children.

The second stage of this project produced similar results to Gunter *et al.* (1991) in that it found the shared nature of television is a large part of its appeal. Children can be watching at home and yet are simultaneously linked into a common experience with friends. This provides children with a rich source of material for discussion at school; it can also give status to the child who identifies a new cult programme ahead of time. Sports programmes, in particular, are a rich source of material for playground discussion for boys. Knowing the scores and the important tries in the rugby/rugby league games are vital for some conversations, however, it is basketball with its hype, energy and good production standards that is especially appealing to children of both sexes. An additional source of appeal for basketball is that, in Australia, it is a sport that most parents don't follow, so the language and heroes of the game are known and belong to children alone.

The children in the second survey were attracted primarily to comedy, drama and variety programmes. They were attracted by action/adventure, humour, the portrayal of contemporary social issues and teenage/adult relationships, the 'right attitude' and good acting. Those programmes that were boring were those without humour; without action and adventure; those they had outgrown (such as preschool programmes); some news programmes and programmes with 'grown-up' humour that children did not understand. For example, children wanted more 'child focus' in the news.

Children aged 5 to 12 years had a wide-ranging vocabulary and were enthusiastic communicators with regard to television programmes. At times they had difficulty articulating what 'boring' and 'good' programmes were beyond these one-word descriptions but they were readily able to identify programmes that fell into each category. Boys and girls of all ages were television literate and were aware what certain cues meant. They understood well, for example, the use of scary or romantic music in building tension in scenes and this often helped them avoid scenes they did not want to watch (i.e. they closed their eyes, hid behind a pillow or else they chose that moment to leave the room). They were well-versed in the use of techniques such as flashbacks, dream sequences, special effects and lighting. In fact, generally, children appeared to be more discriminating, active and literate as viewers than they are often given credit for by some adults. They were, in fact, closer in their reported behaviour to a view expressed by a producer/director who in earlier consultations indicated that, 'Kids [today] are more intelligent and sharp, they have TV grammar, they are TV literate, they know all the TV tricks'. In fact, the final word should go to a writer/director/actor who said: 'Kids don't watch what people think they should watch. A lot of shows are what adults think kids are interested in, not what they are interested in . . . it's like taking a spoonful of medicine'.

Acknowledgments

The author would like to thank Milica Loncar, formerly with the ABA and currently with the Australian Tourist Commission, who was a co-worker and author on both the studies described in this chapter. She would also like to acknowledge Frank Small and associates who undertook the fieldwork for the first study and assisted with the questionnaire design and analysis.

Notes

1   The ABA is the regulator of television, pay TV and radio in Australia. The ABA was created in October 1992 by the Broadcasting Services Act (the Act). The philosophy behind the Act was one of industry self-regulation based on codes of practice. Research is regarded as a primary way of monitoring community attitudes to the implementation of these codes. Research into community attitudes to programme issues provides information about the way broadcasters are meeting their obligations. In the past, classification

issues of sex, violence and offensive language have been found to represent areas of particular concern to the Australian public. The ABA believes that research must also include the child's perspective about their broadcasting needs. The research also informs the ABA in developing policy in relation to television for children. This includes determining standards for children's programmes on commercial television, assessing compliance with those standards and monitoring whether the commercial television code of practice is working to protect children from potentially harmful programming material. The research results are widely disseminated to assist programme makers and broadcasters to understand and serve the interests of children.

2　The full report of the results of this research have been published in the ABA monograph, Sheldon *et al.* (1994). The qualitative results have been published in Sheldon and Loncar (1995).

3　The results of this research have been published in the ABA Monograph, Sheldon and Loncar (1996).

4　The children who were participants in these studies have all been given code names.

5　This research summary is based on Bow *et al.* (1995), a report commissioned by the ABA.

6　Since this qualitative research was conducted, the classification system has changed. In September 1993, the Commercial Television Industry Code of Practice came into effect. An important feature of the Code of Practice was that it brought into line the classification systems for film, video and television. The television classifications are now G, PG, M and MA. Material classified 'M' (mature) is recommended for viewing only by people aged 15 years or over. Material classified 'MA' (mature adult) is suitable for viewing only by people aged 15 years or over because of the intensity and/or frequency of violence, sexual depictions, coarse language, or because violence is central to the theme. At the time of publication the commercial television industry had begun a comprehensive public review of its 3-year-old Code of Practice.

References

Bow, A., Wale, K. and Gillard, P. (1995) *Children Watching Television: An Annotated Bibliography and Literature Review*, Melbourne: Telecommunications Needs Research Group.

Burton, L. (1991) *Children's Responses to Television*, Incorporated Association of Registered Teachers of Victoria (IARTV) Seminar Series, No. 4, Jolimont, Victoria, June.

Chung, K. M. (1990) 'Developing a "needs-based" media education programme for infant children', unpublished PhD thesis, University of Tasmania.

Comstock, G. and Paik, H. (1991) *Television and the American Child*, San Diego, CA: Academic Press.

Edgar, P. (1977) *Children and Screen Violence*, St Lucia: University of Queensland Press.

Gillard, P., Haire, R., Huender, S. and Meneghel, M. (1993) 'Children's recollections of television coverage of the Gulf War', *Media Information Australia*, **67**: 100–106.

GUNTER, B. and MCALEER, J. L. (1990) *Children and Television: The One Eyed Monster?* London: Routledge.

GUNTER, B., MCALEER, J. and CLIFFORD, B. (1991) *Children's Views about Television*, Aldershot: Avebury.

LUKE, C. (1990) *TV and Your Child*, Sydney: Angus and Robertson.

MCCANN, T. E. and SHEEHAN, P. W. (1985) 'Violence content in Australian television', *Australian Psychologist*, **20**(1): 33–42.

NOBLE, G. and FREIBERG, K. (1985) 'Discriminating between the viewing styles of the commercial and ABC child TV viewer', *Media Information Australia*, **36**, May: 22–33.

PALMER, P. (1986) *The Lively Audience*, Sydney: Allen & Unwin.

ROBERTS, S. (1989) 'Violence on television – how are children affected?', *Rattler*, Spring: 16–18.

RUSSELL, A. L. (1993) 'Television: Interesting stuff for life', address to Visual Media in Education Conference, Friends of the ABC, Brisbane, August.

SHEEHAN, P. (1980) 'Television violence', *Scientific Australian*, July: 27–33.

SHEEHAN, P. W. (1983) 'Age trends and the correlates of children's television viewing', *Australian Journal of Psychology*, **35**(3): 417–31.

SHELDON, L. and LONCAR, M. (1995) 'Cool stuff and slimy stuff – Children and classification issues', *Media Information Australia*, **75**, February: 139–49.

SHELDON, L. and LONCAR, M. (1996) *Kids Talk TV – 'Super Wickid' or 'Dum'*, Australian Broadcasting Authority, Monograph 7, Sydney: ABA.

SHELDON, L., RAMSAY, G. and LONCAR, M. (1994) *'Cool' or 'Gross': Children's Attitudes to Violence, Kissing, and Swearing on Television*, Australian Broadcasting Authority, Monograph 4, Sydney: ABA.

SIGNORIELLI, N. (1991) *A Sourcebook on Children and Television*, New York: Greenwood Press.

TULLOCH, J. and TULLOCH, M. (1992) 'Tolerating violence: children's responses to television', *Australian Journal of Communication*, **19**(1): 9–21.

ZOHOORI, A. R. (1988) 'A cross-cultural analysis of children's television use', *Journal of Broadcasting and Electronic Media*, **32**(1): 105–13.

Chapter Six

Video game culture:
Playing with masculinity, violence and pleasure

Nola Alloway and Pam Gilbert

The impact of the multi-million dollar video game culture on children and young adults is now clearly acknowledged – but generally its impact is viewed negatively. Parents, teachers, politicians and the clergy have all voiced concerns about the time children spend playing video games, about the violence and aggression apparently legitimated within such games, and about the possible links between increasing social violence and lawlessness and the popularity of the new gaming culture (see Senate Select Committee 1993). Attempts to assess the effects of video games on young people have been extensive, and have come from a variety of research domains and research methodologies (see Durkin 1995). Typically, however, studies have sought to show causal links between children's behaviour and the images that dominate in the narratives and practices of game playing. And, typically, it seems, they are unable – unequivocally – to do this.

Surprisingly, however, very few of the studies have started with what seems to be one clear and interesting feature of this culture. Video game culture is a strongly male-focused and intensely masculinist, aggressive and violent culture (Braun and Giroux 1989). There are many more boys than girls who play video games and visit video game arcades, and there are far more aggressive themes, male figures and male voices on screen in video games than in television (Durkin 1995). Even the video game arcade – the physical site for social game playing – has become a domain in which girls and women are likely to feel uncomfortable. The arcades are frequented predominantly by boys and young men and seem not unlike the pool hall or the Aussie hotel public bar as arenas for the public display of competitive, aggressive and sometimes violent masculinity.

Just as the Barbie doll culture constructs a highly gendered representational field targeted at girls, which includes multimedia cultural texts, images and objects, the world of video games offers much the same to boys and young men. Through participation in the practices associated with video gaming, boys and young men enter into a discursive field within which constructions of hegemonic masculinity dominate. Little wonder that girls and young women become non-players; that they see themselves as bystanders or spectators in this highly masculinized field. Little wonder, also, that the field becomes eminently desirable and attractive to boys and young men as an arena within which to learn and to practice the 'doing' of masculinity.

Discussions about the effect of video games on young people can often bypass this significant aspect of its impact. It is not uncommon, for instance, for researchers to treat 'children' as an homogeneous group, bypassing the interplay of gender, class and ethnicity in the ways in which children take up positions in relation to cultural pursuits; representing children as equally and commonly positioned in cultural meaning-making (see Kline 1996). In analyses of video gaming, a focus on 'childhood' at the expense of the social and discursive construction of the child as a gendered, classed and ethnic subject, can blind us to the ways in which participation in children's and youth culture almost always involves participation as a gendered, classed and ethnic subject. Video gaming is certainly no exception, and this chapter will argue that research which seeks to unravel some of the complexities associated with participation in the practices of video gaming needs to address this issue.

Initially the chapter presents a case for an appropriate theoretical framework for considering video game culture and its practices – a framework that can take account of the complexity of cultural texts and textual practice, particularly, in this case, ways of reading and working with constructions of gender and of violence within video game culture. The chapter then examines the construction of gender and violence within one site of this culture: the magazine texts that are produced to accompany it. Having developed a lens through which to make visible the gendered practices of video game culture, the chapter then presents findings from a small research study in which teenage boys talk about their attitudes to gaming and game narratives. The boys' lack of access to discourses through which they could describe or reflect upon the gendered practices of this culture, or the gendered violence implicit within it, are discussed. In conclusion, the significance of this 'blindness' for educators is considered, particularly in terms of how we might work with video game culture within the context of the classroom.

Discourse, Subjectivity and Positioning

What people say about violence is just junk and that. It's on TV, it's everywhere. You can't avoid it. So I mean, you know.

(David, 15 years)

The dilemma in attempting to research the effect of video game culture on children and adolescents is almost exactly as David warns. Video game narratives and the practices associated with video game culture form part of a complex interplay of discursive practices. They do not stand alone. They are part of a network of discourses and social practices that similarly construct violence, aggression, gender relations, ethnicity and power. It is because they dovetail so easily into other meaning-making regimes that they become so easily 'naturalized' in cultural practice.

Violence is not just a feature of video game culture. Violence is, as David says above, 'everywhere. You can't avoid it.' We can plug into violence on television, popular film, the Internet, radio, advertisements, brochures, magazines, newspapers, novels, theatre, MTV . . . The video game site is but one site within a complex set of sites. The violent narratives common to video game texts are only 'readable' and recognizable because they repeat narratives written elsewhere. Attempts to isolate the effects, say, of video game culture upon children's behaviours and attitudes, cannot ignore the ways in which children and adolescents, as contemporary social subjects, learn how to understand themselves through the intertextuality of a broad range of cultural texts and images.

This understanding is semiotically marked out in terms of difference and opposition: an understanding, for example, of what it means to be a male or female subject; to have dominant ethnic or racial status; to be privileged or silenced. Young people take up positions within their social worlds according to how they are situated and constructed as gendered, classed and ethnic identities, although the interplay between these positionings is always complex. In simple terms, young people do not 'read' video game texts in identical ways. Rather, they enter into the discursive world of video game culture already positioned in a number of – sometimes – competing and contradictory discourses. How they take up the stories and practices on offer in the cultural texts associated with video gaming will be dependent upon this social positioning.

However, for boys and young men, the draw and power of hegemonic discourses of masculinity must be compelling. Davies (1990) reminds us of the seductive way in which 'desire' serves to hold together discourses on gender; of the way in which, as gendered social subjects, we learn to desire the characteristics and qualities that come to be associated with socially endorsed versions of femininity and masculinity. Video game texts operate powerfully within this sphere. Many of these texts align masculinity with power, with aggression, with victory and winning, with superiority and strength – and, of course, with violent action. They offer positions for young male game players that promise success as masculine subjects. The video game arcade thus becomes a social arena within which hegemonic masculinity can be experienced and practised. Other elements of difference can perhaps be sublimated to the strength of this discourse. In the virtual reality on promise within the video game, maleness is frequently associated with the attainment of power and success through violent action.

Defining Violence

In highlighting the need to consider media representations of violence, Giroux (1995: 300) argues:

> While the relationship between representational violence and its impact on children and youth is not clear, the culture of violence spawned by television, videos, and film is too pervasive to be ignored or dismissed.

In this chapter we consider the culture of video gaming as another contemporary media form that feeds into the culture of violence. Perhaps because it is less attractive to an adult than to a youth market, the video game culture is often overlooked as a media source that peddles particular kinds of messages to the young about what it means be male or female, what it means to relate as gendered beings, and ultimately, what it means to be human. Since the video game industry has ridden high on a youth market and sales, parents often have little detailed knowledge about what their children are playing at, even when the parents themselves purchase the goods.

In theorizing the relationship between representational violence and the processes of meaning making, Giroux draws distinctions between the kinds of violence represented in popular cultural texts. He focuses specifically on cinematic representations of violence. However, his distinction between ritualistic and symbolic violence is particularly helpful in examining the potential impact of video game violence on discourses of masculinity, on gendered subjectivity, and on desire as discussed in this chapter. The distinction between the two forms of violence revolves around the presence/absence of moral dilemmas and decision making, and around the ways in which the audience is invited to either accept as commonplace, or to reject as unacceptable, violence as expressed through the narrative and semiotic features of the texts.

Giroux identifies ritualistic violence as characteristically banal, predictable, stereotypically masculine, superficial in content, and ultimately, as pleasure seeking. In conceptualizing ritualistic violence, he argues:

> Audiences connect with such depictions viscerally, yet they are not edifying in the best pedagogical sense, offering few insights into the complex range of human behavior and struggles . . . [The violence] does not recast ordinary events or attempt critically to shift sensibilities. On the contrary, it glows in the heat of the spectacle, shock, and contrivance, yet it is entirely formulaic.
>
> (Giroux 1995: 301)

In weaving a closer alliance between violence and masculinity, Connell (1987) also argues that some forms of popular cultural texts promote versions of masculinity that are based on unquestioned and unproblematic expressions of violence. This is not to say that such texts are necessarily amoral. They are often intensely, although simplistically, moral. However by disconnecting action from emotional complexity, the 'killer-heroes and cardboard cut-outs' depicted in such texts fail to pose moral questions associated with masculinity and violence, and so associate hegemonic masculinity with emotional alienation and dissociation.

By contrast with ritualistic violence, symbolic violence 'attempts to connect the visceral and the reflective':

> Symbolic violence does not become an end in itself . . . It serves to refer-
> ence a broader logic and set of insights. Instead of providing the viewer
> with stylistic gore that offers the immediacy of visual pleasure and escape,
> symbolic violence probes the complex contradictions that shape human
> agency, the limits of rationality, and the existential issues that tie us to
> other human beings and a broader social world.
>
> (Giroux 1995: 303)

And so, within this framework, it is possible to distinguish ritualistic cinematic representation of violence – paraded in movies like *Die Hard* (1988), *Blown Away* (1994), *The Terminator* (1984), *Speed*, *Robocop* (1987) and *Bad Boys* (1995) – from symbolic violence represented in movies like *Schindler's List* (1993), *The Crying Game* (1992), *Dead Man Walking* (1995) and *Once Were Warriors* (1994). Ritualistic violence invites the respondent to bask in the excitement of destruction; symbolic violence asks for more complex, critical, and intellectual engagement with the issues. By associating the pleasure principle, ritualistic representations of violence naturalize the narratives that simultaneously reflect, create and maintain reality. In stark contrast, by evoking more complex emotional responses, symbolic representations of violence challenge the reader to resist, to contest, to denaturalize cultural and textual practices that legitimate violence and that betray our potential for human connectedness.

While Giroux examines ritualistic violence in contemporary cinematic repres-entations, it can be argued that the same kinds of formulaic, knee-jerk, pleasured responses to violence are programmed within the narrative and semiotic features of many video games. Like Bruce Willis- and Arnold Schwarzenegger-style movies, video game culture invites players to engage viscerally with the action, to disen-gage the critical faculties, to take pleasure in the vicarious experience of gratuitous violence. More so than violent movies, video games are directed at a male youth market. In the following section we look at the kinds of magazine texts available to video game players, most of whom are boys and young men. We look more particularly at how these texts produce versions of masculinity, of femininity, of gender relations, and of male culture that come to represent desirable expressions of being and relating.

Gaming Magazines

At first reading, it is apparent that gaming magazines are aimed at marketing games, offering players independent reviews of available and forthcoming software and hardware, giving game-players a voice through editorials, and trading hints on how to improve game scores. While the magazines achieve these explicit aims, it is possible to see that, implicitly, they market much more. What we argue is that, overwhelmingly, the texts produce and make available versions of masculinity, of femininity and of gender relations that are narrow, restrictive and regressive with respect to contemporary moves to encourage more expansive identities and democratic relationships. A politics of gender is articulated in the texts – a politics that constitutes gender as asymmetrical relations of power. The asymmetries of power are worked out in relations between men and women as well as between hegemonic and other versions of masculine identity. As we will discuss, the sexual politics spelt out in the narrative and semiotic features of the texts are consistently patriarchal, sometimes misogynist, and intrinsically homophobic.

The gaming culture too easily passes as entertainment alone. But like other forms of entertainment, it implicitly speaks a politics of gender. As Giroux (1995) argues, entertainment cannot be divorced from its representational politics. This point is critical when we acknowledge how learning occurs outside of the classroom, through texts other than school texts, and through practices other than those endorsed by schools. The gaming culture, internationally successful with large numbers of boys, has the potential to instruct, just as teachers do. Arguably, for particular groups of boys, video game culture may wield more instructional authority than that exercised by teachers in classrooms. Popular cultural texts of these kinds operate as cultural and community pedagogies; they offer sites for meaning-making and pleasure; they market representational politics; and at the same time, they pass as apolitical entertainment.

Texts that advertise, promote or review video games almost invariably target a young male market. Images of boys and young men dominate. There are few images of girls and young women. Use of language exclusively directed at boys is familiar in video game texts. For instance, with the Nintendo Game Boy™, the merchandise itself is male identified. And with Sega, a typical advertisement pictures a young boy in jeans, sneakers and sideways-tilted baseball cap wondering, 'What's a boy to do if he don't have a Sega Master System 11?' (1993 Sega advertising material). The boy is invited to flick peas at his sister if he is too long frustrated, or alternatively, to tempt his grandmother's affections so that she cannot resist satisfying his desire and paying for his pleasure. In this instance, female representation is considered only as it serves to gratify the boy – the subject of the narrative of wish-fulfilment.

Thus the gender-exclusive narratives are maintained. For instance, most readers would recognize the anticipation of a male player in the text of a recent advertisement for Access software:

> The Roswell UFO crash.
> A package.
> A serial killer.
> A government cover-up.
> A mysterious woman.
> A missing man.
> A terrible secret.
> And you need to shave.
> It can't get any worse . . .
>
> (*Computer Game Review*, April 1996: 78)

Semiotic features of advertising texts also remind us that video games represent male terrain. One Game Boy advertisement identifies a boy in a bath playing *The Hunt for Red October* on his Game Boy (*Hello*, December 1992). The dominant images in the visual text are of the Game Boy and of an erect object rising above the bubbles of the bath, from between the boy's legs. The image invites us to make the intertextual connection between the movie and the video game so that we know that the object represents both a submarine periscope and the phallus. The phallic symbolism asks us to unmistakably identify the game, the game machine, and the game player with an exclusively male world. Similar semiotics are used in an advertisement for a Fighter Stick, an input device for the Sega and Super NES. In this advertisement a young man straddles a crocodile which raises a dangerous-looking, open-jawed, erect head between the boy's legs. The verbal text reads: 'Never loan out your stick.' (*GamePro*, June 1994: 2). Narrative and semiotic features combine here to mark out the machismo of video gaming culture.

When players are offered a voice in gaming magazines through letters to the editor or trouble-shooting columns, the space sometimes becomes the site for struggle between male and female writers over language usage. In tying the gaming culture to racy images and texts, editors and writers generally opt for the informal language of the streets. Sometimes this translates into language that seems more appealing to boys than to girls. Throughout the magazines there are endless references to which games 'suck', to what information is a 'load of crap' and to which competitors should 'Go suck the farts out of dead seagulls' (see *Megazone*, October 1993: 32). Some girls attempt to register their dislike for the language practices of male subscribers and male editors. But rather than disturb the established order, their complaints often feature as a source of levity and as an opportunity for the editor to further display his command of street-wise language. Carly's letter and the editor's response quoted here offer an example of how girls' protests can become the object of belittling humour and patronage:

Dear *Megazone*,
I got the latest issue of *Megazone* today and I have a complaint to make. I am totally sick of you swearing in your magazine. If you don't stop the foul language, you will have one less person to send your magazine to. Apart from that, I like the rest of your magazine.
Carly

Well, you can $#@% off, then. Just my little joke, Carly, and sorry you've taken offence. While I must agree that the swearing has been getting a little out of hand, I'm not totally against the odd 'rude' word for emphasis. But we certainly won't use swearing for the sake of it.
(*Megazone*, October 1993: 33)

Continuing a theme of deliberate and contrived unrefinement, a spate of advertisements in gaming magazines capitalizes on images of toilet rolls and pedestals that promote a lavatory humour, more closely aligned with social constructions of boys' than of girls' culture. In such ways, language and images employed in these magazines serve to mark out the gaming terrain as more appropriate to male than to female players.

Despite any rhetoric to the contrary, it is clear that boys are identified as the major potential consumers of the culture. Given that boys have been targeted, perhaps the most disturbing feature of the gaming culture is the way that it so powerfully and seductively coalesces images of masculinity and violent action. Consistent with Giroux's theorizing of ritualistic violence, the games invite visceral response and associated pleasure. Testifying to its popularity and its potential to deliver pleasure, a game like *Mortal Kombat* can net millions of dollars soon after its release. In this game, the screen action is embedded in violence. The challenge is for players to identify with a screen character and to outdo one another in the exercise of violent action. In *Mortal Kombat,* all the characters are violent. Given the opportunity, Sub-Zero tears off his opponent's head while Kano punches through his opponent's torso and rips out a still-beating heart. Sonya Blade, the only female in the cast of eight, engages in battle with male characters and specializes in eroticized violence – the 'burning kiss of death'.

It seems that even as portrayed in sports games, masculinity is inevitably inscribed with violence. Games that invite the most violent expression receive the highest star ratings in reviews in these magazines. And so *Speedball 2* earns its parodic review:

> This Bitmap Brothers game is a futuristic *tour de force*. Taking the best elements from both sci-fi films and every ball sport imaginable, with a liberal sprinkling of extreme violence and tactical gameplay, *Speedball 2* is extremely playable . . . *Speedball* mixes soccer and senseless violence. One day, all games will be played this way.
>
> (*Megazone*, July 1995: 37)

Gaming texts are often quite explicit in making links for players between violence, pleasure and desire. A review of *Cosmic Carnage,* for instance, heralds the game as 'a fun-to-play beat 'em up for all walks of life (as long as you like extreme violence, bloody effects, are over 15 and have a 32X!)' (*Megazone*, July 1995: 32). Similarly, a review of *True Lies* interweaves narratives of violence and pleasure. The game is reported as 'basically just a killfest', 'a rough, tough, grit-your-teeth-and-party shoot 'em up/platformer with enough action to quench the most bloodthirsty of appetites!', a 'blasting good time' where there is 'plenty to do, see and kill' (*Megazone*, July 1995: 22). In what can be read as a conflation of violence and pleasure and as a defence against critical reflection, *True Lies* moves into the realm of bizarre humour. Offering the promise of the pleasures of play, the magazine review claims:

> To give the game a bit of strategy, innocent bystanders litter the playing area and seem to have the uncanny ability of getting in the line of fire. Shoot three of them and those ever-frustrating words appear . . . GAME

OVER! Besides being real pains in the holster, they also display funny antics to give senseless violence that comedy feel, with old men taking your photo, waiters offering you a drink, a karate class training in the park and one chicken s#%t who dives for the ground covering his head with a newspaper!

(Megazone, July 1995: 23)

Likewise, *Sega Saturn Magazine* introduces *Street Fighter Alpha*, a revamped version of the old *Street Fighter*, in an article entitled 'A Street Fight Named Desire'. In reading the review, potential consumer-players are textually engaged with messages about desire and the challenge of violent action:

Suckers these days are all coming from the pocket ya know? What happened to the noble art of beating the crap out of someone with your fists eh? Or doing them with a swift boot to the jaw?

(Sega Saturn Magazine, March 1996: 50)

While such texts may be naively driven by the simplest of marketing strategies, it seems that they may produce more complex social outcomes than are perhaps intended. In targeting a predominantly male market and capitalizing on the sale of pleasure, the texts produce narratives that inform young men about the intrinsic relationship between hegemonic masculinity, violence and desire.

It can be argued that desire for the violent masculinity produced in these texts is powerfully affirmed through intertextual connections with cinematic versions of the games. For example, the video games *True Lies* and *Terminator* call on references to Arnold Schwarzenegger, *Die Hard* to Bruce Willis, *Lethal Weapon* to Mel Gibson, *The Hunt for Red October* to Sean Connery. In each instance, the Hollywood protagonist guarantees vicarious hegemonic male status to the game-player. Desire and pleasure are deeply implicated in these textual productions of what it means to be successfully male.

Hegemonic Masculinity, Femininity and Other Masculinities

Hegemonic masculinity is not produced in isolation. As Connell (1987: 183) explains '"Hegemonic masculinity" is always constructed in relation to various subordinated masculinities as well as in relation to women.' At the same time as producing a violent masculinity, gaming texts often marginalize and inferiorize those associated with the feminine or with non-violent masculinities and position them as 'other' to hegemonic male characters. Hegemonic masculinity is assured ascendancy as gaming texts range easily from narratives that attribute male characters with dominant status, to mild expressions of contempt for that which represents the 'other', to outright misogyny and homophobia.

While many print-based texts have been analyzed over the past two decades for sexist representations, the more recent genre of gaming texts seems to have escaped critical scrutiny. As an example of its reinvestment in female dependence and male heroics, one gaming magazine provides a table of the 'Top Ten Damsels in Distress' (*Electronic Gaming Monthly*, July 1993: 44). Even in games where men do not hold monopolies on warrior positions, there appears to be a palpable determination in the texts to mark out differences between male and female characters and to sexualize and eroticize the woman warrior. As previously mentioned, in *Mortal Kombat,* Sonya Blade's specialist combat strategy is the burning kiss of death. A more recent game, *Fighting Vipers* has nine characters, three of whom are female. A sneak preview of the characters reveals the heterosexist politics that underpins the inclusion of the women and ensures their subordinated status in relation to the male warriors. Presumably, the male warriors can revel in eroticized violence as Grace – who is 'deadly in the ring. Strong and fast too' – is recognized as a 'bit of a babe'. As for Candy, she is known as 'the most fashionable member of the posse'. Through some fanciful feat of physics, Candy manages to do what any athletic woman would find a daunting task – she fights in a red dress as she 'uses her posterior and long stilettoed legs to defend herself against stronger opponents'. Jane ('Plain Jane'?) is the only female character whose name does not reference a virtue or a consumable product, who is not explicitly sexualized, and who is tokenistically described as having 'the strength of ten men' (*Sega Saturn Magazine*, March 1996: 17).

While it can be argued that the eroticizing of women warriors serves no worse purpose than emphasizing femininity and constructing gender as difference, the narrative patterns of the texts play into a more deprecating politics for women. Derogatory humour is sometimes used to dismiss female characters included in the games. For instance, in a review of *Legends of Valour* players are advised that there is a 'chatting up section of the game'. The review warns that although 'many of the Mitteldorf women belong to Satanic cults and bizarre radical feminist organisations, they will respond to the correct advance'. Once again, the text slips from any pretence at inclusivity of audience through its presumption of male players. Some of the 'correct' advances that players are invited to choose are 'Hello, luv. Nice dress.' 'Do you sacrifice here often?' and 'Is the halitosis all part of the ensemble?' (*Games Master*, April 1993: 113). The derogatory-style humour serves to camouflage a politics of gender wherein masculine identity is made dominant through the subordination and denigration of female identity.

To argue the point further, some gaming texts play with inclusive language in mocking ways. As an example, in a review of *X-Men: Children of the Atom*, inclusive language is associated with derision. In clarifying the purpose of the game, players are told:

> The idea is you, the heroic player, take control of one super-being and take him (or her, equal opportunity chick fans) into single combat against another super-type.

> (*Sega Saturn Magazine*, March 1996: 62)

As another example of derisive, albeit inclusive language, players are introduced to Psylocke, a female psychic gaming ninja: 'Given her mistressy [*sic*] of the martial arts . . . she's a force to be reckoned with' (*Sega Saturn Magazine*, March 1996: 63). In a final gesture of inclusivity the question is posed: 'So what make these X-Men so darn "X" then? How come they get a cool prefix like "X" when the rest of us are just known as (wo)men?' (*Sega Saturn Magazine*, March 1996: 65).

Throughout the review, maleness is understood to be the uncontested centre. There is no need to mark male inclusion through bracketed information and asides. By contrast, the language practices adopted in the article locate femaleness as other than at the centre since women's inclusion must be marked by parenthetic information, by qualifying and explanatory notes, and by derisive language play. Contrived inclusion of this kind suggests that there is a need to identify the conditions and occasions for considering female, but not male, consumers of the culture. Incidentally, no such derisive humour is aimed at the title of the game, only at those to whom the unassailable title might not apply.

In some texts, the progression is from mild derision to straightforward contempt for women. Editors for some magazines choose to feature misogynist expressions from male contributors as evidenced in the following extracts from Megamouth Letters:

> What a mob of bludgers you all are, do you pull yourselves and dream about mega babes all day long? By the way, Agatha is no mega babe. She is an ugly mole and looks like my dog's ass with its nuts hanging through. Get a life boys.
> Scott, Django, Clint
>
> *(Megazone, July 1995: 14)*

> I love your mag but I am so pissed off at the people who send in so much crap about Cammy and Mileena when Kitana and Chunners are the best! I mean Cammy's just a wedged little pom with a flat chest and Mileena, well, she's the ugliest bitch I've ever seen.
> Lachie
>
> *(Megazone, July 1995: 16)*

As the instances accumulate, it is difficult to continue to dismiss such humour as apolitical. Editorial space devoted to letters like these amplifies a gender politics that strays beyond patriarchal domination to the borders of misogyny.

Gaming magazines also introduce players to the pleasures of sexual domination. Given the targeted market of male players, this usually means domination by men of women. *Virtual Valerie,* for instance, offers the opportunity for players to have Valerie perform at their pleasure. Players are invited to act out their fantasies in a virtual world where almost any sexual desire can be accomplished. Interactive CD versions of 'sexploits' are available through titles like *Babe Patrol, Hot Dog Girls in Florida, Luscious Ladies in Lingerie, Extasy Suites, Striptease, Hot Slots* and *Hump Towers* (*Computer Game Review*, April 1996: 39). In these games, women's interests and bodies are subordinated to male desire. As testimony to the patriarchal rule embodied in such games, *Crystal Fantasy* invites players to 'interact with the sexiest young jewels of the Mac Daddy harem. Take snapshots of the girls and play with them in your own private portfolio. Six highly interactive, three dimensional gorgeous babes!' (*Computer Game Review*, April 1996: 39). The texts of the games and of the magazines that support them combine powerfully to produce and to sell a sexual politics founded in asymmetries of power that hold men in ascendant, and women in subordinate, relations to one another.

Hegemonic masculinity is not only marked out in relations of power with women, however. It is also identified in relation to subordinated masculinities as well as to the environment. Games advertisements and reviews, and the games themselves, link intertextually to indelibly mark the parameters of hegemonic male status. As an example of marking out acceptable/unacceptable masculinities, prospective players are told – through both narrative and visual representation – that Lester, the bespectacled protagonist of *Anatomy of a Hero* is a 'bit of a nerd'. However, the game promises sufficient adventure – including romantic entanglement with a 'jungle babe' – to 'make a man out of him' (*GamePro*, June 1994: 135). Here it would seem that being a man, and not a nerd, is identified in relation to risk-taking adventure as well as to heterosexual endorsement. The same issue of the magazine provides other instances of textual delineation of hegemonic masculinity. An advertisement for *MegaRace* challenges reader-players to identify masculinity through the imposing image of a scarred punk with dilated pupils and demonic facial expression. The text reads:

No Cops
No Laws
No Wimps
Are you a Girlie-Man or a Megaracer?

(*GamePro*, June 1994: 127)

Such an advertisement invests in the textual construction of masculinity as oppositional to representations of the law, to less violent masculinities, and to the feminine. Through textual constructions like these, hegemonic masculinity can be understood as unfettered, unregulated, lawless, and dissociated from those – both male and female – who do their gender otherwise. As the threads of such texts are pulled together the contradictory nature of hegemonic masculinity becomes apparent; that is, hegemonic masculinity at once seeks heterosexual endorsement and separation. It seeks out women and seeks to avoid them. It is also intrinsically homophobic in its rejection and fear of manifestations of masculinity that do not reflect a like image. It seems that hegemonic masculinity can be so fragile, so tenuously held that non-hegemonic versions of masculinity must be constructed as oppositional to identity as a real man. The threat of identification with a hybridized 'girlie-man' is avoided as the boundaries of acceptable maleness are drawn through the discursive and social practices of gaming. Homophobic separation and rejection are implicit themes of games that seek to create and to reflect hegemonic masculinity.

Without further analysis of specific visual and narrative representations, allow us to say that our overall impression of gaming texts is that they produce and market hegemonic masculinity that is predicated on fierce individualism, competition and rivalry, domination and control of others, violent action, and a disregard for all forms of life other than for the self. Games like *Cosmic Carnage* and *Stellar Assault* offer self-aggrandizing opportunities, not only to control human others, but ultimately to control the universe. As one advertisement says, participation in the game is 'just like being God, except the graphics are better' (*Electronic Gaming Monthly*, July 1993: 73).

Embodying the Game

The distinguishing feature of video gaming is its interactivity. As the industry becomes more sophisticated in its productions, so do the games promise a more realistic walk on the wild side. Gaming texts eagerly promote the idea of full sensory, embodied experience. To illustrate the point, a review of *Cosmic Carnage* pledges the experience of realistic violence for the prospective player:

> The main graphical difference you notice is the use of the 32X's panning capabilities . . . The effect is similar to watching a movie where the camera zooms in for a close-up, catching an R-rated view of that head being ripped from its shoulders.
>
> (*Megazone*, July 1995: 32)

Similarly, a review of *Terror TRAX* (Trace, Research, Analyse, eXterminate) claims that the game 'features live actors in ultra-realistic, full-screen, full-motion video for a truly horrifying interactive experience' (*Computer Game Review*, April 1996: 44). Likewise, Microsoft promises 'a lethal cocktail of heightened graphics, magnified sound and cornea-burning speed'. Microsoft boasts that players would 'have to ride bareback on a screaming bullet' to be connected any faster to the heart of the game (*Computer Game Review*, April 1996: 35). In pumping up the reality stakes, hardware is designed to allow players a more fully embodied game. Peripherals like the 'Menacer' – an input device shaped as a pistol – require players to shoot at the screen in executing their moves and taking out their screen opponents. The *Aurora Interactive* and the *Force Vest* allow players to strap on interactive vests whereby sound from the game translates into vibrations into the vest for an amplified embodied experience. More and more the body itself merges with the peripherals, blurring the boundaries of body/machine/game/device.

Better graphics, better technology, and the advent of virtual reality offer young men, and the few young women players, the opportunity to know, to practise, to play at and to embody gender and sexual politics as suggested through the narrative and semiotics features of games and gaming texts. However, as the third section of this chapter suggests, the pleasure gained through this embodiment of powerful masculinity makes it difficult for many young men to make critical and reflective readings of the gender relations on offer within the discursive and social practices of gaming.

Boys Talk about Game-Playing

The small research study that we describe in this section was conducted with 22 boys aged between 15 and 17 years. The boys were all video game parlour participants who were asked if they would be willing to talk on tape for 20 to 30 minutes about video gaming. Boys could participate in pairs if they preferred, and four boys did take up this option. The interviewees were therefore all volunteers, and the main selection criteria for participation in this study were the boys' presence in the parlour, and their willingness to be part of the study. The interviews followed a structured set of questions. We were interested in the social aspects of game culture, as well as how the boys could talk about the games and about game-playing; about good and bad games, about boys' game preferences, about the skills and social practices associated with game-playing.

A strong issue to emerge from these interviews was that the video game parlour and video game playing are clearly recognizable social sites within which to practise masculinity. However the male participants in this study had little access to discourses about masculinity or gender relations that might have given them an understanding of links between learning how to 'do' masculinity, and being an arcade video game player. While the boys could talk about the rather odd role girls played in the parlours, and about the pleasure and excitement of playing games like *Mortal Kombat* and *Virtual Cop* with their mates, they were uncritical and unreflective of gaming practices.

The boys were aware that game-playing and game arcades were both predominantly male spaces and male pursuits. As Martin said, 'It's sort of like a boys' thing. Like girls have like knitting and riding horses . . . I think computer games are more of a guy thing'. Or as Brian similarly remarked, 'It's definitely male dominated, you know'. While the boys were quite happy to have girls come to the parlours – and some of them were happy to have older people come as well – the space was clearly regarded as male space within which girls were visitors or spectators. The boys' comments here certainly did not reflect the misogynist undertones about girls found in the gaming magazines.

Interviewer:	Do many girls come here?
Tim:	Nah – I don't see any.
John:	Compared to boys there's not that many.
Interviewer:	Well, say you did see a couple of girls, Tim, what sort of girls would they be? . . . like gamers . . . would the girls be in that category do you think?
Tim:	Nah, I reckon they would just be friends of people who come here.

Interviewer:	Do you think they would be playing games while they were here or what?
Tim:	Not sure. Probably not. They would probably just watch their boyfriend or whatever.
Interviewer:	John, what do you think?
John:	I don't think they play that much. Probably what he said. Just sorta hang around, hang around waiting for their boyfriends.

Other boys made similar remarks about girls' positions within the games arcades.

Nathan:	When we go to the movies I say, 'Let's go to Timezone'.
Interviewer:	They do or you do?
Nathan:	Oh I do. They tag along.
Interviewer:	They tag along?
Nathan:	Yeah, nothin' better to do.
Interviewer:	When they come in here what do they do? Do they play games with you?
Nathan:	Nah. Usually watch and have a Coke.

Several other boys also described how girls would 'tag along' and watch. 'They're not really here to play,' said Danny, although two of the boys thought that girls who did play probably did so because they were 'tomboys'. Generally, however, the comments were more like this, where the exclusivity of gaming culture was invisible.

| Interviewer: | Why do you think mainly guys play? |
| Danny: | I don't know. I guess it's not a thing girls get into as much. Mm, I dunno. |

Only one of the boys offered any suggestions about why girls weren't interested in game-playing.

I just think they enjoy different types of games. Like most of these games are pretty monotonous. They just play a game of basketball or race around a track or kill a couple of people. I reckon girls are probably more creative. They prefer more games like you can get on your personal computer at home and stuff. No, I don't think they really enjoy coming here. Some of the things need actual physical skill like the basketball shootout or the table hockey.

(Dylan)

The girls were just a backdrop to the boys' action. Most of the boys knew little about the girls who were in the arcades, had obviously not noticed too much about what the girls did, and assumed that if girls were there they must have come in with their boyfriends. When Danny was asked about what sort of girls came to the arcades, he was obviously stuck for an answer: 'I don't know. Just girls. I don't know. Girls are girls.' The space seemed clearly designated as male – and for male pursuits.

Game-playing was obviously pleasurable. Almost all of the boys talked about the enjoyment they got from game-playing and the arcade context was part of this pleasure. It was clearly a social site for boys – a place with an atmosphere that they didn't get at home with their home systems. 'It's definitely social. There's all kids your age and that. There's not that many places around to go' (Brian). Almost all of the boys went with male friends or met up with male friends at the arcades.

Interviewer: Do you come here by yourself or mainly with friends?

Nathan: Mainly with friends. It would be pretty boring if you came by yourself.

Interviewer: Why is that?

Nathan: No one to talk to and say 'Wow – look at that!'

Interviewer: So how many friends would you bring with you?

Nathan: Two or three, just a little group.

However the social activities the boys engaged in were gender-stereotypical. The style of play amongst groups of boys was usually parallel rather than collaborative play, and the noisiness of the arcade parlour would have contributed to this. It is hard to hold conversations in arcade parlours. The sociability was about playing *beside* rather than with one another – or about playing *against* one another in competitive play: 'if you play with another three of your mates that's just like really fun, you know. Just smash each other up sort of thing' (Brian). There was obviously little cooperative play, and little conversation or discussion between players. Almost all of the boys preferred two-player games and the competitive drive was high: 'When you're playing with your mates it kind of gets more competitive' (Brian). This was seen as a problem for girls, because as Brian also added: 'Ya know men are naturally more competitive and they want to like . . . kill like 30,000 people, ya know.' Nathan remarked: 'Ya don't picture girls playing those computer games, saying, "Oh fuck – I lost again".'

The competitive aspects of the games were enhanced by what many of the boys regarded as very realistic qualities of the better arcade games, another attraction of the parlours. In their descriptions of 'good' games, there were comments like these: 'It's fun, it's virtual, it's 3D, and it's real good. You got a gun and you reload and you just shoot' (Peter). Arcade games were seen to be more 'realistic', and therefore more fun to play, than were games at home:

It's really realistic. You've got different viewpoints to view the car from and the wall fights you when you go around a corner . . . You can't get that sort of realism anywhere else really. You can't get it at home.

(Brian)

Implicit in the boys' description of this realism was a recognition of the enjoyment of being physically involved in playing: of the pleasure of using the body as a peripheral. The opportunity to engage their bodies in the game-playing added to a sense of realism which excited the boys.

> It's good, it's fun, it's realistic. You can slide and crash and stuff like that . . . You're actually in the driver's seat.
>
> > (Tim)

> You can use your hands and you get to use your eyes and targeting and they're running past.
>
> > (Peter)

> In the arcades you actually sit in the seat with the pedals and the steering wheel.
>
> > (Brian)

> You're actually in the driver's seat.
>
> > (John)

> When I'm playing the game, I'm there . . . and you get like demented. Like . . . I can't switch off. Like I mean like when I go for a block in the game I actually physically jump up in the air. It's really quite annoying . . . It's just, I don't know, maybe your brain short circuits or something. You feel like you're there. Ah, it's weird.
>
> > (Dylan)

However, the boys implicitly recognized that this physical engagement with game-playing was not shared by girls.

Interviewer: Do you think girls enjoy playing games?
Alan: Ah – not as much as guys.
Interviewer: Why do you think that?
Alan: Ah, I don't know. They don't really get into it as much as guys do. We get a lot more involved.

None of them, however, offered explanations for why this might be so.

The excitement in the realism and physical engagement with the games was linked to the storylines and narrative progression of the games, the best of which were seen by the boys to have good graphics and to be action-packed, fast-moving, challenging, competitive and, often, violent. Gary, for instance, claimed that a good game had to have 'like action in it. Lots of action . . . and if you shoot a person and they fall over a bridge or something, it's good'.

Most of the boys had difficulty providing any critical reflection on the games they played in terms of storylines or violence, and the violence in the games was naturalized and made commonplace within their speech. Nathan, for instance, talked about 'the good killing action' as well as 'the blood, the violence' in *Samurai*

Showdown, and Wayne described the story of *Mortal Kombat,* his favourite arcade game, like this:

> I like the storyline behind it . . . Twelve combatants [are] trying to beat each other up basically. Like it gets into depth about each character and why they are there, and other characters are trying to kill that particular character and stuff like that.

While the violence seemed to have become so commonplace to the boys, many of them described how it was not commonplace to their mothers or to girls. There seemed to be an implicit linking of violence to men and masculine activity. Two of the boys commented on how the violence in the games stopped girls from playing. Several of them, however, said that their fathers enjoyed playing the games – and sometimes did so in the arcades. None of them thought that their mothers would ever want to.

> She hates them. She really hates computer games . . . Too violent.
>
> (Peter)

> Like my mum has seen me play *Doom* and she despises that game. She just really does not like it at all. It's like 'What do you do in this game? Just kill things? Yeah. Yeah. That's all right son, see the therapist.'
>
> (Dylan)

This seemed to account for the boys' ambivalence about letting younger brothers play violent games – about allowing them entry as apprentices into masculinist culture. When asked whether young boys should be allowed to play these games, the majority of the boys were non-censorious. They saw few problems with younger boys playing the more violent games like *Virtual Cop* and *Mortal Kombat.*

> Most of the regular games would be all right. I think that violence is all talk. If they want to be wild they'll be wild.
>
> (Kevin)

> . . . as long as they know the difference between fighting on the computer screen and fighting outside in the real world. Otherwise, don't let 'em play it.
>
> (Seamus)

> *Interviewer:* Do you think it would be OK for little kids to play these games?
>
> *Peter:* Yeah, they like 'em.
>
> *Interviewer:* Say for example you had a 6-year-old brother and you brought him in here one day. Do you think it would be OK for him to play *Mortal Kombat?*

Peter:	Yeah.
Interviewer:	Why is that?
Peter:	'Cause little kids like guns, like racing cars and all that.
Interviewer:	So they like cars and guns. Do you know why they like cars and guns?
Peter:	Like they've never driven a car or shot a gun.
Interviewer:	Is that the same reasons for you?
Peter:	Yeah.

What was lacking for almost all of the boys was the possibility of working more reflectively and critically with the activities associated with game-playing, as well as with the stories and actions authorized and legitimated as 'masculine' through the game narratives. The links in particular between violence and masculinity needed to emerge more explicitly – and the boys needed opportunities (and language) with which to discuss this. Their almost egalitarian approach to game culture (they seemed to think that anyone could come and play if they wanted to) blurred and masked the strongly gendered features of game culture, and helped to soften and naturalize the excessively violent images and actions implicit in this culture.

Conclusion

It is important to recognize that popular cultural texts and practices like those associated with video gaming, whether by intent or by default, produce and market a politics of gender under the guise of apolitical entertainment. It is equally important to recognize that many of the boys and young men who are attracted to these textual and cultural practices may have little understanding of how they are positioned through the texts, how gendered subjectivity, pleasure and desire are deeply implicated in the narratives – and how they may come to know and to desire themselves within the terms of the texts. Neither might they have much motivation to change.

The point with gaming texts is that their narrative and semiotic features compound understandings of masculinity and gender with violence and pleasure. The issue, therefore, is not one simply of censorship. It is also, we argue, about critical and reflective analysis of cultural practice. Where critical citizenship is honoured as a goal of education, classroom practice should be about enabling students critically to read the processes wherein they take up personal, relational and cultural meanings. Given that the gaming culture is largely directed at boys, it seems particularly important that boys and young men have the opportunity to understand and to contest a masculinity that is expressed in terms of domination and control of others, gratuitous violence and institutionalized warfare, competitiveness at any cost, disregard for others and the environment, and self-aggrandizement through conquest. Boys' gaming culture, like any other, offers the possibilities of resistance and contestation. The pedagogical danger lies in the uncritical acceptance of the discourse that can be practised through the personally absorbing, highly interactive, populist culture of gaming.

We must be careful that the task for educators is not seen as a simple one of objectively deconstructing texts and practices. We must keep in mind that video game texts deal not only in knowledge about what it means to be and to relate as a gendered subject – but in pleasure and desire and subjective experience. For the educator, the challenge may not reside solely in identifying the politics of the texts, but in mobilizing boys' desire to do their gender otherwise. Given the complexity of the task we must remind one another that: 'This is a challenge for all of us who believe that transformative teaching and learning are central to the development and functioning of critical public cultures' (Giroux 1995: 313).

References

BRAUN, C. and GIROUX, J. (1989) 'Arcade video games: Proxemic, cognitive and content analyses', *Journal of Leisure Research*, **21**: 92–105.

CONNELL, B. (1987) *Gender and Power: Society, the Person and Sexual Politics*, Sydney: Allen and Unwin.

DAVIES, B. (1990) 'The problem of desire', *Social Problems*, **37**: 801–16.

DURKIN, K. (1995) *Computer Games: Their Effects on Young People. A Review*, Sydney: Office of Film and Literature Classification.

GIROUX, H. (1995) 'Pulp fiction and the culture of violence', *Harvard Educational Review*, **65**(2): 299–314.

KLINE, S. (1996) 'Technologies of the imaginary: Evaluating the promise of toys, television and video games for learning', Paper presented at the Sixth Australian and New Zealand Conference on The First Years of School, Hobart, Tasmania, January.

Senate Select Committee on Community Standards Relevant to the Supply of Services Utilising Electronic Technologies (1993) *Report on Video and Computer Games and Classification Issues*, Canberra: Parliament of the Commonwealth of Australia.

Magazine References

Computer Game Review, April 1996.
Electronic Gaming Monthly, July 1993.
GamePro, June 1994.
Games Master, April 1993.
Hello, December 1992.
Megazone, October 1993.
Megazone, July 1995.
Sega Saturn Magazine, March 1996.

Chapter Seven

'It's different to a mirror 'cos it talks to you':
Teenage girls, video cameras and identity

Gerry Bloustien

The most important thing I have got from making this video is the chance to analyze myself a bit . . . and that means to see myself the way others see me. It is also a chance to look at myself and my morals and see whether that is how I really want to be portrayed.

(Fran)

Introduction: An Alternative View of the City

Janine, Wanda and Janelle, members of an Aboriginal all-female teenage rock band, had been videoing themselves in the park. In the Botanic Gardens, where they chose to start their film, they had practised interviewing each other and playing with the camera. We had been there all day in 40 degree heat and now, hot and tired, we were wandering back to the train station to go home. We set off down North Terrace, Adelaide's aesthetically fine main boulevard, lined with museums, galleries and marble statues – reminders of the city's rich and formal colonial past. Suddenly the seriousness of their earlier videoing changed. Wanda gave us an alternative view of the city, directly addressing the camera which was still held by Janelle:

'Here,' she said to the camera, *sotto voce* and beckoning with her finger, 'I'll show you something!' She led the camera over to the war memorial fountain, an impressive monument with its solemn stone angels and its martyred immortal soldier. ''Ere is where you come when you're a bit stuck for the fare home after a night out and you've been experiencing too much alcohol'. She led the camera around the back of the fountain to the small wishing well. 'See?' Wanda winked knowingly at the camera and still in a slightly hushed voice, as though she were sharing a secret between friends, 'You come 'ere, lift up the wire and take enough to get 'ome'. She shrugs exaggeratedly. 'It's easy!' She then led the camera further down the street, serious purposeful demeanour – investigative journalism perfected – while Janelle continued to film. She stopped before some young women at a bus stop. 'Excuse me. Would you like to be in a documentary?' The camera caught their nervous expressions. 'What is it on?' they asked. 'Women and sex,' replied Wanda, before sweeping onwards majestically towards the station.

Theoretical Frameworks

The anecdote about Janine and her friends encapsulates, for me, the basis of my argument in this chapter. Before my eyes, these young women subverted what had been a serious attempt to capture themselves 'authentically' on video, by turning it into a very funny parody of the whole difficult exercise. In speaking (with winks and nods to the camera) of 'experiencing alcohol', of being at the railway station at night or stealing money from the war veterans' fountain, the girls were deliberately overturning at least two discourses: first, the documentary mode itself and second, a racist/sexist discourse. Articulating the very stereotypes that would usually be used against them as young Aboriginal women – underage drinking, petty crime and vandalism (''ere's where you get your fare home') and overt sexual activity ('women and sex') – the girls appeared to be taking control of these negative images. Yet none of these depictions appeared in their final footage, neatly edited for public consumption. There, we only see a group of young Aboriginal women who show us the fun of practising in their rock band with friends or being with a large extended family at home. What is happening here? Why the gap? In what way does the camera allow a play with image and identity to occur, a play that is both unsettling and liberating at the same time?

This chapter is about subjectivity and performance and their relationship to play, fantasy and the media. It also explores the place that the transformative power of play held in the lives of the young women in this study. For these young women, fantasy constituted self-making. It was the essential ingredient in reflexivity, in experimenting with and exploring gendered personhood. Further, the role that popular culture played in the production of that fantasy was salient, for television, music, film and magazines were the sites of the production of play and fantasy, not simply the means of consumption. In other words, the production of fantasy through play and, thus, the constitution of identity itself, is a very active exploratory process.

What I am exploring in this chapter is one aspect of that process, the effect of self-recognition and self-creation through the mechanism and power of the camera lens. I am looking at how that process integrates and meshes with everyday experiences – but first, a flashback to the genesis of this research and its methodology.

Research and Methodology

In the wider ethnographic research from which this chapter is drawn, I was exploring the everyday lived experiences of 10 teenage girls *through their own eyes*.[1] The participants, deliberately drawn from diverse ethnic and socio-economic backgrounds, were invited to document on video any aspects of their lives that they considered important.[2] They were assured that they would have complete control over the selection, filming, style and editing of the video footage and that if they wished we would screen their edited videos publicly at a student film festival.[3]

The girls were given no funding nor specific direction on ways of using the camera beyond the fundamentals.[4] The point was emphasized that they were free to video what they liked and how they liked, although I would be willing to show them specific video techniques if they requested them. No one did. The camera was a compact Hi8 'superior' domestic camera, deliberately chosen for its low-light capacity, its near-broadcast video quality and its small size. The camera's compactness was important because I wanted it to be as unintrusive as possible in the girls' lives.

The research examined the way each girl chose to interpret, negotiate, challenge and explore her developing sense of self and her relationships with the various social institutions of which she was a part. The range of stylistic approaches that they seemed to explore at different times was quite wide; one could see aspects of music video, parodies of David Attenborough-style documentaries or mock current affairs formats. At other times, there were more serious attempts to document the fun, the movement and excitement of their social engagements by using hand-held camera techniques. Here the camera was in the middle of the activity rather than standing off, objectively recording events.

What emerged from the videos and the filmic processes were the perceptual frames and boundaries the individuals placed upon themselves. The insights into the ways in which the girls acknowledged their particular social and cultural constraints became clearer. For the teenagers, the camera became a tool for interpreting and redefining their worlds. Not everything in their world was for public viewing. Not everything was selected for recording in the first place. Not everything was recorded in the same way. The selection, the filming and the editing processes highlighted the way the girls struggled to represent themselves in ways that cohered with their already established social and cultural frameworks. On the surface, such attempts at representation seemed like 'just play' but under closer scrutiny we can see specific strategies, 'the human seriousness of play' (Goffman 1970; Handelman 1990; Levi-Strauss 1966/1972; Turner 1982), providing insights into the way gendered subjectivity is performed and simultaneously constituted. To understand this we need to see identity as process (Hall 1987), with popular culture (especially television, film and music) playing a vitally important role in its production.

Identity as Process: Play and Mimesis

Engagement with popular culture, especially for young people, is a complex dialectic activity, one that oscillates repeatedly between total engagement and a balancing, knowing distanciation. From my observations and understandings of the young women in this study, I perceived this involvement with popular culture to be a deeply engrossing, embodied play – a 'deep play' (Geertz 1975, 1983), an experimentation with aesthetics, form and image that was infused with meaning. There was no total unthinking abandonment to pleasure, although there were moments of disengagement with the everyday. Nor was it the play of people who believe that their actions could be, in some way, ultimately politically subversive. A legitimate scepticism interfused this play – the scepticism of those who know that they too can create images and knowledge but that ultimately the illusion is, after all, just play. The concept of play being used here is not so much about changing the rules, or of calculatedly implementing strategies, but rather, having 'a sense of the game' (Bourdieu 1977, 1980/1990; Bourdieu and Wacquant 1992). Seen in this light, we can see that play has a very serious function indeed.

Here, then, I am using the concept of play to describe a particular process of representation and identification; strategies that incorporate, reflect on and depict the individual everyday experiences and perspectives of growing up female in Adelaide, South Australia, in the mid-1990s. The introduction of the camera during the fieldwork offered a 'symbolic' space to play, to experiment, as I shall detail below, but simultaneously it highlighted the usual difficulties and constraints the girls experienced in their search for 'alternative selves' (Schechner 1993: 39).[5]

Take 1: Play in Action

There seemed to be an awareness by all the girls that the camera was an exciting way of simultaneously exploring and constructing themselves, discovering and constituting 'the real me' and emphasizing difference. Hilary, for example, wanted to show how '*other* girls acted and behaved' and that 'not everyone is the same. We are all individuals'. She was aware of the power of media representation and was annoyed that, as she perceived it, teenagers were so often depicted in a negative light, especially in the tabloid press.[6] In this way, then, she and some of the others saw the potential of the camera as a political tool, a vehicle for presenting alternative points of view to a wider audience. This did not mean, however, that the girls always approached their films with any obvious generic formula in mind, rather there seemed to be an experimentation with form as well as content in their footage.

Initially, there did tend to be an attempt to stage formal interviews and to generalize for the audience about teenage behaviour. The narrative form was drawn straight from those television programmes which best seem to 'capture reality' – news and current affairs. Many of the girls were eager to be the 'television host', the mediating authority figure, keen to interview *others* on what *other* teenage girls like and feel, rather than be the focus of attention themselves. Several went around their school yards like investigative journalists, armed with microphones and camera to ask their friends and acquaintances 'significant questions':

Girls wanted to be 'host'

'Do you think boys should tell their girlfriends how to dress?'
'How do you feel about smoking and alcohol?'
'Do you think boys are only after one thing?'

It was an interesting distancing of themselves as 'subject' and initially my frustration was intense as I realized that the girls saw themselves as investigators of *others*, not the object of scrutiny themselves. I then began to understand that this was the initial testing out of space and possibilities – to see what was 'permissible' in their own eyes and in their own worlds – to explore what their world would look like through the more seemingly 'objective' lens of the camera.

Apart from this 'straight' interview form, where the questions were deliberately open-ended, such play with the camera also provided an opportunity to encourage others to articulate what the investigator already knew or suspected.

Pointing the camera and microphone at her friend Marika, Janine asks 'What do you do in your spare time?' Marika looks a bit incredulous at the question. 'Hang around. Run away from the cops'. 'What were you doing?' asks Janine sternly. Marika looks uncertain, laughs nervously, looks at the camera and then back again at Janine. 'Mucking around. Drinking beer,' she says. 'Oh so you *drink* do you?' asks Janine. 'Nah not me!' replies Marika quickly – one eye on the camera again – 'it's the other fellas'.

entrapment

Experienced journalists would recognize this as entrapment! So, on one level the girls were using the interview and related documentary style to find out things for themselves – to discover what other young people their age did and didn't do. The camera and microphone could either provide a licence to confirm what they already suspected of their friends and acquaintances or it could provide a forum for such discussion. Again, we need to see such activity as strategized play.

Such play is closely tied to identity, notions of self and ways of dealing with uncertainty. It is a concept of embodied play that equates with pleasure but not triviality (Handelman 1990). This type of play has taken a very particular form since the advent of the camera, the phonograph and now the complexities of even more elaborate technologies of mechanical reproduction. Michael Taussig (1987, 1993) drawing on Walter Benjamin's (1936/1973) insights, developed further the concept of *mimesis*, the embodied ways of becoming *other*; the innately human way of attempting to gain mastery over that which we do not understand.[7] Taussig describes the way colonized or dominated groups appropriate for themselves the representations of the dominant culture of their societies, and in accepting for themselves the stereotypes laid upon them, they 'become' other. With the invention of highly-technologized means of representing self and other, and of understanding the other through the self, the fusion between the two has become greater. Mimesis, or embodied mimicry becomes a way of becoming other 'wherein the representation shares in or takes power from the represented' and 'the capacity of the imagination [can be] lifted through representational media . . . into other worlds' (Taussig 1993: 16). Thus the dominated take on board the means of subordination, often reaffirming the process of domination through their attempts to understand, to resist, to self-empower. It is a way of attempting to appropriate the power of the dominant and has been seen by many as a (sometimes misplaced) strategy of 'resistance' (see for example, Lewis 1990, 1992; McRobbie 1991, 1994; Willis 1977, 1990).

After this more hesitant beginning, this strategy of play or mimesis, this attempt to see themselves as other, developed more forcefully. A greater experimentation occurred in the mode of documentary itself. In an attempt to articulate and test their own feelings and the constraints of their world, the girls turned the camera on themselves by making *themselves* the overt, acknowledged subjects of the investigation in two related ways. Either a technique I called 'ask me questions' was used, or the girls used 'the fly on the wall' technique, pretending the camera did not exist. Sometimes both techniques were used by the same person at different times. Both were techniques of distancing or *othering* in attempts to gain some kind of mastery over both the situation and the representation. Yet both strategies also rapidly brought a blurring of 'porous realities' (Schechner 1993) in their wake. The resulting portrait seemed 'smudged', like an Impressionist painting, as I shall illustrate below – 'the real me' is suggested, but tantalizingly just out of reach.

Take 2: Ask Me Questions!

Several of the girls asked me to film a section of their video by acting as camera person and interviewer. Grace, for example, asked me to come to her house on particular afternoons or early evenings when she knew her mother and her younger brother would not be at home. This, she informed me, was to ensure privacy. After we had set up the camera in her room, she would sit in front of it and say, 'Ask me questions!' In situations like this I often found that the period when I asked the questions – 'What is your name? Tell me about yourself. What kind of a person are you?' – didn't last very long. The questions seemed to be used as starting points for the young person to then launch into descriptions or accounts of significant aspects of their lives. Perhaps to be 'asked questions' in this way offers licence to be personal. So much of our culture, especially for women, emphasizes the inappropriateness of talking about oneself so that a space has to be created in order for one to 'objectify' oneself, in order to be other. Although these conversations were recorded, I emphasize again that it was always understood that the resulting raw footage was under the control of the subject. In other words, whatever the person said and did in front of the video could be removed or, if it were retained, it could be used for the final edited video, or left aside. This strategy seemed to provide the freedom to play with confidences and important information, a licence to unsettle and unravel conventionally controlled behaviour, to create and constitute reality at the same time. In this way, aspects of the girls' lives that perhaps would not have been revealed to an adult researcher were talked about relatively openly on the video.

Although all of the girls talked about illicit drug use – either their own or even if they did not use, the difficulties they faced when with friends, as drug-taking was so common – I did not expect anyone to commit themselves to discussing their own involvement on camera. They were all quite candid, specific and detailed in their discussions with me – *off* camera – as they talked about their various social activities and mused about friendships, parties or other events. Yet one afternoon, Grace spent several hours chatting in front of the camera about her own and her friends' experimentations with illegal drugs. She told me where and how they obtained the substances, the cost, which ones she had tried and which ones she was too afraid to try. She told me about the large cross-section of friends she had and how they would often meet up in the city. The main activity they had in common was their shared use of a combination of alcohol and amphetamines; 'I can't imagine a world without drugs. It'd be so boring,' she said. She told me that her group regularly took 'Dope, acid trips [LSD] and Rohypnol'. I met many of these friends during my fieldwork, several of them repeating this information to me in their casual conversations with each other. Although off camera, she had chatted about these activities before, on video Grace was very careful not to name names of those friends who had actually taken some of the harder drugs and she announced that she certainly would not select those sections of her video for public viewing. She made, however, no attempt to wipe the material completely off the tape by recording over it. I understood that perhaps this was to be a record for herself.[8]

The 'ask me questions' mode thus seemed to provide an opportunity for the young people to talk about very personal, often difficult, problems through this method of distanciation. This was 'serious play', an opportunity to simultaneously explore and portray themselves as other. In this mode, Sara talked about her unpleasant experiences of racism at school, Fran talked about her difficult and antagonistic relationship with her father and nearly all the girls talked about the difficult balancing act of being simultaneously both child and (female) young adult:

> They say these are the best years of our lives. [short laugh of exaggerated mock despair] I think I'll just *die* when I get out of school!
>
> (Grace)

The fact that the girls talked about these 'risky' things is less interesting than the fact that they chose to reveal them on video tape as part of their documentary footage. It seemed as though actions and thoughts performed on tape, but not in front of a visible audience, could create a space for experimentation. Something recorded can be watched, examined, understood as though it were someone else's experience. As Fran, at the end of film-production time affirmed, the camera was a means to constructing the desired image:

Since I started making this film . . . I'm seeing myself through other people's eyes, how other people see me. It's been good though, because if you see something you don't like, you can change it. It's different to a mirror 'cos it talks to you.

The reference to the 'talking mirror' highlights again the difficulty of maintaining a secure sense of self, an awareness that the self can be changed and that that change is part of its constitution. The gap between the 'performing me' and the 'inner me' becomes blurred.

Take 3: Fly on the Wall

Another blurring of spheres through the utilization of a documentary style was when the camera was used to record usual events but was not acknowledged during the filming. Mary was quite specific about this. She wanted the camera to show her usual activities of collecting her social security cheque, going shopping and so on while pretending that the camera 'was invisible'. She led the imaginary camera audience through the mall, chatting to acquaintances as she went to window shop at her favourite sports clothing store. The clothes there were way out of her price range but she directed the camera to show her judiciously scrutinizing the items of clothing, feeling the quality and checking the prices and chatting to the staff as though she were a regular purchaser. She certainly was a regular *visitor* to the sports store but she was not able to afford the prices of these expensive brand-name clothes. At no stage did Mary attempt to talk to the camera. She behaved as though the camera were invisible and had just captured her usual activities on film.

As was the case with several of the girls there were events and aspects of Mary's life that she decided to portray very differently. For example, there were events that were not recorded or talked about *on* camera at all. Away from the camera, Mary had talked about her experiments with drugs including 'magic mushrooms', fungi with hallucinogenic properties that grow wild in the local hills. On another occasion, she had given me a detailed account of shop-lifting and car theft and chases in the city. These activities were narrated again to me later by several of her friends, through their conversations with each other in my presence, and later by Mary's social worker.[9] Most of Mary's friends were boys and some were known offenders, frequently appearing before the courts or spending time in the detention centre, yet these details of petty crime or 'offending' did not appear in Mary's footage. In front of the camera, it seemed that Mary was anxious to portray a respectable, socially responsible self for others to see and understand. It was also, as I realized later, a way of constructing a portrait of herself that she could feel good about.

I felt through making this film I could acknowledge myself. I can see some very good parts of me.

(Mary)

Frequently the 'fly on the wall' technique alternated between objective and subjective mode so that initially the event may have been recorded without acknowledging the camera and then suddenly the video and assumed audience were acknowledged and included in the diegesis. In this manner, several of the girls filmed their own or other people's parties. During these times the camera was often acknowledged and experimented with by other guests who used deliberately shaky hand-held and tracking shots, extreme close-ups, unusual angles and direct address. Sometimes it caught self-conscious conversations or physical jokes that highlighted the usual concerns of young people. Grace and her best friend chatted resignedly about sexual double standards as they cooked together in Grace's kitchen. At Fran's party, one of the boys planted a deliberate smacking kiss on another boy for the benefit of the camera while another put on lipstick and then pouted and kissed at the camera lens. Amid the resulting hilarity one of the boys asked aloud, 'Will you respect me in the morning?'

Pat was very involved with techno-rave culture and so filmed quite a number of dances. Her material detailed the crowds, the ritualized performances of the DJs and the MCs and, through a strobe facility on the camera, she managed to express the mood of the dances and the effect of the lights and the music extremely impressionistically. The strobe effectively meant that the dancers were shown moving slowly and rhythmically like automatons, while the music and the background chat of the dancers continued at their normal pace. Again, there was no direct gaze to the camera during these scenes – the operator was effectively invisible and ignored as she recorded the event. However, when she filmed some scenes at a techno community radio station where she helped out occasionally or when she filmed the preparations behind the scenes for a number of techno-raves, the people she was filming then responded by laughing, chatting and showing a self-conscious awareness of the camera lens. Publicly, Pat seemed to be portraying herself as very much part of the 'scene', describing herself as a raver and distinguishing between the 'real thing' and the many 'try hards', those who attempted to be authentic but failed. It was only *off* camera she talked angrily about the sexism and double standards she perceived in the ravers' scene.

So these were moments of gaining distance, of 'seeing myself as others see me, of analyzing myself a bit' (Fran), of attempting to grasp 'the real me'. Yet, simultaneously, the camera provided an awareness that 'the real me' was not readymade but available to be constructed – the self and identity are not simply reflected upon and represented but constituted in the very act of representation, in the very act of play. In some cases, direct address to the camera, as a kind of confessional, was used as a way to pin down this elusive self.

Take 4: 'Authority' and 'Authenticity' Through Direct Address

Of all the girls, Diane used the camera most personally as a form of diary. Several times after an important evening, a special party or event, alone in her room, Diane would record her feelings, excitements and anxieties on the video. The self she portrayed and projected on these occasions was primarily someone who, in her own words, 'enjoyed partying totally' but simultaneously was concerned about difficulties of friendships, the pressures from peers and parents concerning appropriate social behaviour and the difficulties of negotiating relationships with the opposite sex without incurring the reputation of a 'slut'. Her monologue was punctuated every now and again with qualifications in case the camera should think she were being too forward, obsessed with boys or even too self-absorbed. 'Have I bored you yet?' she would ask of her imagined audience. Towards the end of the fieldwork time, she was to articulate the pleasure of using the camera as a diary because 'It became like my best friend. I knew if it got bored or didn't like what I said, it wouldn't get huffy or run away.'

Such use of the camera again points to an awareness of the elusiveness of an 'authentic self' and a need to manage and control the uncertainty (Goffman 1959). It was a way in which the girls created boundaries of certitude, marking off what was private and what could be considered as constituting 'the real me'.

> That's why some people keep diaries. A diary can be more important than a best friend. Sometimes, you can't tell a friend what you are thinking because you may not know whether you really believe it. How can you tell someone something when you don't know whether you know it yourself yet?
>
> (Belinda)

Earlier in this chapter, I described Mary's video footage where she had behaved as though the camera were invisible and had just captured her usual activities on film. On a separate occasion, however, but clearly not intended for a wider audience, she gave a detailed verbal account on video – totally unsolicited – of the physical abuse she had undergone as a child when she first was brought into the country by her adoptive parents. This account was later repeated to me by her social worker. Before she began to speak, she dressed herself in her best clothes and created on the kitchen bench a display of photographs of herself as a small child with her biological parents. This aspect of her life seemed to be recorded for herself – a way of *othering* or distancing the events, of enabling her to gain a new perspective on them. These were not to be shown to others, she said. As a companion and a friend in her actual world, which was obviously more than that which was portrayed on video, I was permitted to be privy to the less conventionally acceptable aspects of her life. On the parts of the video that were to be selected for showing to a public audience, however, the representation of her life and her identity was more carefully and, in some ways, 'creatively' drawn.

What is clear here, then, is that both Diane and Mary's public performances were drawn with far more certitude and confidence than their more 'private' selves. It is the slippage that appears between the shifting subjectivities, the possible and the enacted selves, that becomes the problem, the aspect of everyday life and representation that has to be 'managed'. Identity is as much about exclusion as inclusion; who we are requires a delicate and continual drawing up of shifting boundaries. Perhaps an effective metaphor would be a kaleidoscope. In contemporary western culture, perceptions and interpretations of social reality are potentially endless. With each twist of the cylinder another pattern clicks into focus. A similar understanding of reality or realities has been suggested as a multidimensional mosaic created over time (Becker 1987). This could be an even more appropriate metaphor when we consider that the 'reality' we see on the television or the video screen is made up of thousands of tiny moving dots, 'never quite complete and certainly never static' (Haag 1993: 115). Out of these random patterns we impose order, but our hold on what is order and what makes sense can be very shaky indeed. We have to hold tenuously onto quite contradictory notions of reality, switching from one to another as we feel appropriate. Play enables us to do this for 'playing . . . [is] . . . the underlying continuum of experience' (Schechner 1993: 42).

Locating 'The *Real* Me'?

The camera provided not simply a reflection of the participants' sense of identity but its use enabled that identity to be constituted. Shaviro, drawing on Walter Benjamin's understanding of the experience of film, referred to the tactile cinematic image and the effect on the observer. The blurring of what is observed and the observer becomes, he argues, a moment of mimesis. How much more so is this when the subject of that depiction is also the object – for example, when the girls turned the cameras on themselves, on their own sense and portrayal of self. The resultant 'real me' is hard to grasp, impossible to pin down.

> Following Benjamin and Taussig, we must radically redefine the very notion of identification, and say rather that the subject is captivated and 'distracted', made more fluid and indeterminate, in the process of sympathetic participation. Mimesis and contagion tend to efface fixed identities and to blur the boundaries between inside and outside.
>
> (Shaviro 1993: 53)

My observation of Fran's attempt to capture herself on camera provides an interesting example of this. As was often the case with the other girls, I felt there was an interesting gap between the ways I frequently saw her off camera and the way she tailored her portraits to play with her camera image, to experiment with different identities.

I had arranged that Fran should have the camera to video some quieter sections for her film in her home. I knew her as 'Fran' in full swing at Cirkidz, energetically taking part in the workshops or in performance at shows.[10] I had been present when, in Sara's film, Fran had been part of her friendship group and I had also viewed Sara's video of her party where Fran had been a guest.

I saw her as ebullient. Her verbal and body language were effusive and totally unrestrained, irrespective of whether there was a camera present to catch her moods and behaviour or not. At Cirkidz workshops she dominated the conversation with loud comments, bawdy or insulting jokes and raucous laughter. The most agile of the members, she performed backflips and bodily contortions with ease and with superb skill and dexterity. She carried her body with an unrestrained ease and was extremely physical with her close friends, both male and female; sometimes this caused some comment and certainly her physical intimacy with most of the boys in the group had disturbed some of the girls from time to time. On Sara's video, where she had taken film of her friends in the city, there were several shots of Fran doing multiple somersaults on the lawn outside the Adelaide Museum, totally oblivious to the stares of passers-by; at Sara's party, she was shown on camera dancing wildly while calling attention to another girl's dancing movements by yelling, 'Hey look everyone. M's fucking a pole!'

So this was the girl I knew. This was the first time, though, that Fran had suggested that she would like to video her own world, be director of her own film, as it were. I was totally unprepared for the Fran I met at her house on this occasion. She arrived at home about 10 minutes after I arrived, entering relatively quietly and immediately apologizing for being late. She was dressed in a short skirt with black leggings and a large black felt hat – a far cry from her usual casual outfit of shapeless T-shirts and baggy shorts or patchwork pants. She kept the hat on the whole time I was there and throughout the videoing session, so she was obviously proud of it and liked the way she looked in it.

In her room, in front of the camera, she sat upright and quietly poised on her bed asking me if I had had a good week and generally making 'polite conversation' for a few minutes. After she adjusted the bedside lights so that a dull blue light shone on her face from a striking angle, she talked about who she felt she was, her ambitions, her likes and dislikes. It was in this context that she told me that she particularly enjoyed her quality of childishness and her ability to play. It high-lighted for me the very self-consciousness of her pose and the awareness that her more mature serious stance was just as much a play with image and style as her earlier expressions of frivolity and fun.

Michael Taussig asks rhetorically, 'Is it conceivable that a person could break boundaries like this, slipping into Otherness, trying it on for size?' (Taussig 1993: 33). The answer lies in part in our limited conception of identity. Although we have rejected, for the most part, the concept of identity as a 'unified essence' (Hall *et al.* 1992: 65), we haven't yet fully understood the notion of identity as a process, 'who one is to become'. Ultimately, identities are narratives – stories we tell about ourselves – and they are fictional, 'the necessary fiction of action, the necessary fictions of politics' (Hall *et al.* 1992: 66). Such a moment of awareness, of trying to understand who we are, leads not just to a knowing of the self but also to an 'interrogation' of the self. It becomes 'the discursive space from which "the real me" emerges initially as an assertion of the authenticity of the person and then lingers on to reverberate – the real me? – as a questioning of identity' (Bhabha 1987). In more prosaic terms, Hilary addressed just this issue in front of the camera stating, 'I look at my video and think, my goodness! That is *me*!'

Actions and thoughts performed on tape, but not in front of a visible audience, create a space for experimentation, a moment of blurring of what are designated private and public worlds. A fascinating moment illustrating this was when Grace suddenly told me that she wanted to dance. She had been filming and talking about her bedroom in my presence and then she suddenly asked me to leave the room. Once alone, she played her favourite tapes and danced by herself in front of the video for about 10 minutes. Then I was allowed back into the room and she continued her more mundane filming. It seemed as though here was an instance of music enabling the 'saying' of what was, perhaps, usually unsayable. This anecdote leads us on to another rich area of speculation – the symbolic roles and utilization of music.

Creating the *mise-en-scène*: Music and Mimesis

Music played a central role in footage taken by all of the girls. In fact, their inclusion of the music and its importance caused problems when we later completed the documentary and considered where and how the film could be distributed; we had a great deal of music copyright to pay for. However, the issue raised here is the question of why music was so central to the way the girls constituted their senses of self.

The centrality of the home in the girls' videos and the various ways in which it was depicted, indicated both the 'investment' (Hollway 1984) and the ambivalence that the participants felt towards this 'private' aspect and locus of their lives. It seemed to me, as I looked again at the girls' footage, that music continually served as a cultural thread and an effective link, moving between the worlds that we would popularly designate as private and public. Although the participants sometimes videoed their rooms without verbal commentary, music was frequently played in the background to provide a particular ambience. In cases where it became a vitally significant component of the *mise-en-scène*, the music was chosen quite deliberately to match a particular mood or to tie in with a specific poster of a pop or rock-star. As in all drama and film, the music integrated the characterization and themes of the scene. At other times, if the participant was in front of the camera, talking about herself, she often had some appropriate music playing softly – and sometimes not so softly – in the background. In those situations, the music was often selected, seemingly to underscore an aspect of her sense of group identity. So, for example, Grace deliberately selected music from the Violent Femmes, 'a kind of 90's folk punk,' she explained to me. Mary, from Papua New Guinea, played reggae music while she was taking the imaginary 'visitor' on a video tour of her house. It appeared as though the girls were making the music another symbolic aspect of their sense of self along with the posters and other cultural icons in their rooms and their homes.

Even when the music was not being played, the importance of its wider status as essential commodity was present in the record sleeves, CD covers, posters and T-shirts that frequently decorated the wall spaces. As indicated above, it was not simply the obvious significance of fan-group membership that the music implied, but the wider meaning that such an icon emitted. For example, in the bedrooms of Janine and her Aboriginal friends were posters of Bob Marley and, sometimes, Aboriginal musicians. Mary also had photos of Bob Marley and many posters of Jamaican and African-American basketball stars. For these girls, obviously the skin colour of the stars and personalities on their wall posters was significant. What their choice implied was not simply their own fandom of these cultural groups but that such membership cohered with their immediate familial and community values and expectations. Their choices suggested an awareness of the constraints in their performed subjectivity and of their investments in these chosen positions.[11]

The third way that the music was combined with the girls' camera use was through dance and music video. Several girls recorded their own dancing to their favourite musicians but when it was 'serious play' it was recorded as either 'fly on the wall' (as in Pat's depictions of the rave scene) or as a secret activity (as in the case of Grace). In any other recording, the girls tended to exaggerate their movements, using humour to stress their ironic stance. So, for example, when Diane filmed her two friends, Helen and Jane, dancing in front of her TV to one of Peter André's songs, their movements echoed exactly those of the dancers on the television screen in the pop clip. The girls swept in front of the screen, shoulders raised, gazing with sophisticated disdain over their shoulders, back at the camera.

Helen: This is how sluttish models walk.
Diane: [From behind the camera lens as she filmed] Oh very sluttish! Remember to smile. You'll be famous.

This kind of exaggeration, or mimetic excess, always hinted at the moments when 'contradictory realities coexist, each seemingly capable of cancelling the other out' (Schechner 1993: 36). It is to a closer look at this mimetic excess that I now turn.

Playing with (Self) Identity

The different uses of the documentary form allowed the girls to record themselves as investigators, seekers of 'Truth' and to create themselves in their own images of socially acceptable, mature young adults. But play, to return to my premise at the beginning of the chapter, can be exciting and dangerous because it is unpredictable. Play can expose the lack of containment – the inability to maintain a fixed, carefully controlled self. The carefully drawn mask can slip.

Such moments of slippage, moments of heightened awareness of the (lack of) management of identity, often were dealt with on video through mimetic excess and humour.[12] This was when the more usual serious recording of experience was abandoned in favour of exaggeration, a very clear excessive posing or ironic stance. The example of Diane with her friends, above, is one such moment. Perhaps a less immediately obvious example of mimetic excess, but a poignant one nevertheless, was revealed in Kate's video. She and a friend began by seriously asking each other about leisure time and school. After a while, they began to stage the interviews, deliberately placing the interviewee in deep shadow to 'conceal' her identity while asking emotive questions about school, parental and peer group expectations and so on. The interviewee would pretend to cry and the interview would finish by the interviewer saying softly and with a great show of concern, 'Would you like to end the interview now?' Because, in actuality, the girls attended different schools and because they saw Kate's school as the more academic, their video personae differed accordingly. So, in the first scenario, Kate pretended to suffer distressing teasing by her peers because her B grade average was not high enough. When they swapped roles, her friend pretended to be distressed because *her* friends teased her for her *high* academic achievements. This portion of the video was an extremely elaborate parody of a current affairs programme but it also resonated with their own concerns and awareness of class differences and familial expectations. After a while, they tried to return to the same interviews in a more serious vein but they soon switched off the camera, perhaps aware that the scenario was too unsettling to discuss or portray without humour or intense role-play.

Conclusion: Getting Ready for Distribution?

In this chapter, through obvious limitations of space, I have only explored one aspect of the whole research – the use of the camera by the teenage girls as a means to 'play with' and 'explore' possible identities through particular generic styles and televisual forms. When the participants came to edit and condense their footage in the edit suite, the exercise proved even more liberating because sound and image could be separated and new selves could clearly be created in the final video product. Images could be removed as though they had never been. Old 'selves' could be revisited and scrutinized for their 'authenticity' at representing 'the real me' or 'the me as I am now'. Sara expressed the difficulty of the exercise in the following way, grinning ironically:

> I've changed a lot over the three years which made editing hard. Sometimes looking at myself was like looking in a mirror at a great big zit.[13]

The usual way of analyzing film texts, even such home-produced artefacts, would be through film theory which draws on semiotic and psychoanalytic concepts as, for example, in the work of Modleski (1988), Penley (1989), Williams (1983, 1989) and many others. However, while these approaches are valuable and insightful, here I am drawing on postmodern concepts of identity, specifically the concepts of play and mimesis; I seek to emphasize the phenomenological and physiological factors that underly film-making and viewing. The cinematic apparatus in this paradigm is not creating 'an impression of reality' (Baudry 1986) but a palpable and disturbing power. Walter Benjamin calls this 'the physical shock effect' which 'disrupts the traditional, historically sedimented habits and expectations of vision; it undoes the transcendental and phenomenological structures that claimed to regulate perception and to ground and unify the ego' (Shaviro 1993).

Childhood and adolescence usually allow space to play and play, as we have seen, is a very serious, often desperate, venture – a testing and stretching of boundaries to harness a sense of certainty. For the teenage participants in this study, their engagement with narrative style, genre and form in their own film-making indicated their searching for and struggle with their sense of shifting possible identities. At the end of the filming process, Hilary states: 'The film has shown me change is the only certainty in life.'

Elsewhere (Bloustien in press), I employ the metaphor of 'threshold braking' to describe my teenage film-makers' efforts to hold on to certainties. Threshold braking is a strategy used to control a car under situations of potential danger. It involves learning how to develop a feel for the situation, adjusting one's foot on the brake, applying just enough pressure to avoid a skid. Taussig's comment reminded me of this:

> As in so many moments of the mimetic, what we find is not only matching and duplication but also slippage which, once slipped into, skids wildly . . . This slippage is its 'secret' so . . . that 'secret' equals slippage.
>
> (Taussig 1993: 115–116)

Taussig refers here to the manageability of attempting to control the uncertainties of one identity by appropriating another – one more certain, more powerful, with more status. Frequently, that can involve accepting the identity imposed upon one by others. The girls could see the possibilities of alternative gendered identities in their world. Their language was replete with references to images from advertising, film, television, magazines, and music videos suggesting the opportunities and possibilities for change, transformation and control – but the girls also knew simultaneously that such 'freedom' was romantic and fantastic. In spite of the media hype, self-making is hard work. Identity is not like a fashion item that can consciously be put on or off at will. For these girls, as for all of us, there were many taken-for-granted aspects of their lives, symbolic boundaries, which were non-negotiable because they were 'unsayable'. In this very serious process of playing, the girls retained their 'feel for the game' (Bourdieu 1980/1990), an awareness of symbolic constraints. There was too much at stake to contemplate anything other than what was already known, what was safe. When self-scrutiny became too intense, and the boundaries too terrifyingly blurred on or off the camera, then the play slipped into mimetic excess. It is through this delicate process of self-making that our sense of identity emerges. It is through the serious process of play, of exploration and representation, that the self is constituted. In the late 1990s, the camera, and related technologies, have proved a particularly powerful tool for young people in their search for, and creation of, that elusive 'real me'.

Notes

1 Here I use the term 'everyday' to describe the way individuals perceive and engage in their worlds. It is a perception of the world rather than just a sphere of existence. Drotner summarizes it thus: 'Everyday life is a means to create some certainty in a world of ambivalence' (1994: 352).

2 The names used here are, of course, not their real names. In their videos, where they had complete control over what would be portrayed for an audience and what would not be revealed, they have retained their real names.

3 The festival was held in December 1996. The video was awarded two prizes – best documentary and best editing out of 140 entries.

4 As a production 'company', Femco (Female Cooperative), formed for the express purpose of making the documentary, the young women and I were able to attract funding from the Australia Council Community Arts Project, purely to cover the cost of postproduction.

5 Elsewhere Schechner (1985: 110) reminds us that other theorists have also recognized that through play 'transitional phenomena take place'. The child and later the adult recognize certain situations and events as 'not me . . . not not me'. During the process of this recognition, however, a blurring occurs, the 'dance goes into the body' (Schechner 1985: 110).

6 The daily newspapers are regularly full of articles about teenage violence, crime and vandalism. In such articles, youth becomes synonymous with a threat to the ordered control of society. For example, *The Adelaide Advertiser* (6 August 1994) under a headline reading 'Designer theft the new fashion' ran an article beginning: 'A thriving black market in stolen fashion clothing is being run throughout Adelaide schools by "highly organised" teenage groups.'

7 He calls this the modern form of 'sympathetic magic', wherein 'the model, if it works, gains through its sensuous fidelity something of the power and personality of that which it is a model' (Taussig 1993: 16).

8 Grace was also quite adamant, whenever I brought her video footage into her house, that I hand it directly to her and not to her mother. She obviously had more concerns than other girls, but all the girls treated their 'raw' or 'wild' footage (untreated material) as private and confidential, only showing it to very trusted others.

9 These stories were also repeated in conversations with the authority figures involved – the police, social workers and the magistrate when later Mary herself was brought before the courts.

10 Cirkidz was originally called the Bowden Brompton Youth Circus, an organization formed for disadvantaged youth in Adelaide. It is now open to many different young people from diverse socio-economic and ethnic backgrounds from all over the metropolitan area.

11 Wendy Hollway (1984) argues that particular subject positions are taken up over other possible conflicting ones, at specific times, according to the amount of 'investment' that a person perceives is placed therein. 'Investment', here, is conceived as both emotional commitment and vested interest. I would argue, further, that that investment stems from

the familial and community framework within which the individual develops her sense of self and thus her possible range of subjectivities. See Bloustien (in press).

12 Schechner (1993) refers to these moments as 'dark play' and, indeed some of these moments can be entirely without humour.

13 Obviously, one of the worst scenarios for a teenager is discovering that the face in the mirror has a blemish that she hadn't noticed before. However, highly significantly, 'zits' can be covered up and eventually they disappear as though they had never been.

References

BAUDRY, J-L. (1986) 'Ideological effects of the basic cinematic apparatus' (trans. Aslan Williams) in P. ROSEN (ed.) *Narrative Apparatus and Ideology: A Film Theory Reader*, New York: Columbia University Press.

BECKER, S. (1987) *Discovering Mass Communication*, Glenview, IL: Scott, Foresman.

BENJAMIN, W. (1936/1973) 'The work of art in the age of mechanical reproduction', in W. BENJAMIN *Illuminations*, London: Fontana.

BHABHA, H. (1987) 'Interrogating identity' in L. APPIGNANESI (ed.) *The Real Me: Post Modernism and the Question of Identity*, ICA Documents, no. 6, London: ICA Publications.

BLOUSTIEN, G. (in press) 'Ceci n'est pas une jeune fille' in H. JENKINS, T. MCPHERSON and J. SHATTUE (eds) *Hop on Pop: The Pleasures and Politics of Popular Culture*, Durham, NC: Duke University Press.

BOURDIEU, P. (1977) *Outline of a Theory of Practice*, Cambridge: Cambridge University Press.

BOURDIEU, P. (1980/1990) *The Logic of Practice*, Cambridge: Polity Press.

BOURDIEU, P. and WACQUANT, L. J. D. (1992) *An Invitation to Reflexive Sociology*, Chicago, IL: University of Chicago Press.

DROTNER, K. (1994) 'Ethnographic enigmas: the "everyday" in recent media studies', *Cultural Studies*, **8**(2): 341–57.

GEERTZ, C. (1975) *The Interpretation of Cultures*, London: Hutchinson.

GEERTZ, C. (1983) *Local Knowledge*, New York, Basic Books.

GOFFMAN, I. (1959) *The Presentation of Self in Everyday Life*. Harmondsworth, Middlesex: Penguin Books.

GOFFMAN, E. (1970) *Strategic Interaction*, Oxford: Blackwell.

HAAG, L. (1993) 'Oprah Winfrey: The construction of intimacy in the talk show setting', *Journal of Popular Culture*, **26**: 115–21.

HALL, S. (1987) 'Minimal selves', in L. APPIGNANESI (ed.) *The Real Me: Post Modernism and the Question of Identity*, ICA Documents, no. 6, London: ICA Publications.

HALL, S., HELD, D. and MCGREW, T. (eds) (1992) *Modernity and Its Futures*, Oxford: Polity Press for The Open University.

HANDELMAN, D. (1990) *Models and Mirrors: Towards an Anthropology of Public Events*, Cambridge: Cambridge University Press.

HOLLWAY, W. (1984) 'Gender difference and the production of subjectivity', in J. HENRIQUES, C. URWIN, C. VENN and V. WALKERDINE (eds) *Changing the Subject*, London: Methuen.

LEVI-STRAUSS, C. (1966/1972) *The Savage Mind*, London: Weidenfeld and Nicholson.

LEWIS, L. (1990) *Gender Politics and MTV*, Philadelphia, PA: Temple University Press.

LEWIS, L. (ed.) (1992) *The Adoring Audience: Fan Culture and Popular Media*, London: Routledge.

McROBBIE, A. (1991) *Feminism and Youth Culture*, London: Macmillan.

McROBBIE, A. (1994) *Postmodernism and Popular Culture*, London: Routledge.

MODLESKI, T. (1988) *The Women Who Knew Too Much: Hitchcock and Feminist Theory*, New York: Methuen

PENLEY, C. (1989) *The Future of an Illusion: Film Feminism and Psychoanalysis*, Minneapolis, MN: University of Minnesota Press.

SCHECHNER, R. (1985) *Between Theatre and Anthropology*, Philadelphia, PA: University of Philadelphia Press.

SCHECHNER, R. (1993) *The Future of Ritual*, London: Routledge.

SHAVIRO, S. (1993) *The Cinematic Body*, Minneapolis, MN: University of Minneapolis Press.

TAUSSIG, M. (1987) *Shamanism, Colonialism and the Wild Man*, Chicago, IL: University of Chicago Press.

TAUSSIG, M. (1993) *Mimesis and Alterity: A Particular History of the Senses*, New York: Routledge.

TURNER, V. (1982) *From Ritual to Theatre: The Human Seriousness of Play*, New York: Performing Arts Journal Publications.

WILLIAMS, L. (1983) 'When the woman looks', in M. DOANE, P. MELLENCAMP and L. WILLIAMS (eds) *Revision: Essays in Feminist Film Criticism*, 83–99, Frederick, MD: University Publications of America.

WILLIAMS, L. (1989) *Hard Core: Pleasure and the Frenzy of the Visual*, Berkeley, CA: University of California Press.

WILLIS, P. (1977) *Learning to Labour – How Working Class Kids Get Working Class Jobs*, Farnborough: Saxon House.

WILLIS, P. (1990) *Common Culture: Symbolic Work at Play in the Everyday Cultures of the Young*, Milton Keynes: Open University Press.

Chapter Eight

The friendly phone

Patricia Gillard, Karen Wale and Amanda Bow

'Teenage romance seems to be ending Australia's love affair with the mobile phone' announces a recent newspaper article. Parents, horrified at the cost of their children's conversations, are exhorted to make rules which limit children's use of mobiles and 'make clear their purpose' as 'communication and business tools' (Rollins 1996). The article implies that teen conversation is not a legitimate use of the phone, though it does not suggest that mobiles should be confiscated. No wonder. It goes on to describe mobiles as the 'fastest growing area' of tele-communications, with people under 30 making up over half of the customer base. The industry itself, however, is ambivalent about this emerging group of consumers.

Despite these dramatic changes, there is a complete lack of research in the public domain about telecommunications in the lives of a new generation of users. This chapter explores the roles telecommunications play in teenagers' lives and their views about a communications future. The findings draw on two different forms of research and have been prompted by the question of whether or not today's adolescents are a distinctive group in their understanding and use of information and communications technologies (ICTs). In this account, we call those between 13 and 19 years, teenagers or teens (which reflects the ways they refer to themselves) and in our own work, the term 'household' is used in preference to the more value-laden term 'family'.

Media Use within Families

Research about teenagers and telecommunications is almost non-existent. There have, however, been studies about the family context for children's media use which provide a framework for considering telecommunications uses. An early study of teenage girls (Palmer 1986) mentions the phone as an adjunct to media use at home. A passing reference was made to phone calls between close friends, who were co-viewers of favourite TV programmes, even though they were not present in the household: 'some girls would even telephone each other in commercial breaks to make comments to each other straight away' (Palmer 1986: 33).

Observation research within households pointed to the influence of family rules and practices in providing a context for media use (Bryce 1987; Bryce and Leichter 1983). In one study, the 'micro-culture of the family' was documented by researchers who lived in three households, for periods of up to six weeks (Bryce 1987: 136). The interdependence of physical space and social behaviour were what emerged most clearly from this research; spatial boundaries between such activities as eating and viewing, the personal control or ownership of TV spaces and even auditory boundaries proved to be significant to some family members who, in the latter case, complained if the media activity of others violated their 'auditory privacy'. Of special importance was the 'time culture' of the families. Families who emphasized schedules, segmentation and promptness were termed 'monochronic'; 'polychronic' families were ones where several things, including TV viewing, happened at once (Bryce 1987).

Gillard's ethnography of 23 children viewing television at home established the importance of parental rules and control of family routines in affecting how, when and what children viewed on television. In families where parents imposed rules and practices about amount of time spent viewing and, possibly, the content of what was viewed, children were more likely to watch fewer hours of television and to watch non-commercial programmes. It was members of this 'controlled' group who were intent viewers of TV (Gillard 1992).

By contrast, when parents supervised the content of programmes, but not the amount of viewing time, or when there were no rules but only the usual family routines, children watched more commercial TV and for longer hours. These children did not watch intently, but engaged in many other activities while the TV was on – a finding that was confirmed in a survey of over 500 children the following year. Longer hours of viewing meant greater activity around the set (Palmer 1988).

Until recently, studies of media use within the family context have overlooked teenage children. We do not know whether the 'time culture' or the patterns of parental control act to influence teens' media use at home in the same ways that they do with younger children. A renewed interest in adolescents and media use, however, has been shown in recent times. In two articles, the bedroom emerged as a most significant location for teens because it was here that they engaged in solitary media use to 'cultivate a newly discovered private self' (Larson 1995: 535). While television was used to disengage, music was used to 'directly engage with issues of identity' (Larson 1995: 547).

Phone conversations and computer games as well as Internet use were not mentioned in Larson's account. Presumably these activities also contribute to teens' emotional lives, although they might alter the picture he draws of 'solitary bedroom lives where media has [*sic*] some of its most significant functions, where the private and public are woven together' (Larson 1995: 536).

Information and Communication Technologies

Very little is known of teenage use of the phone and other ICTs in the household context. Singh *et al.* (1997) studied the meanings of information and communications technologies in the lives of household members and found that parents saw children and teenagers as key motivational influences in the purchase of new ICTs because often these items were claimed to be educational necessities. They also found that teens were deeply concerned about the social impact of new technologies and believed that huge lifestyle changes, due to new ICTs, were bound to occur and be out of their control.

Detailed studies of ICT use in 16 English families has yielded theoretical descriptions of the nature of domestic consumption and its complex links with both the public economy and the 'moral economy' of the household. The moral economy is a 'set of cognitions, evaluations and aesthetics which are themselves defined and informed by the histories, biographies and politics of the household and its members' (Silverstone *et al.* 1992: 18). Although the language of economics overshadows some of this theorizing (see also Livingstone 1992, who speaks of 'accounting practices' in explaining the role of domestic technologies), its emphasis on the dynamic interplay between household members and other social institutions, as expressed in technology use, provides an additional perspective on teenager's ICT uses at home.

The possibilities offered by creative multimedia, networked to households, lend new importance to understanding the influences of domestic social practices. Frameworks developed to study telecommunications uses at home will also be able to chart the interactive uses of new media. Miller (1994: 280) has suggested an approach which brings together ethnography, ethnomethodology and discourse analysis to study 'the ways in which setting members use discursive resources in organizing their practical actions, and how member's actions are constrained by the resources available in settings'. The call for a combination of cultural and sociological approaches, in theory and method, is not new (Denzin 1992; Jacka 1994; Vorderer and Groeben 1992). However, an interdisciplinary approach is now necessary to adequately understand the phenomenon of networked media. The impetus is practical as well as theoretical.

Research Design

The research to be reported here is firmly located in the tradition of analytic ethnography (Lofland 1995). The two studies were quite different in that the methods used, the people involved and the contexts in which they communicated their views were quite distinct and separate. In the first study, information about teenagers was part of a larger project and was framed by its overall purposes. Called 'Telecommunications Cultures', the project described ways of living with the phone for 11 individuals, deliberately chosen for their differences in terms of age, gender, ethnicity, sexuality, employment, city/country location and social roles. There were only three teens in the group. The second study, which is given more prominence in this account, was designed to look carefully at the ways teenagers used telecommunications in their social relationships and to explore their views about a telecommunications future.

The first study used in-depth interviews with 11 people, each of whom was asked to keep a diary of phone calls over a week. People were asked to show interviewers the way they held the phone and the way they normally sat to talk. If a call came through, which often happened, a note about body language and the way people answered was recorded unobtrusively. How the individuals 'managed' the phone in their lives, the networks of friends they maintained through tele-communications and the kinds of conversations and relationships they conducted through them were all features of each interview. As the aim of the project was to include wide variation in social experience and uses of telecommunications, the participants were selected because of their differences, rather than because they were representative of larger groupings (Gillard *et al.* 1994).

Of the three teenagers included in this study, two were interviewed at home and one at school. Natalie (age 16) lived with her parents and sister on a farm in rural Victoria, Australia, travelling a long distance to school every day. Peter (age 18) lived in state-supported accommodation, attended school for a few hours each week and worked part-time in an electronics shop. Joanne (age 17) lived in suburban Melbourne with her mother, brother and sister, and attended the local high school.

The aims of the second project were twofold. First, we wanted to find out the place ICTs have in young people's lives and how they use them to communicate. Second, we wanted to explore the types of telecommunications that young people desire, need or expect in the future. The sample consisted of two age groups, 13 to 14-year-old and 16 to 17-year-old girls and boys. Eight single-sex focus groups, based on existing friendship groups, were conducted in school settings, including private, state and rural schools. The first part of the discussion concerned teenagers' communication with each other and the role of telecommunications and the house-hold environment in these relations. The second part explored reactions to a video produced by Telstra which showed a middle-class family living with new and futuristic telecommunications such as the video phone, home education and home shopping.[1] A short survey was used to gain demographic information.

What follows is our interpretation, drawn from results across the two projects, of the role of telecommunications in young people's lives now and their thinking about its place in future society.

The Interview Study

The overall purpose of the interview study was to seek regularities in the ways people defined and used telecommunications in their lives. We concluded that tele-communications' main significance was to provide a 'major line to the outside world from the house' (Gillard *et al.* 1994). Patterns of use reflected individual values about privacy and whether people welcomed or restricted telecommunications contact at home. The three teenagers stood out in their uses of telecommunications as a form of entertainment. Their 'outside line' was crucial for continuing conversations with friends when they were no longer present. 'Privacy' was not defined by them as being at home, but as having private conversations not overheard by other members of the household.

For the three teenagers, household rules and practices supported their extensive phone use and their preference for private conversations. Natalie's household on a farm was geared for telecommunications contact. A touch phone near the computer in a separate room was 'for us girls when we're doing school work', and Natalie claimed sometimes to 'talk for hours' even though the long distance calls were timed and therefore expensive. The phone was both a source of private, intimate talk and a means of contact with the family. When her boyfriend called he would 'do the rounds' and say hello to each member of the family before talking to her.

Joanne's phone was more basic and shared with other family members, but she could choose to move away from the others into a private space because there was a very long cord. The TV would be turned down if she stayed in the lounge-room and complaints were only made by siblings if she spoke for over an hour, because they eventually wanted the TV sound turned up again.

Peter did not live with his parents. He had three handsets in his bedroom, carefully wired in to the one line by himself and constructed for particular purposes. For example, the 'hands free' phone was used when he was doing intricate electronics work and the cordless phone was used in other parts of the house when he was relaxing and did not want to move from his comfortable position. Calls were mainly to stay in touch with his father and girlfriend or to be contactable by his boss at work. Privacy was an issue with Peter's CB radio. He enjoyed talking to the regular identities but was concerned to maintain anonymity on that medium so that they did not know where he lived. Phone calls in all cases were accompanied by drinking coffee, smoking (Joanne took the phone on its lead outside for this), homework and eating snacks.

The three teenagers used the phone in different ways to spend time pleasurably, as a form of entertainment. Natalie's main phone conversations were about clothes, music and football. While talking and drinking coffee she often played solitaire on the computer. Natalie told two stories of tricking people using phone devices. The first involved entering a number so that the phone rang back after a call was made, and this tricked her sister. The second was a series of calls made to a friend's mother during a party. Natalie and her friends did not speak each time the call was answered but their laughter gave them away, and they were rebuked for doing it.

The conversations Joanne enjoyed were about local bands or her pet rat. She would take the phone outside and have a smoke as she conversed. Peter deliberately searched transmissions at different frequencies for his amusement. Through his work at an electronics shop, he had recently purchased a scanner which he could also use while riding his pushbike. He used it to listen in to different kinds of transmissions, especially police car chases, the progress and conclusion of which he liked to trace in his street directory 'to see how far they get and what damage they cause'. Unlike the others, Peter did not enjoy long conversations on the telephone. He was more entertained by the unfolding dramas scanned from the airwaves.

Telecommunications provided the means of extending contact with friends into the times when teens were in their own homes. The time spent on the phone and the content of calls reflected their desire to continue engagement with friendship networks. This also happened when they were feeling 'bored'.

Natalie was active in a number of sporting and community groups in the town. The phone extended these contacts and allowed her to continue the day's conversation with friends. School holidays in particular were 'dead without the phone'. As Natalie commented:

> I love the telephone. Being out on a farm, 'cause it's sometimes, during school holidays you don't see your friends quite as much as you would like to, so you call them up or get help with your school work or I don't know, teenage gossip.

Joanne's conversation with friends was also about 'what we've done during the day'. In her interview, Joanne made fine distinctions between the topics of conversation with particular friends, including her boyfriend Allen:

> With Allen and Ellie, I'll be talking about little things because we talk all the time you know like say, oh like walking the dog and the dog got off the lead and having to catch him again. And just little things like that . . . If I was talking to Sue or something we will be talking about bigger things, like say if Allen and I have had a fight. I also talk to Brian about things like that as well, but I don't talk as in-depth with Ellie cause we tend to do homework and hang around. Yeah that's it.

Peter used his CB radio to talk to friends:

> I just use that for finding my friends . . . and if I'm bored sometimes I'll, I'll turn it on and see who is on there if anyone I know is on there . . . I don't know, just strike up a conversation anyway, if somebody is around. I have met so many people through it.

Sometimes he arranged face to face meetings:

> Generally you work out what they are like and everything and then go for what you call a mobile which is just when you meet up with another person off the CB. Usually, make a time and a place.

The main uses of telecommunications by the three teens in this study were for active socializing, homework and planning further contact. Households were supportive of teens' phone uses, including their extensive 'teenage gossip'. Peter's use of CB technology, instead of the phone, was for similar purposes, confirming the importance of available technologies for contact and engagement.

The Teenage Group Study

Parental rules influence the way the phone is used by teens; parents who work at home, for example, often have more structured and strict rules around phone usage because the phone is an important tool for their employment. Work, parental usage and homework were big influences on time spent phoning – simply having to share the phone with siblings placed restrictions on teenagers who wanted to chat for long periods of time.

One of the girls, Gloria (age 17), had her own phone line. This enabled her to make calls whenever she wanted. She was a frequent long distance caller and realized the benefits of setting her own limits because she paid her own bills. It was she who pushed for an independent phone, not her parents. Gloria explained:

You don't have to get your parents' permission to use the phone and like, I pay for everything myself so I know that, say, if I've been on the phone to Sydney for, I don't know, couple of hours or whatever, then I know that I have to pay for it and that's sort of, just my problem.

A pattern of priorities emerged in the use of the phone in the household. If one or more parents worked from home, work calls had priority. If a work call came through, whoever was using the phone must automatically end the call. After work priorities, the phone was secondly the parent's phone and thirdly the children's. Most teens, like Jill and Jason (both age 17) here, said that if they were on a call and their parents wanted to use the phone they would end the call straightaway.

Um, well, I can never use it, if Dad's um, got business and he's got a business at home so, he has to make all these calls, that's it, I can't use it [laughter] . . . it's like, 'no', you know 'cause he knows that, and um, if I've got to ring someone, my family, see if they want to ring anyone because I'm on there for hours! [Laughter] I have to cut my call short for that. I can't work easy call.

(Jill)

Interviewer: Do your parents have any rules that they've made?
Jason: Get off the phone when they want it.

Cost was also an issue for most parents. John (age 16) was made to pay for one overseas call that went on for too long. However, as the comments from Beau and John (both age 13) below indicate, restrictions were usually made at the outset concerning 0055 numbers (which are expensive service calls) and long distance or international calls.

No overseas calls and no prank calls.

(Beau)

I'm not allowed to ring up them [0055 numbers] because when I ring up the competitions that sort of sit on the phone and keep on ringing, ringing, ringing putting my name back in and ring, ring, ring. I've only won a pair of socks.

(John)

Most teenagers mentioned that they spent considerable time on the phone. There was some family resistance to this, including restrictions on the amount of time, but teenagers commented that parents didn't usually enforce this.

Interviewer: So do your parents have any rules?
Cheryl (16):   No. Not effect[ive] ones.

The younger boys mentioned that parents did not necessarily want to be asked for permission to use the phone, but they wanted to know the purpose of the call. This was so they could judge whether the phone call was appropriate or not, especially on weeknights which were supposed to be set aside for homework. One group of girls mentioned parental concern about the content of phone conversations:

Emily (16):   Oh, we've got a cordless, and I'm not allowed to take it upstairs into my bedroom, I'm not allowed to take it outside on the verandah because they don't want the neighbours hearing what I talk about 'cause apparently it's embarrassing. [Laughter]
Jesse (17):   Oh yeah, that reminds me of mine, I'm not allowed to shut the doors so my parents can eavesdrop.

The different concerns of parents, about time spent talking as against the purpose or content of calls, seems to parallel the findings for children's television viewing described above (see Gillard 1992). From the small group studied here, it seems that parents are flexible about their teens' phone use, but time (sometimes in relation to homework), content and cost are areas of rule-making and restrictions. While this exploratory study cannot establish the broad patterns of use relating to parent's rules that the earlier television research found, it seems likely that families with rules restricting phone use inhibit the development of elaborated uses of the phone – that is, uses where simultaneous activities are involved.

From the teenagers' perspective, the most important feature of household practices concern the possibilities of holding private conversations. Ideally, teenagers want privacy for all conversations but especially for discussions involving the opposite sex or secret activities:

I think mainly for private calls it would be talking 'bout stuff that your parents don't want to really hear about, like stuff you've been up to.

(Ted, age 17)

Unlike televisions which usually have a fixed location, the portability of some phones makes it possible to adopt tactics for not being overheard. These include avoiding visual surveillance as well as adjusting the network connection or the equipment, as Will and Josh describe:

> If you want privacy you probably take, actually I take my mum's cordless phone and walk into my room . . . I always have to go with the other phone, and then I've got to unplug the top phone so that she wouldn't be listening in . . .
>
> (Will, age 14)

> Like from up where one phone is you can see the other one, so if I'm sitting on mum's bed, see the other phone, that's pretty safe . . . But then my mum will close the door just because she wants privacy.
>
> (Josh, age 14)

Teenagers had a detailed understanding of the restrictions their friends faced at home, indicating that it had been a topic of conversation between them. Some had adopted strategies and codes to signal when a conversation was being interrupted by parents walking past or listening in. The following excerpt was a re-enactment between friends who knew each other well outside school. When one party was no longer able to speak freely, the other would construct a conversation that needed one word answers to proceed.

Cheryl (17):	Do a re-enactment . . .
Sophie (16):	Like I might be . . .
Cheryl:	Go, go!
Sophie:	Um, OK.
Cheryl:	How was last night?
Sophie:	Um, good, good.
Cheryl:	No, what happened, seriously?
Sophie:	Um.
Cheryl:	Oh, OK, your dad's in the room.
Sophie:	Keep going. Getting there.
Cheryl:	Your mum's in the room?
Sophie:	Yep and . . .
Cheryl:	And your dad.
Sophie:	Yeah . . .
Katie (17):	I just say hang on, and I say what do you want? . . .
Cheryl:	And you do yes, no, hot, cold, warm and . . . [laughter]

Placement of the phone influences its use and limits the possibility of private conversations. Although teenagers would prefer to use the phone in private, the phone is often installed in places over which they do not exercise much control. In homes of the teens in this study, the primary phone was placed in a communal area such as the kitchen and the secondary phone was placed in a semi-private space. Most often this was a study or parents' room and so the teenagers were subject to limitations in these spaces.

One girl complained that she used to use her father's study to call but was constantly being reprimanded for making herself comfortable by putting her feet on the desk. The shared spaces can also be subject to constant interruption:

> Mmm in my parent's room especially, like sometimes my sister walks in and I say Becky go away blah, blah, blah.
>
> (Anna, age 17)

Mobile phones were not yet in evidence for most in this group. Their flexibility has the potential to give more privacy to teenagers because they can use them away from home. On the other hand, additional rules may accompany new telecommunications, as seems to be the case for Emily quoted above, who was not allowed to take the cordless phone into her bedroom.

Teenagers phone their school friends for long periods even though they spend a considerable amount of time with each other during the day. They speak of the content of their talk as fairly unimportant but what is important is making contact with friends for company, support and to relieve boredom. Some, like Rod (age 17), described parents' opinion of teenage telephone talk: '. . . 'cause when you call up people you will waffle on and talk about [nothing], they just think you're wasting time.'

Use of the phone for talk with friends was as true for boys as for girls. This confirms Skelton's earlier finding (1989) that teenagers in Australia were distinct from other groups in showing few sex differences in their uses of telecommunications. A survey of Australians over 13 years old has also shown that gender differences are not significant (Gillard *et al.* 1996). The idea that males do not talk at length to friends or use the phone for socializing has been dispelled by the fact that large numbers of Australian men and boys use it precisely for these purposes. Gender stereotypes will have to be modified in this area.

When pushed to reveal the content of calls teens, like Liz (age 16) and Gail (age 17), generally describe chatting about everyday matters:

Interviewer:	So what kinds of things do you talk about when you're on the phone?
Liz:	Anything.
Gail:	Um.
Liz:	Normal things.
Gail:	Just talk about like you know, I don't know like um,
Liz:	Anything that's happening in your life.
Gail:	Anything.
Liz:	Problems or . . . Holly's just 'oh my god this happened.' Holly's the drama queen.

Most often teens ring each other to talk about common interests such as school, girls/boys, sports, homework or pastimes. As Michael (age 14) indicates below, they are a support network as well as a sounding board for ideas which cannot be shared with family members:

Sometimes we talk about computers and stuff. Games. Well just, every-thing like, just what was on our minds, say if we've got to tell something and you can't tell anyone in the family, sort of ring someone and just tell them what you . . . Like we were about to talk about um, basketball, ref-ereeing, girls um, lots of things.

Some groups spoke as if telephone conversation was quite different from face to face conversation. They spoke of it as being more private and also less inhibiting, which is especially good for phone-dating (discussed below).

Interviewer: OK, you say it's different being on the phone than being together?
Tom (17): Yeah.
Matt (16): It's an uninterrupted thing, you can talk about anything, without worrying about anyone overhearing.

Some boys, like Brett (age 13) and Todd (age 13), said they were much more sure of themselves on the phone and saw the phone as integral to developing close friendships:

Brett: [If we didn't have telephones] I don't think we'd be as good friends as we are.
Todd: Yes, 'cause we sort of found things about each other and . . . spoken to each other on the phone, we sort of, you sit there and you talk about . . . you sort of have two personalities, over the phone per-sonality, like you're talking and you're just talking about things you want to talk about, instead of . . . shying yourself at school.

Close personal talk requires privacy. Yet teens mentioned that parents and siblings tried to overhear or even listened on another line and tried to be part of the interaction:

I hate it when my parents are there. I was talking to my boyfriend, we had a huge fight on the phone, this was not long ago, well, it was kind of the breaking up point, got off the phone, my dad goes 'Oh, having a hard time with a fellow are you?' [Laughter] Dad, he'd pretend to be asleep [laugh-ter]. In the study, sitting down reading a book you know, the book's down and 'Oh having a hard time with a fellow are you, do you want to talk about it?' 'No, it's OK'. Not with you, Dad, I can't think of anything worse than talking about personal things.

(Jacqui, age 14)

Talking to the opposite sex and about the opposite sex, took up much of the calls:

Interviewer: So what do you usually talk about?
Matt (16): Um, usually girls. Girl stuff . . . I think.

Because it was a central issue, interviewers sought to clarify with groups of teens when they would and would not use the phone for personal talk, and whether they preferred face to face discussion for some types of situations. There was no broad agreement about when the phone would and would not be used for these purposes. No doubt parental restrictions, the placement and mobility of the phone operated as external constraints which were then negotiated and used to the extent possible.

In their exploration of whether face to face or phone conversation was more personal, limits were reached in what could be expressed in language. It was clear that teenagers valued the visual clues they received when face to face and yet they were sometimes awkward and liked to be free of such scrutiny:

You picture it yourself and on the phone sort of just ring up and . . . just be yourself and people can't tell what you're doing or you can just say things.

(Josh, age 14)

The discussion with two blind girls, who were close friends, expressed similar concerns and in the same language, even though 'face to face' would not give them the visual information it would provide for others:

Annette (16): If I have anything really personal to talk to anyone about, I rather see them and talk to them somewhere, like you know, face to face, like I wouldn't really say many things like that over the phone. Unless I have to.
Interviewer: Why do you think that is?
Annette: I don't know, I just like to have my own kind of personal things, I guess.
Interviewer: What do you think, Ali, do you think the same or what?
Ali (19): Um, yeah well, I don't know, I sort of use the phone for personal things so I don't know . . . it's probably easier to say it over the phone I think but anyway, to me.

What is striking is the way issues to do with intimate communication using newer phone technologies are being explored by teens. Their effort to articulate uses of the phone and preferences for being physically present or absent parallels theoretical discussion about bodies, gender and identity that are being provoked by newer forms of online communication, such as the Internet. These issues, it is clear, need extensive exploration.

Considering that the group discussions took place with young adult researchers in a school setting, this probably defines the limits of what teens were willing or able to disclose. It seems likely that, if teens can be confident of their privacy, they will use the phone for detailed, intimate discussion about matters they wouldn't discuss with adults. Particularly in these content areas, where parents also want to make rules and 'listen in', the relationship between teenager and researcher itself may have played out the power relations between teenagers and adults. On the other hand, the researchers were in their mid-20s and there were a number of occasions where the group conducted its own extended discussion without intervention by the interviewer. Nevertheless, our information about teens and the phone must be considered a 'partial' account, both in the sense of being incomplete and of being coloured by our own and their interpretations. The crucial role of the phone in enabling teenagers to articulate joint concerns and examine them with close friends, however, has emerged very clearly.

All the male focus groups and most of the female groups spoke of the role of the phone in relating to the opposite sex:

Interviewer:	Who do you usually talk to on the phone?
Tom (17):	Um, girlfriend.
Matt (16):	Yeah, members of the opposite sex generally.

The phone is used to conduct these relationships partly because the phone takes away the embarrassment of meeting face to face.

Interviewer:	Do you think it's a way of asking girls out?
Tom (17):	Yep, they can't see your face!
Matt (16):	Yes [laughter].
Joe (16):	Can't see your face.
Interviewer:	So why is it good?
Tom:	Oh well because, you go all bright red, you start to get embarrassed about asking.
Interviewer:	So do you normally, would you normally ask girls out face to face ever?
Tom:	No.
Matt:	No. The only time I've done it was on the phone.

Speaking on the phone is a big part of dating for teens, especially those from single-sex schools. Getting a phone number and talking to a boy or girl on the phone is the equivalent to getting to first base: 'One thing leads to another and then you're on the phone' (Josh, age 14).

They spoke of using long extension cords or going outside, in cars or bedrooms with cordless phones to conduct phone dating in privacy. In response to the video of a futuristic household, teenagers like Glenn (age 16) and Peter (age 17) were concerned about the impact of video phones on dating:

Glenn:	If like you talk to your girlfriend everything and then you just broke up or whatever, you're thinking, 'oh yeah, hi.' It's like you

> know, you don't really want a video sitting there filming your performance.

Peter: It's getting to the point where you start going out on dates over the computer, that's just going to be so . . .

Glenn: I'd like to see that.

Some of the younger boys, like Todd (age 13), thought the video phone might be good:

> because I've been given phone numbers by other girls saying, ring this girl, she wants to talk to you. I'd really like to know what she looks like.

Teenagers think that changes to their lives due to new telecommunications are inevitable:

> While we're all objecting to it I mean, from Telecom's point of view, I mean it's gonna happen because it's going to be available and therefore you know people are going to get it and then it's going to become more widespread, so it's going to happen. But, um, whether it's a good thing I think still needs to be worked out.

> (Neil, age 16)

They were extremely concerned about the social impact of these changes, with the major fear being that technology will replace much of the social and face to face contact that they have now. In response to the video, they pictured a future where everyone became totally isolated, 'turning into vegetables sitting in our tracksuit pants in our lounge-rooms' (Gloria, age 16). They feared that no one would get any exercise and become fat and lazy because the need to physically go out of the home would be removed. They affirmed the need for 'human in-the-flesh kind of contact' (Phoebe, age 17).

Teenagers do see positive effects of new telecommunications in two main areas: those which relate to specific people who have particular needs, such as the housebound or the disabled, and for specific circumstances, such as illness, distance and emotional distress. Some groups struggled with the positives and negatives of new technological possibilities during the discussion, articulating difficulties and paradoxes that are not yet expressed in mainstream media or even in research. They commented, for example, that it was unfortunate that the more 'you get connected, the more isolated you are in a way' (Jenny, age 16). One of the boys in a rural school expressed his wishes for the future:

> If there was a way to keep all the technology and to keep a good grasp on the community at the same time, then it would be all right.

> (Colin, age 16)

Conclusion

For teenagers, future communication technologies are seen as a possible threat to the social interactions with peers which at this age are intensely important. The negative scenario of people being isolated and withdrawn in their own homes was rejected. At the same time, new ICTs make it possible to 'carry' friends with them into their private spaces at home and, through the advent of mobile phones, into public spaces.

Teenagers are very enthusiastic about those new technologies which connect them to friends. A national survey of future services confirmed the orientation of teenagers to the socializing and recreational uses of telecommunications; 67 per cent of those under 15 and 33 per cent of those between 15 and 19 years approved of a hypothetical service described as enabling the user to 'talk to a group of friends at once, when you're out'. Older age groups showed very little interest (Gillard *et al.* 1995).

The telecommunications industry is particularly interested in teenagers because they see them as an entirely new generation of consumers, whose adoption of advanced technology and new kinds of interactive, entertainment-oriented con- texts represents a potential new market. The absence of research on teenagers and 'old' communication technologies makes it impossible to know whether the current teenage interests in interactive technologies will persist into adulthood or instead reflect the more social concerns of these short years.

In relation to rules and practices, the household provides both the material conditions and the social contexts which influence telecommunications use. The type and amount of equipment, the attitude to costs, the spaces where equipment is installed (or able to roam) and the rules and practices governing all of these aspects present the teenager with possibilities and problems to be negotiated. On the evidence presented here, parents seem to be accepting of extensive uses of telecommunications for conversations with friends, though sometimes this may only be tolerated because teens describe it as help with homework.

Punishments or narrow restrictions were not found, nor statements that long conversations were a 'waste of time'. This is surprising, considering the denigration of phone talk noted in previous research (Moyal 1989), which also recurs in current industry and media discussion (Rollins 1996). It is possible that the institutions of the press and the telecommunications industry, both patriarchal in their corporate cultures, are reproducing the prejudices of a generation who have not themselves used telecommunications to enhance the broader social aspects of their own lives. Their opinions may be out of step with the enthusiastic socializing many people organize or conduct on the phone.

As with television viewing (see Gillard 1992), the household practices which do exist in relation to telephone use are concerned about content (of conversations, in this case) as well as restrictions on time. With mobile phones or long distance calls, time raises the additional factor of cost. A more representative study would show whether households across different social groups in Australia are as accepting as those reported here. The group situation of the research method adopted may also have prevented teens admitting to each other the kinds of restrictions they faced.

In relation to adolescent identity issues, Larson (1995) has highlighted the importance of the bedroom for an adolescent's emotional development. With telecommunications, the bedroom need not be a place of reflection in solitude. Instead the bedroom (or other place of reliable privacy, where teenagers are not overheard) can become an extension of peer group relations and close friendships that at other times are conducted away from home. For teenagers, the combination of a private space at home and intimate talk with friends may mean that friends become more influential in their emotional development and well-being.

This gives a different emphasis to what has been described as the 'doubly articulated biographies' of ICTs. On the one hand teenagers use media consumption 'literally as a ticket into peer group culture'. Their media exchanges blend the 'moral economies' of the household with the public economy and the bedroom is one site where the exchanges take place: 'within the household, the private rooms of both male and female teenagers provide the locus for converting activities, as friends with similar interests are drawn into the cultural "mint"' (Silverstone *et al.* 1992: 26). With telecommunications, friends need not be present to be involved in these exchanges.

Telecommunications ease a difficult transition time, when friends are important but much time is spent in a household with family members. Murray (1994: 7) has described close telephone conversations as a 'theatre of the self' where individuals 'can define and refine perceptions of their own lives, through interaction with the judgements of sympathetic others'. For teenagers, the implications of this greater closeness for individual development and the fostering of peer cultures have yet to be explored.

Note

1 'Telstra' and 'Telecom' both refer to the publicly owned telecommunications carrier, previously called Telecom Australia and now Telstra. Until 1991 it had monopoly supply of Australia's telecommunications services.

References

BRYCE, J. W. (1987) 'Family time and television use', in T. R. LINDLOF (ed.) *Natural Audiences: Qualitative Research of Media Uses and Effects*, Norwood, NJ: Ablex.

BRYCE, J. W. and LEICHTER, H. J. (1983) 'The family and television. Forms of mediation,' *Journal of Family Issues*, **4**: 309–28.

DENZIN, N. (1992) *Symbolic Interactionism and Cultural Studies*, Cambridge, MA: Blackwell.

GILLARD, P. (1992) 'A new theory of parental control of children's television viewing', in B. TICEHURST (ed.) *Communication Australia: A Search for Meaning in Changing Times*, Sydney: Griffin Publications.

GILLARD, P., BOW, A. and WALE, K. (1994) *A Major Line to the Outside World From the House: Defining the Significance of Telecommunications in Social Contexts*, Royal Melbourne Institute of Technology, Melbourne: Telecommunications Needs Research Group.

GILLARD, P., BOW, A. and WALE, K. (1995) *Privacy and Control: Social Indicators of Interest in Future Telecommunications*, Royal Melbourne Institute of Technology, Melbourne: Telecommunications Needs Research Group.

GILLARD, P., BOW, A. and WALE, K. (1996) *Ladies and Gentlemen, Boys and Girls: Gender and Telecommunications Services*, Royal Melbourne Institute of Technology, Melbourne: Telecommunications Needs Research Group.

JACKA, E. (1994) 'Researching audiences: A dialogue between cultural studies and social science', *Media Information Australia*, **73**: 45–51.

LARSON, R. (1995) 'Secrets in the bedroom: Adolescents' private use of media', *Journal of Youth and Adolescence*, **24**: 535–48.

LIVINGSTONE, S. (1992) 'The meaning of domestic technologies: A personal construct analysis of familial gender relations', in R. SILVERSTONE and E. HIRSCH (eds) *Consuming Technologies: Media and Information in Domestic Spaces*, London: Routledge.

LOFLAND, J. (1995) 'Analytic ethnography. Features, failings and futures', *Journal of Contemporary Ethnography*, **24**: 30–67.

MILLER, G. (1994) 'Toward ethnographies of institutional discourse. Proposal and suggestions', *Journal of Contemporary Ethnography*, **23**: 280–306.

MOYAL, A. (1989) 'The feminine culture of the telephone. People, patterns and policy', *Prometheus*, **7**: 5–31.

MURRAY, G. (1994) *How's the World Been Treating You? Telecommunications Cultures and the Autonomous Call*, Royal Melbourne Institute of Technology, Melbourne: Telecommunications Needs Research Group.

PALMER, P. (1986) *Girls and Television*, Sydney: New South Wales Ministry of Education.

PALMER, P. (1988) 'The social nature of children's television viewing', in P. DRUMMOND and R. PATERSON (eds) *Television and Its Audience: International Research Perspectives*, London: British Film Institute.

ROLLINS, A. (1996) 'Teens ring up costs on cellular phones', *The Sunday Age*, 16 June: 8.

SILVERSTONE, R., HIRSCH, E. and MORLEY, D. (1992) 'Information and communication technologies and the moral economy of the household' in R. SILVERSTONE and E. HIRSCH (eds) *Consuming Technologies: Media and Information in Domestic Spaces*, London: Routledge.

SINGH, S., BOW, A. and WALE, K. (1997) *Centre for International Research on Communication and Information Technologies (CIRCIT) Research Report*, Melbourne: CIRCIT.

SKELTON, F. (1989) 'Teenagers and the telephone', *Australian Journal of Communication*, **15**: 21–24.

VORDERER, P. and GROEBEN, N. (1992) 'Audience research: What the humanistic and the social science approaches could learn from each other', *Poetics*, **21**: 361–76.

Chapter Nine

Dear Anne Summers:
'Microfeminism' and media representations of women

Sue Turnbull

In March 1995, Anne Summers, editor of *The Age Good Weekend* published an essay in her own magazine supplement entitled 'Shockwaves at the revolution' (Summers 1995).[1] In this article, she took young Australian women to task for (in her opinion) failing to embrace feminism; for resting on the laurels won by their mothers; and for being reluctant to rush into print with their own 'passionate perspectives' on contemporary feminist issues. By way of criticism she pointed approvingly to a new generation of American public/populist feminists including Naomi Wolf, Katie Rolphe and Rene Denfield. Summers' grumpy criticism echoed the tone sounded in the final chapter of a revised version (in 1994) of her seminal work of feminist history, *Damned Whores and God's Police* (first published in 1974). In a new introduction to this update, Summers duly acknowledged that her descriptions of society written some 20 years earlier might seem 'quaint and outmoded'. However, what seemed even more 'quaint and outmoded' to the young female students I was then teaching was Summers' militaristic metaphors: her rhetorical call to arms. They could not conceive of themselves as a united front of feminist 'warriors' banded together under the same 'banners and slogans' fighting shoulder to shoulder for any particular feminist cause.[2]

The *Good Weekend* article by Summers was only one text discussed in the context of a 13-week course about women and the media, directed to second and third-year undergraduates majoring in Media Studies within a general BA programme at La Trobe University in Melbourne. It was, however, this text more than any other which focused my attention as a media educator (and a conflicted *fin de siècle* feminist myself) on a range of issues to do with how to teach about the media; and in particular, how to teach about 'feminist' responses to the media in contemporary social and media contexts.[3] What follows is therefore an attempt to explain how I approached this task in relation to a specific group of students: a group whose frequent ambivalence about feminism echoed the more cautious critiques of feminism and the media taking place within, what might be called for want of a better term, academic feminism. Such debates generally receive much less attention in the media since they largely occur in academic books and journals with small circulations, rather than in the pages of the *Good Weekend*.[4] The article by Summers may therefore stand for a nostalgic moment (which may never have existed) when things seemed clear: when feminists knew who they were and what they stood for – and everyone could tell a sexist image when they saw one. The passing of this imagined moment leaves me as a media educator with this problem: if there is no longer (if indeed there ever was) any unified feminist position or response, then how should I teach my students to read media representations of gender?

To be fair, the course I was teaching, Women and Media, would hardly have been possible without 20 years of feminist writing about the media and women. The course came into existence at the end of the 1980s on the crest of a successful bid to get Women's Studies acknowledged as a legitimate area of academic study within the academy.[5]

Women and Media, which is modified every year, included in 1995 such issues as representation, power, sexuality, essentialism, employment and violence against women in relation to diverse media texts such as advertisements, soaps, television news, women's detective fiction and the British television sitcom, *Absolutely Fabulous*. The first session involved an overview of feminist politics in Australia, drawing on an essay by Ann Curthoys (1994) covering the period from 1970 to 1994. The 'classic' (and arguably reductive) taxonomies of liberal, Marxist and radical feminist approaches were delineated and the possibilities of poststructuralist feminism and postmodern approaches to popular culture foreshadowed, before I invited the students to write about their own experience of, and relationship with, feminism. This task, I explained, was not for assessment. What I wanted them to think about and tell me was how they 'situated' themselves, at that moment, in relation to feminism before we tackled the issues raised by the intersection of women, media and feminist theory. I knew where I was coming from (even if I didn't know where I was going), but I had no idea about them either way. I wanted to know something about the group I was addressing.

The 19 responses I received revealed a diversity of experience and positions ranging from those who had imbibed what they imagined as feminism with their Vegemite on toast, to those who described having it thrust in their faces at university and hating it. In between were the 'there's no way I'm a feminist but I support them 100 per centers' – and the simply confused. What is interesting about these responses is that they inadvertently constitute a critique of Summers's 'big picture' feminism, or what the students came to describe as 'macrofeminism'; and how what is revealed is a much less ambitious feminist response to the everyday business of negotiating a place in the world. This practice of feminism in the context of everyday life was termed in the context of our course 'microfeminism'.[6]

I would like to suggest that in embracing the concept of microfeminism with its emphasis on the local, the immediate and the tactical, the students were implicitly rejecting a macrofeminism based on the presumption of a coherent female identity and shared political agenda. If this prospect is alarming for feminists like Summers, for feminists like Mouffe, questioning the coherence of an essential female identity and common interest is a necessary precondition for the construction of what the latter describes as a 'radical democratic politics' (Mouffe 1995: 317–18). Such a politics would encourage allegiances to be formed which may not depend on shared identities (such as race, gender or ethnicity) but on shared political interests in specific social contexts.

I shall attempt to characterize the students' positions in relation to feminism by quoting from their responses (with the authors' permission, although I have changed their names). The outcome of this characterization (caricature?) is a story which I readily acknowledge as my own. I have constructed a version of events from my experience of the course, my encounters with feminist theory, the media, and my selective interpretations of the students' perspectives. I can only hope that this description will prove helpful to others who are trying to address the issues of personal experience, theory and practice, in that singular encounter we call teaching.

Taking It All for Granted?

If Summers was 'horrified' and 'mortified' to encounter young women who regarded feminists like her as utterly remote from themselves, a number of students acknowledged a debt to women of her generation, including Lillian:

> Last night I had dinner with my mother, four of her friends and their daughters. We all laughed and carried on and discussed our grand plans, just as a table of eight women tend to do. I looked around at one point and noticed four or five groups of women; all of us enjoying the increasing significance of International Women's Day. We then went to the opening of an all-women artists exhibition which was awful, but we had fun none the less. I was brought up in very much a *Women's Room* environment. Divorced career women bringing up their kids seemed to be the norm to me ... Besides the obvious need for personal achievement, I have been able to take an extended education and access to an imminent career for granted, as have most women of my age, something for which I am grateful to those women before me who have taken on careers and higher education in environments which haven't been so conducive to them.
>
> (Lillian)

Taking it all for granted? I don't think so. Lillian and those who shared her perspective are clearly well aware of the political significance of their parents' childrearing practices:

> I am a happy child of the 70s, raised by parents who would claim to be sexually liberated and conscious of non-sexist child-rearing. In fact my

mother used to change the characters in bedtime stories so that Jane helped in the garden and Greg helped in the kitchen. I attended a co-ed state school which would have been considered left-wing and had a diverse class and cultural mix. Girls were always encouraged to participate in Science, Sports, Maths etc. (yet not all did). I have always been a bit of a tomboy and some would say I was a radical feminist, but simply speaking I would call myself a liberal feminist, believing in equality not superiority. I've never experienced any major moments in my life in which being female has held me back, but I have witnessed a lot of sexist behaviour from both women and men.

(Karla)

Never having experienced any moments in which they felt themselves to have been disadvantaged because of their gender seemed a surprising and common theme:

I have grown up in an environment in which I was not oppressed in any way, but rather encouraged to grow, develop and take up my rights as an equal to men. I have never felt that anything was out of my reach because I am a woman.

(Margaret)

Clearly feminism for many of the young women in this study connoted a struggle for equality of opportunity, an equality which they considered they had already achieved. Equality as a feminist goal has often been dismissed as an inadequate solution to women's oppression. However, in this instance, I think it represents for these young women the possibility of a shift in their political horizons. They are no longer so concerned with a politics of identity based on sexual difference as they are in a more general notion of equality of opportunity. In Mouffe's terms, 'sexual difference is no longer the most pertinent distinction in their lives' (1995: 373).

Indeed, only two students mentioned any conflict at home over issues which they implicitly defined as feminist. Chris complained about the 'use' of beautiful women in the media and her arguments with brother, boyfriend and father about the 'exploitation' of women's bodies. Ann mentioned arguments with her father over her desire to manage a career in conjunction with marriage and childrearing: 'I've always felt I could successfully juggle both (although admittedly with a lot of hard work)'. In each case, male relatives were portrayed as wildly out of touch, and the student herself had no doubt that she was right and they were wrong.

Even if the student rejected or questioned feminism, it was clear she had assumed a political position with regard to equal rights:

When I think of the word feminism, I am greatly confused. Does it mean the women who go to protests, burn their bras and have 'girlfriends'? Or is it the ones who think it is their husband's turn to cook the dinner? What about all the ones in between? Am I a feminist because I think I am of equal status to the boy next door? Even the dictionary definition does not help: 'Feminism: the principle or practice of social and political advancement or liberation for women.' I come from an all girl family. I have four sisters – full, half and step – who have lived in and out of the house for as long as I can remember. I went to an all-girls' school from the age of 10 until university and have come from a middle-class background. Now as I have entered the university system, I have been bombarded with 'women's rights' and feminist perspectives. And I have no idea how to respond to my ideas of feminism. To me I think feminism is having the chance to further my education, having a career and choosing when – if I ever want to – to have a family. I have never come up against a male who has told me that I can't do something, because I am a girl; God forbid if it happened now. I would probably give him a few punches that I learned in self-defence, throw a few 'derogative male' terms at him and then write a letter to the local paper. Does this mean I am a feminist?

(Yvonne)

For Andy, feminist labels were to be avoided because of their reductiveness:

Feminism to me means many things, and as there are many different feminist theories, it is understandable that with some of them I agree, and with others I do not. I do not call myself a feminist although I have in the past been called one. The reason I do not call myself one is that to be called feminist is to be labelled, hence put in a stereotype. However, I do believe in equality.

(Andy)

The picture I have painted thus far is of a group of white, predominantly Anglo-Australian middle-class young women who have few doubts about themselves or their value. Anne Summers should be proud. They are the beneficiaries of what she describes as her generation's struggle to create a new world of opportunity for women, often at the expense of their own relationships and happiness (Summers is inclined to martyrdom). What bothers her is that these young women are not prepared to carry on where she left off. She cannot understand why they are not embracing the causes she identifies including: violence against women, employment discrimination and ubiquitous sexism 'in conversations, in advertising, in the media, in the arts and in most areas of our lives' (Summers 1994: 527).

The young women in Women and Media acknowledged the importance of these issues in principle, but argued that they felt no desire to respond to them in the very public ways Summers suggested. A particular sticking point appeared to be their vision of feminism itself – a vision coloured by their encounters with an older generation of feminists like Summers and the vocal feminists at university, who embodied a militancy and absolutism they rejected:

My Italian parents brought me up in what I consider to be the perfect blend of discipline and freedom. Moderation, balance and compromise have ensured constant happiness in my upbringing. The issue of feminism never really interested me until I started Uni three years ago. At this point I was made aware of feminism by the radicals. Pamphlets shoved in my face opposing every little inconsistency between men and women. The thing is, men and women are different. Every woman is different. Different opportunities are going to cross people's paths at different times. However, I do believe in equality between the sexes.

(Barbara)

Teaching around the 'But' of Being A Feminist

It is interesting to note that it is a student who draws attention to her ethnic background who picks up on the significance of difference above (a significance also noted by Andy). As Curthoys points out, during the 1980s and 1990s, it was Aboriginal and immigrant women who forced a recognition of difference in both women and their political goals by objecting to a white Anglo-Australian feminist agenda which ignored their experience (Curthoys 1994: 25). More recently, Ien Ang (who is well known in the field of audience research and cultural studies) has also spoken out against an insistence on the stable Anglo-Western subject of feminism. As a woman of Chinese descent, she is even more suspicious of a new brand of 'multicultural' feminism which seeks to embrace difference in order to colonize new subjects and territories for feminism:

Feminism must stop conceiving of itself as a nation, as a 'natural' polit-ical destination for all women, no matter how multicultural. Rather than adopting a politics of inclusion (which is always based on a notion of communality and community), it will have to develop a self-conscious politics of partiality, and imagine itself as a 'limited' political home, which does not absorb difference within a pre-given and predefined space but leaves room for ambivalence and ambiguity.

(Ang 1995: 57–58)

Ang's ambivalence and partiality, her insistence that 'I'm not a feminist but', echoes that of the students in the group I was teaching, many of whom also questioned feminism as a 'natural' political destination (even though they might recognize its significance as a point of departure). It is, however, on the word 'but' that the relevance of feminism to Ang and to these students turns. As it emerged, these Media Studies students already seemed to know how to read these texts and what was expected of them by me in a course called Women and Media. This prior knowledge, which entailed an assumption of what they imagined as accept-able feminist critical positions with regard to the media, revealed the 'lie' in their rejection of feminism. As one of the two American exchange students explained:

How do you relate to feminism? How do you situate yourself in feminism? For me, these questions almost seem to be stated backwards. Feminism for me isn't a once in a while political position, protest or march. It is much more. Feminism relates to me, my experiences, beliefs and ideas. It shapes the way I view the world, experience life, and interact with others. I don't find myself situating myself in feminism but rather feminism has situated itself in me.

(Jody)

One consequence of this 'situated' feminism was that Jody (like the rest of the young women) had very definite ideas about how to read a media image. My problem as a media teacher was that the approaches they used were oversimplistic, emerging from what has become a populist version of feminist media theory assuming a particular ideological position with regard to the text thereby necessitating a disavowal of its ambiguous pleasures. If a sexist image is a sexist image, then what more is there to say?

Addressing this group of students in the subsequent weeks, I therefore found myself confronting an interesting set of contradictory desires as a media teacher with feminist tendencies. How could I challenge the majority conviction that feminism might have little to offer in terms of politics or theory, even as I unsettled their preconceived notions about how to produce a feminist reading of a media text? In other words, how could I teach a course around the 'but' of being a feminist while teaching them to be critical of feminist media theory? Like thousands of media teachers before me, I turned to advertising as the way in.

Selling Women

It is ironic to note that advertising has served a number of feminist causes extremely well (particularly during the 1970s and 80s). The representation of women in advertising, that most conspicuous manifestation of rampant capitalism, has constituted an easily accessible platform from which to launch campaigns about women's role and position in society, participation in the labour force, 'false' body images, exploitation etc.; issues which have often been brought to public attention in the context of a vocal critique of advertising. The problem for me as a media teacher is that while I can recognize the value of advertising as a political platform, the traditional critical approaches seem inadequate when dealing with the emergent forms of advertising which have already taken on board the critiques of the past, letting the public know that the advertisement knows they know. In other words, advertising is no longer an innocent discourse with regard to the political implications of its address and imagery; there are no innocent consumers and no innocent images left, if indeed there ever were.

However, in order to give the students some sense of how the critique of advertising had evolved, and how closely such critiques were related to feminist politics, the second session of the course began with a consideration of Patricia Edgar and Hilary McPhee's pictorial account of gender display in advertising in 1974, *Media She*. My intention was not to condescend to the past by suggesting that things were simply more obvious then, but to suggest that the representation of women may indeed have changed in the last 20 years, probably in some measure as a direct result of such feminist interventions. *Media She* knew exactly what it was about: 'This is a book about distortions perpetrated on women by those employed in mass media organisations'(1974: 1). Advertising images of women, it was argued, perpetuated an image of women as sex symbols and inferior human beings. The book concluded with a set of role reversal images in which two hirsute males adopted the bimbo/cutesy poses of the advertising pin-up to satiric effect.

The students roared with laughter; both at the quoted images of women which they considered to be so blatantly sexist as to be comic, and the hairy men cavorting with or without their jocks. 'But', they argued, 'many women now choose to be housewives, and many women choose to wear sexy underwear – just for themselves'. What we then discussed was the question of choice, since what constitutes choice in these instances is a complicated matter. It could be argued, I pointed out, that a woman only 'chooses' to be a housewife because she knows her husband can make more than her or she can't get reasonable child care; or wearing sexy lingerie is a narcissistic exercise in consumer behaviour whereby a woman constitutes herself as an object of desire with implicit reference to an imagined but absent 'male gaze' (Radner 1995: 55). This latter suggestion, however, doesn't get us very far since it effectively undermines any possibility that a woman can act out of her own desire, or derive any pleasure from self-adornment, since every impulse she may have is revealed to be motivated by false consciousness.

My next strategy was to try and outline the history of Mulvey's overworked thesis of 'the male gaze', which migrated from film theory in the 70s, in order to colonize, in subsequent years, every imaginable discussion taking place about the representation of women, including advertising (Mulvey 1975). Briefly, since this thesis has been so exhaustively rehearsed elsewhere, Mulvey uses Lacanian psychoanalytic theory in order to argue that women in Hollywood films of the 1930s, 40s, and 50s were constructed as the passive objects of an active male gaze constituted at the intersection of three 'looks'; that of the camera, that of the characters in the film and that of the spectator in the audience. Although Mulvey subsequently modified her position (1981), the formulation of the 'male gaze' was seized upon as a valuable weapon in an argument about power and the media which effectively denied any pleasure a woman might have in looking at other women or even men on screen. As Barbara Creed has pointed out, there is no place for female desire in the concept of the male gaze; nor is there any place for gay men or women whose desire must always be assumed to be displaced by that of the Oedipally fixated male spectator (Creed 1994: 161–4).

The set reading for the session on advertising I had chosen precisely because it demonstrated an attempt to tussle with the issue of the male gaze in relation to advertising addressed to young women in the mid-1980s. In a discussion focused on a set of advertising images featuring young women in an urban setting wearing raincoats over their designer underwear, Janet Winship attempts to tease out some of the contradictions involved. The advertising image in question, she suggests:

> implicitly references the men-in-dark-raincoats brigade, flashing and getting off on women. Yet here that relation is reversed. It is young women who flash their bodies, and with their gaze and pose coolly confident, they express less the customary passive sexuality of woman than an assertive strength. Their sexuality is constructed around difference, between the 'masculine' cropped hair and firm body, clumpy boots and dark mac – and the 'feminine' shiny pink lips and lacy camisole. Maybe it isn't a sexuality which wholly breaks from the oppressive codes of women as sexual commodities but neither does it straightforwardly reproduce them. The conventions of gender and sexuality are, it seems to me, being actively tampered with. If on the other hand as feminists we refuse that representation and reject the imagery of these pages, we need to be careful that we are not simply outlawing a sexual representation of women.
>
> (Winship 1985: 25)

Ten years down the track, I am tempted to suggest that if Madonna hadn't existed, advertising would have invented her, since the description above anticipates the look of that particular pop icon in at least one of her many manifestations. Madonna has achieved her success precisely by tampering with the conventions, exploiting the contradictions of female presentation and representation. One such contradiction became the subject of an *Independent* article in 1993 by Catherine Lumby entitled 'Sexist or Sexy?'

In this piece, Lumby puts her finger on a perceived rift opening up between young women and older feminists in relation to the portrayal of women's sexuality. Lumby suggests that what the old feminist guard, including the pro-censorship lobby, have failed to take on board is the fact that younger women are much less likely to accept the argument that sexual objectification is wrong, or that women are always the victims in heterosexual encounters. Furthermore, this television generation is well aware of the role of parody, irony and fantasy in contemporary culture and highly unlikely to mistake momentary appearances for universal reality. Like Winship before her, Lumby therefore points to a generation of young women who have the knowledge and strength to act in the world (as a legacy of their mother's feminism), but who can also laugh and enjoy those images which a preceding generation found troubling and offensive.

The Body in Question

Everyone was invited to bring in a pictorial advertisement for discussion in this Women and Media class. We duly passed around the images of beautiful models with artfully displayed bodies drawn from a range of women's magazines, promoting everything from exercise gear to whatever it is Dolce and Gabbana actually sell (I hadn't a clue and the ad didn't help). We talked about the aesthetic of the female body and whether these images were directed to a male gaze, or (more likely, given the context) a narcissistic female gaze. So far, no surprises. The students had each chosen an advertisement which appeared to exemplify what they initially described as the 'objectification of women'. I then presented the class with the image I had selected precisely because I believe it challenges the adequacy of those theories of the image they had happily been invoking.

The advertisement for Calvin Klein underwear was pulled from the March edition of *Vogue Australia* in 1995. It shows Kate Moss, famous for being a 'waif' supermodel (of which much more anon) in a piggy-back pose with an anonymous male model whose torso is exposed from the knees up. He is wearing the Calvin Klein Y-fronts, and a shirt that is hardly on. His neck is exposed while his face is scarcely in view. The face we see is that of Kate Moss; of her body we see only a naked leg and arm. The image, in stark black and white, recalls the 'high art' portrait photography of Helmut Newton or Richard Avedon.

I asked the students to whom they thought this ad was addressed. Problem number one: if the product being advertised is men's underwear, is it the presumption of the advertisers that men read *Vogue*? In which case why show the man's body and not that of Kate Moss? Could it be that the male body is on display for a desiring female gaze? The same gaze which buys the underpants for her partner? In which case, what happens to the argument about narcissism? Could it be that the beautiful male body is in fact addressed to gay men who might also read *Vogue* in which case could this ad also be construed as an appeal to what has been called 'the pink dollar'?

The substitution of an eroticized male body in a space formerly occupied by women has not gone unnoticed in popular and academic discussion of advertising. In his book, *Promotional Culture* (1991), Andrew Wernick suggests that such innovations reflect changing male and female social roles and a consequent unsettling of the whole symbolic system within which images of masculinity and femininity are projected (Wernick 1991: 48–68). We should not rejoice too soon, however. Wernick concludes that while male and female roles may have become interchangeable, this equalization merely amounts to a levelling process in the sphere of consumption itself. What we have produced is an equality of 'self-absorbed, and emotionally anxious personalities for sale' (Wernick 1991: 68). Under the conditions of late capitalism we are all simply commodities or 'promotional subjects'.

Wernick's left-wing (arguably Marxist) critique of consumerism (I pointed out) fails to take into account the complex and contradictory ways in which women's (and men's) relative status and power has been enhanced by their role as consumers. In other words, consumption (which necessarily entails a degree of economic freedom and control) has offered to women:

> new areas of authority and expertise, new sources of income, a new sense
> of consumer rights; and one of the consequences of these developments

has been a heightened awareness of entitlement *outside* [my emphasis] the sphere of consumption.

(Nava 1987: 208)

Nava's conclusion is salutary; she suggests that consumerism is much more than economic activity and that like sexuality 'it consists of a multiplicity of fragmented and contradictory discourses' (Nava 1987: 209). It is therefore interesting in this regard to consider further the conjunction of consumerism, economics and sexuality which circulate around the body of Kate Moss, the particular 'personality on sale' in the ad under consideration.

Down the Garden Path of Theory?[7]

Everybody in the room instantly recognized Kate Moss and simultaneously acknowledged her as a 'waif' model. What is of interest here, is that the discourse surrounding 'waifness' meant they already knew they were to critique her image as an 'unrealistic' body type. How and why should this be so? Looking back over my newspaper and video clips, I am tempted to suggest, without being able to fix the moment in time, that Kate Moss (like Kristen McMenemy) arrived on the fashion scene as a news story in which concern about waifdom became the basis for an article about the dangers of eating disorders:

Over the last two to three years, models have started to look more normal. Now we have this horrendous trend back to this real anorexic look. It's very frightening. Bulimia has been steadily growing [and] my fear is that this will have an even bigger increase in anorexic and bulimic behaviour, Mrs Robinson [a Melbourne psychologist] said.

(*Age*, 30 March 1993)

In the period when I was writing this paper, the popular magazine *Who Weekly* (27 May 1996) ran a cover story on the latest 'heroin-addict chic' look which included a full page spread (see Figure 9.1) of model Jodie Kidd alongside an 'average size' young Australian woman. This photospread was accompanied by a nutritionist's warnings about the dangers of trying to starve one's body into the new shape. The point I am making here is that media representations of women are regularly debated *in the media* so that contradictory messages are the rule rather than the exception; we are invited to admire the image even as we are warned of its potential dangers.

The students in Women and Media knew that Kate Moss represented an 'unrealistic' body type (even though thin women do exist). What was interesting in the advertisement in question was her body was all but hidden, inviting us to speculate about how thin it might be, even though the elegant leg wrapped around the

Figure 9.1 Contradictory messages in *Who Weekly*, May 27, 1996, No 222, pp. 52–53.

male model looked both solid and muscular – very unwaif-like. However, we were not being invited to look at Moss's body, we were being asked to look at her face and to recognize her *as* Kate Moss, supermodel.

The arrival on the scene of the supermodel is an interesting and much discussed phenomenon. Elle McPherson, Claudia Schiffer, Naomi Campbell and Linda Evangelista are the immediate identities which spring to mind; Moss and McMenemy are later arrivals. What these women have in common is that, above and beyond their role as fashion models, they are treated as celebrities; their romantic attachments, business investments and careers avidly documented in the press and on screen. Linda Evangelista's apocryphal statement that she doesn't get out of bed for less than $10,000 a day has become a catchphrase to be quoted every time the word supermodel is used (*Australian*, 15 May 1996). These are women who sell their image, and laugh all the way to the bank while pro-censorship feminists argue over whether or not their appearance as a centrefold spread in *Playboy* or *Penthouse* constitutes exploitation. Well might we then ask who is exploiting whom? To return to the body in question, however, what (I wondered to the students) was Kate Moss paid for the use of her face, arm and leg in this advertisement – and did this matter?

One year after this class where I had floated the question of economics, I found an essay by Patricia Mellencamp concerned with the history of feminist film criticism in which she makes the following observation:

> I am no longer interested in dream girls, in theories of sexual desire, or in secrets. Warhol was right; with enough repetition, sex becomes boring. I am interested in women's knowledge and in the money, along with the sexual economy – why we have more knowledge and less authority (and money). I suspect we have been led astray – down a garden path of theory.
>
> (Mellencamp 1996: 30)

What Mellencamp suggests is that all that agonizing over the male gaze and Oedipal investments of desire have taken us in the wrong direction; what we've missed is the money. Rather than worrying about Barbara Stanwyck's image on screen, why weren't we asking about her contract negotiations, 'her conditions of production?' (Mellencamp 1996: 25). My point entirely. Why, I asked the students, are we worrying about Moss's image when we should be asking about her contract with Calvin Klein and the degree of power this gives her over the handling and marketing of her image? And who is Calvin Klein anyway?

Of course, it was agreed, we should be doing both. It would be foolish to argue that economic considerations negate the significance and immediacy of the image; but it is also foolish to argue that we can consider the image in isolation from other factors. I pointed out with reference to an essay by Sue O'Sullivan (1994), in these hyperconscious postmodern times, we should never assume that pleasure in the image implies a commitment to what it represents. What we need is a much more nuanced understanding of the intersection of economics, consumerism (in all its contradictions), and symbolic representation.

Reflections

Looking back at this class on advertising, I can only hope that it demonstrates the teaching strategy I tried to employ in the course overall. In each session I attempted to historicize feminist media theory with reference to particular examples (about, say, pornography or romance) without seeking to condescend to a simpler past or by necessarily assuming a more sophisticated present; I therefore wanted to acknowledge the political nature of the interventions made about women and the media and the strategic value of such interventions in the broader debate about women's roles in society. In each class I presented examples drawn from the media which I found problematic and which challenged the adequacy of current media and feminist theory to encompass their address. In this way I tried to suggest that feminist theory in general, or about the media in particular, is not (and never has been) a fixed body of knowledge but is always in process and therefore open to critique or rejection by those who might still – if hesitantly – describe themselves as feminist (Ang 1995).

I wanted the students to conceive of theory as a kind of toolbox and to invite them to test the utility of a range of theoretical approaches on a variety of media texts to see how well they worked in practice and what results (in terms of inter-pretation) they produced. My aim here was not to suggest that one theoretical approach might be better than another, although it was hard to refrain from arriving at provisional conclusions. My primary goal was to encourage the students to participate in ongoing debates about women, the media, theory and politics now (in class) and perhaps later (in some other future contexts). I shall refrain from making any claims about the success of this project, since to quote from students' final essays would merely illustrate how they tried to satisfy the teacher assessing them by telling her what they thought she might like to hear (though the point of the class was to have them assume no right answers – which is, of course, the right answer). I can only hope, therefore, that I did indeed provide them with some perspectives on the conjunction of feminism and media theory and the need to think critically about both.

Perhaps my other major goal was to enable the students to admit rather than disavow what might be called, following Barthes (1975), 'the pleasure of the text' and to provide them with ways of trying to identify and discuss the nature of such pleasure. How we *feel* about a text may be very different from what we have been taught to *think* about it. If I had any larger purpose, it was to suggest that it is this contradiction between our emotional and intellectual responses which both feminism and media theory have largely failed to address when talking about popular culture.

In retrospect, I can only suggest that the reluctance of the students to whole-heartedly embrace feminism as the defining aspect of their political selves (taking the Ang position) may not be such a bad an indication as Summers thinks. Given that each student had a strong commitment to the notion of equality, it may well be that their political interests and energies will take another form. Each of the young women in this class clearly perceived that she *could* act politically (should she feel so moved), either on her own behalf and/or in the interests of others. Such acts might be tactical and small (the microfeminist response to dealing with the private and everyday); or strategic and large (the public macrofeminist response); or not even expressly feminist at all, leaving open the possibility of other political allegiances cutting across gender lines.

Because I think there is no possibility of a real conclusion here, since anything is possible, I will end with another voice and another set of issues which I believe necessitate a change of direction in our thinking about how to teach about feminism and the media. I have hitherto concealed the presence of Keith, the only male in the class (which was indeed open to all male students).[8] Keith was relatively quiet (which was hardly surprising in the circumstances), but attended regularly and submitted two essays, one dealing with the representation of men in sports advertising and the other attempting to deal with his responses to pornography. Asked to describe his own position with regard to feminism, Keith wrote:

> You said we could do this exercise by giving a type of biography. Telling you that I grew up as the fourth of seven kids and that the youngest is a girl (the rest being highly sport-competitive oriented males) may give you some insight into my uncertainty about the term feminism. I remember speaking to my dad last year and he said he regarded himself as a feminist in many respects. My view of my dad as this big strong, masculine fella was not changed, but my image of the typical or stereotypical feminist changed dramatically. I hope that this course assists me in understanding feminism or things relating to it a little better.
>
> (Keith)

I hope it did, Keith, but maybe you've been rather overlooked in this debate about feminism and representation. What do you and your dad know, feel, and understand about representation, feminism and politics? How can we include you in this debate which has so far concerned you but excluded you?

Notes

1   *The Age Good Weekend* is an A4-size colour supplement published to accompany the extensive Saturday edition of *The Age* newspaper in Melbourne, Australia. It regularly contains longer feature articles on all kinds of topics including food, real estate and other regular columns. For UK readers, it is worth noting that Anne Summers is not to be confused with the owner of Britain's leading chain of sex shops.

2   This combative imagery is drawn from the text of *The Age Good Weekend* article (Summers 1995). It is, however, even more striking in the final chapter of the second edition of *Damned Whores and God's Police* (Summers 1974/1994).

3 I must confess that I am attached to this notion of *fin de siècle* feminism. The *Compact Oxford Dictionary* defines '*fin de siècle*' as 'advanced, modern or decadent'; I think this is probably an accurate summing up of my feminist credentials.

4 Although the work of Catherine Lumby who is both an academic and a freelance journalist is a notable exception and is cited later in this chapter.

5 I would like to acknowledge here the much valued contribution of my dear colleague and friend, Dr Ina Bertrand, with whom I co-devised and sometimes co-taught this course.

6 How these terms emerged is intriguing. As I recall, they came into existence during the discussion of Summers' article – fairly late in the course when students were insisting that there were no longer any big unifying issues – only tactical and immediate ones. Someone muttered something about macro and micro which I represented to the class as microfeminism and macrofeminism – terms which were received with some delight since they served as a shorthand reference to this particular moment in our discussions.

7 This phrase is borrowed from Patricia Mellencamp's (1996) essay 'Five ages of film feminism'.

8 It is the rule rather than the exception that there is at least one male student every year who opts to take Women and Media. As they are in the minority, they do tend to be rather quiet but are usually not silent.

References

ANG, I. (1995) 'I'm a feminist but ... "other" women and postnational feminism', in B. CAINE and R. PRINGLE (eds) *Transitions: New Australian Feminisms*, Sydney: Allen and Unwin.

BARTHES, R. (1975) *The Pleasure of the Text*, New York, Hill and Wang.

CREED, B. (1994) 'Queer theory and its discontents: Queer desires, queer cinema', in N. GRIEVE and A. BURNS (eds) *Australian Women: Contemporary Feminist Thought*, Melbourne: Oxford University Press.

CURTHOYS, A. (1994) 'Australian feminism since 1970', in N. GRIEVE and A. BURNS (eds) *Australian Women: Contemporary Feminist Thought*, Melbourne: Oxford University Press.

EDGAR, P. and McPHEE, H. (1974) *Media She*, Melbourne: Heinnemann.

LUMBY, C. (1993) 'Sexist or sexy?' *The Independent*, November: 30–35.

MELLENCAMP, P. (1996) 'Five ages of film feminism', in L. JAYAMANNE (ed.) *Kiss Me Deadly: Feminism and Cinema for the Moment*, Sydney: Power Publications.

MOUFFE, C. (1995) 'Feminism, citizenship, and radical democratic politics', in L. NICHOLSON, and S. SEIDMAN (eds) *Social Postmodernism: Beyond Identity Politics*, Cambridge: Cambridge University Press.

MULVEY, L. (1975) 'Visual pleasure and narrative cinema', *Screen*, **16**(3): 6–18.

MULVEY, L. (1981) 'Afterthoughts on "Visual pleasure and narrative cinema" inspired by *Duel in the Sun*', *Framework*, 15/16/17: 12–15.

NAVA, M. (1987) 'Consumerism and its contradictions', *Cultural Studies*, **1**(2): 204–10.

O'SULLIVAN, S. (1994) 'Girls who kiss girls and who cares', in D. HAMER and B. BUDGE (eds) *The Good, the Bad and the Gorgeous*, London: Pandora.

RADNER, H. (1995) *Shopping Around: Feminine Culture and the Pursuit of Pleasure*, New York: Routledge.

SUMMERS, A. (1974/1994) *Damned Whores and God's Police*, Ringwood, Victoria: Penguin.

SUMMERS, A. (1995) 'Shockwaves at the revolution', *The Age Good Weekend*, 18 March: 26–29.

WERNICK, A. (1991) *Promotional Culture: Advertising and Symbolic Expression*, London: Sage.

WINSHIP, J. (1985) 'A girl needs to get streetwise: Magazines for the eighties', *Feminist Review*, **21**, Winter.

Notes on contributors

Nola Alloway is a senior lecturer in the School of Education at James Cook University of North Queensland in Townsville, Queensland. Her research includes studies of young children's computer play, gender in the early childhood classroom, and masculinity and literacy. One of her major book publications is *Foundation Stones: The Construction of Gender in Early Childhood* (Curriculum Corporation 1995).

Chris Bigum is an associate professor in the Faculty of Education at Central Queensland University. His research and teaching interests are in the implications of new information and communications technologies for educational practice and policy. He has published widely in this and related areas. With Bill Green, he co-edited *Understanding the New Information Technologies in Education: A Resource for Teachers* (1992) and he has written numerous monographs and research papers on education and new information technologies.

Gerry Bloustien is a lecturer in the School of Communications at the University of South Australia and an independent film-maker. Her research interests include gender and representation, and popular culture, particularly the impact of new technologies on the everyday lives of young people. She also has a keen interest in popular music including the use of music in contemporary Australian films. Some of her published work appears in *Continuum* and *Youth Studies Australia*.

Pam Gilbert is an associate professor in the School of Education at James Cook University of North Queensland in Townsville, Queensland. She has researched and published in the areas of popular culture and schooling, literacy, and gender and education. Some of her better known publications in these areas include *Fashioning the Feminine: Girls, Popular Culture and Schooling* (with S. Taylor, Allen and Unwin 1991), *Literacy in Contexts* (with A. Luke, Allen and Unwin 1993), and *Divided by a Common Language: Gender and the English Curriculum* (Curriculum Corporation 1994).

Patricia Gillard is a professor in the Department of Communication Studies and Director of the Telecommunications Needs Research Group at the Royal Melbourne

Institute of Technology, Melbourne, Australia. She was also Head of Research and Development for ABC television for three years. Her own research is in the area of children and television and, most recently, telecommunications consumers. Major publications include *Girls and Television, The Lively Audience* (as Palmer) and *Positioning Telecommunications Consumers.*

Bill Green is a senior lecturer in the School of Social and Cultural Studies in Education, Deakin University, Geelong, Australia. His research and teaching interests range across English curriculum studies, curriculum and literacy, and technology and cultural studies. His publications include two edited collections: *The Insistence of the Letter: Literacy Studies and Curriculum Theorizing* (Falmer Press 1993) and *Teaching the English Subjects: Essays on English Curriculum History and Australian Schooling* (Deakin University Press 1996).

Sue Howard is a senior lecturer in the Faculty of Education at the University of South Australia. She teaches educational psychology and media studies and her research interests combine these perspectives. She is currently working on two projects, one focusing on perceptions of television reality among young viewers and the other on children's perceptions of public power and politics. She has contributed to a number of journals including *Media Information Australia, The Australian Journal of Early Childhood* and *Youth Studies Australia.*

Mark Laidler is currently lecturing in Education at RMIT, Melbourne after 15 years as a primary school teacher. In his PhD studies he is developing a poststructural analysis of children's (possibly) subversive use of the Internet and the popular disapproval this attracts. His work has been published in *Metro Magazine.*

Geoff Lealand is a senior lecturer in Film and Television Studies at the University of Waikato in New Zealand. His research and teaching interests centre on audience theory, dynamics of the global and the local and television as popular culture. His particular interest in children and media has been motivated as much by his two computer-literate children (his daughter made her first connection with the Internet at age 3) as by his teaching activities.

Jo-Anne Reid teaches at the University of Ballarat, Victoria and has a long-standing involvement in language and literacy across primary, secondary and tertiary settings. She has recently completed doctoral work on programming as a disciplinary practice, and is interested in the potential of poststructuralist theories of practice for rethinking teaching and learning in a postmodern society.

Linda Sheldon is a registered child psychologist and worked from 1992–95 for the Australian Broadcasting Authority. She was the Manager of the Research Section for much of that time and was instrumental in designing and undertaking attitudinal research with both children and families. At present, she is working in New Zealand as a psychologist and as a media research consultant. Her current project is with the New Zealand Broadcasting Authority, investigating community views about adult entertainment on pay TV.

Sue Turnbull is a senior lecturer in the Department of Media Studies at La Trobe University, Melbourne. She is co-author, with Kate Bowles, of *Tomorrow Never Knows: Soap on Australian Television* (Australian Film Institute 1995) and is currently working on a project involving women as readers and writers of crime fiction. She is vice president of the ANZ Communication Association, deputy chair of the Australian Cultural Studies Association and in 1996 was a joint winner of the Henry Mayer prize.

Karen Wale and **Amanda Bow** are research associates for the Telecommunications Needs Research Group at the Royal Melbourne Institute of Technology. They have both been involved in researching the social relations of telecommunications for over two years. Both are currently enrolled in Masters degrees at RMIT, studying the social implications of telecommunications.

Index